Clyde A. Milner II is an associate professor of history at Utah State University. His published articles, like the present book, reflect his combined interests in religious history and the history of American Indians.

With
Good
Intentions

With
Good
Intentions

Quaker Work

among the Pawnees,

Otos, and Omahas

in the 1870s

Clyde A. Milner II

University of Nebraska Press: Lincoln and London

The paper in this book meets the guidelines for
permanence and durability of the Committee on
Production Guidelines for Book Longevity of the Council
on Library Resources.

Library of Congress Cataloging in Publication Data

Milner, Clyde A., 1948-
With good intentions.

Bibliography: p.
Includes index.
1. Pawnee Indians–Government relations. 2. Oto Indians–
Government relations. 3. Omaha Indians–Government
relations. 4. Indians of North America–Government relations.
5. Society of Friends–Nebraska–History–19th century. I. Title.
E99.P3M54   970.00497   81-16238
ISBN 0-8032-3066-4   AACR2

Dedicated to
Minnie Mack Pearce Sargent
Carol Ann O'Connor
Ernestine C., Clyde A.,
and Charles F. Milner
for education and inspiration

Contents

Preface

In 1869, as part of President Ulysses S. Grant's Peace Policy, members of the Society of Friends became government Indian agents. One group of Quakers, the Hicksites, took control of the Northern Superintendency, which encompassed seven Indian societies on six reservations in Nebraska. The interaction between three of these native societies and their Quaker administrators is the main topic of this book. Although administrative history is important to this study, it has not been allowed to exclude the ethnohistory of the Pawnees, Otos, and Omahas in the 1870s. In addition, the comparative histories of these three native societies present a nearly day-to-day picture of varied Indian actions within the framework of government policy. A more limited study of only one native society might fail to recognize the rich complexity of this response.

The 1870s were a time of turmoil and despair for American Indians on the Great Plains. Nebraska's native peoples confronted the decline of the buffalo, the outbreak of epidemic diseases, the devastations of grasshoppers and droughts, and the depredations of red and white neighbors. Beyond these developments, the Pawnees, Otos, and Omahas each confronted distinct problems. The Pawnees lost a forty-year war of attrition with the Teton Sioux; the Otos split into two factions; and the Omahas permitted the allotment of their reservation into individual farmsteads. Nonetheless, these three native societies maintained an initiative for adaptation based more on their own cultural traditions than on the desires of government administrators.

As for the Quakers, they brought good intentions to their work as Indian agents. They strove to assimilate the Indians under their care into white society, while, in general, they maintained their personal integrity. Yet, a close examination of the Quaker administration of the Omaha, Pawnee, and Oto agencies reveals a record of frustration and failure which also characterized the Quakers' efforts at other reservations. The presence of honest Quaker agents did not transform these Indians into "civilized" Christians. Indeed, the Quakers often misinterpreted or ignored the problems which plagued these Nebraska natives.

In all likelihood, no other group of white Americans in the post-Civil War period could have prevented the rapid decline of these native peoples into abject poverty and social displacement. Sadly, the example of the Quaker Indian agents indicates how the desire to do good does not always produce beneficial results. By the 1870s, well-meaning white friends could not solve the complex issues which confronted the Omahas, Otos, and Pawnees. Tragically, these Indians found that they had lost control of their own fate as well.

In the preparation of this book, I have been fortunate to gain the support of friends and scholars. I owe many debts of thanks. The largest is to Howard Lamar, who guided my earliest efforts with thoughtful observations and appropriate encouragement. Leonard Thompson stimulated my thinking on various aspects of this work, as did P. Richard Metcalf, Richard White, Peter Nabokov, Sydney Ahlstrom, William T. Hagan, Paul Stuart, and Martin Zanger. Martha Royce Blaine and Paul Olson commented insightfully on specific chapters. The Newberry Library's Center for the History of the American Indian, funded by the National Endowment for the Humanities, provided a one-year fellowship for research and writing. I am indebted to Lawrence Towner, president of the Newberry Library, as well as to Richard Brown and John Aubrey, for their support during my year in Chicago. At other archives and libraries, I wish to thank J. William Frost, Bert Fowler, and Jane Rittenhouse Smiley of the Friends Historical Library (Swarthmore College), Barbara L. Curtis of the Quaker Collection (Haverford), Paul D. Riley of the Nebraska State Historical Society, Mary Lee Ervin of the Oklahoma Historical Society, Richard C. Crawford and Samella T. Anderson of the National Archives, and Herman J. Viola of the Smithsonian Institution.

At Utah State University my colleagues have been generous of their time and sympathetic in their words. I am especially grateful to Ross Peterson, Michael L. Nicholls, and Paul Hutton. In addition, Carol Ann O'Connor, my colleague for life and herself a professional historian, listened and listened and understood. I am happy to announce that her love and patience were never strained by the need to type a single word of this entire project.

With
Good
Intentions

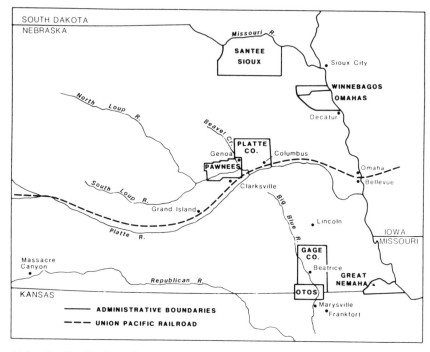

Nebraska: The Northern Superintendency

CHAPTER ONE

The Quaker Policy of U. S. Grant

The Peace Policy and the Quaker Heritage

In November of 1868, Ulysses S. Grant returned to Washington, D.C., from his home in Galena, Illinois, as the president-elect of the United States. In the four months before his inauguration, he said nearly nothing about plans for his new administration. The newspapers speculated about who would be included in the new president's cabinet, but no names were announced. Occasionally, correspondents wrote about rumored policy changes. On February 25, 1869, the *Boston Daily Advertiser* published a front-page article which had been telegraphed from Washington. It claimed that General Grant planned to radically reform the management of Indian affairs. The president-elect, the article maintained, wanted to gather all the Indians on reservations and hoped to root out the gang of thieves and speculators who inhabited the Indian Bureau. The *Advertiser*'s correspondent believed that Grant would not hesitate to fight hostile natives, but added that "all Indians who are disposed to peace will find that the policy of the new Administration is a peace policy." The Boston newspaper further indicated that the general had given the Indian question great study but had not limited his consultations to former military associates. "He is much impressed with the humane idea of the Quakers on the questions lately raised respecting our Indian policy, and will allow this class of citizens considerable prominence in the Indian work of his administration. He has had some correspondence with leading men in this sect, and the probabilities are that no small number of his agents will be Quakers."[1]

The Boston article was substantially correct. Grant did plan to reform Indian affairs. Indeed, many of the efforts of both Grant and the Congress in this area became known as the "Peace Policy"—a term which Grant himself eventually used in his speeches. President Grant's commitment to this reform had grown out of his responsibilities as General of the Army after the Civil War. Not surprisingly, he supported military control over most interactions with the Indians. Since 1866, in his reports to the secretary of war, Grant had advocated the transfer of the Office of Indian Affairs from the Department of the Interior to the Department of War. He also had approved warmly of Gen. William T. Sherman's actions on the Plains, which attempted to settle all Indians on their assigned reservations and keep them there permanently. Sherman described the efforts under his command as a "double process of *peace* within their reservation and war *without.*"[2]

In the matter of what to do with the Plains Indians once they came to the reservations, Grant apparently listened most closely to his aide-de-camp Ely S. Parker, who was both a brevet brigadier general and a Tonawanda Seneca chief. As a sachem among his own people, in western New York, Parker had met Quaker missionaries and other members of the Society of Friends. Indeed, Parker had written to Quaker leaders on February 15, 1869, ten days before the newspaper article appeared in the *Boston Daily Advertiser.* He informed these Friends of President-elect Grant's request "that you will send him a list of names, members of your Society, whom your Society will endorse as suitable persons for Indian agents." In addition Grant, through Parker's letter, assured the Friends "that any attempt which may or can be made by your Society for the improvement, education and Christianization of the Indians, under such agencies, will receive from him, as President, all the encouragement and protection which the laws of the United States will warrant him in giving."[3]

Grant's appointment of Indian agents from a pacifist religious denomination, though unexpected, did not contradict his belief in military control of Indian affairs. The Quaker agents were limited to the Northern and Central superintendencies, which encompassed the Indian lands of Nebraska plus some of Kansas and present-day western Oklahoma. For all the remaining Indian agencies, Grant recommended military officers. In command of these new Quaker and military agents, Grant placed the first Indian commissioner of Indian Affairs, Ely S. Parker, who nonetheless was also an experienced army officer and friend of the president. The new military presence in the Department of the Interior became complete with the appointment as secretary of Jacob D. Cox, a Union general in the Civil War and a former Republican governor of Ohio.

Since the issue of the transfer of the Office of Indian Affairs had remained stalled in Congress for several years, Grant had begun his presidency with an attempt at de facto transfer. He brought some of the army into the Department of the Interior to control the Office of Indian Affairs. In the face of these actions, Congress soon began to modify Grant's "Peace Policy." On April 10, 1869, as part of the $2 million appropriation bill for the management of Indian affairs, Congress established an independent Board of Indian Commissioners. This board was to share control with the secretary of the interior of the disbursement of funds appropriated for the Indians. The ten members of the board were to be outstanding citizens selected by the president, and were to serve without pay. Grant accepted the establishment of the Board of Indian Commissioners because it was not a petty political maneuver by Congress. Nonpoliticians such as Henry Whipple, the Episcopal bishop of Minnesota, and Thomas Wistar, a Quaker leader from Philadelphia, had lobbied for this measure. Another strong supporter had been George Stuart of Philadelphia, one of Grant's personal acquaintances. In fact

Grant relied on Stuart's recommendations when he appointed the first set of commissioners — nearly all of whom were leading philanthropists and churchmen.

Grant also went along with the Congressional act in 1871 which declared that Indian societies would no longer be recognized as independent nations with whom the United States needed to sign formal treaties. The president still supported transfer of the Office of Indian Affairs to the War Department, but on January 23, 1870, Maj. Eugene M. Baker massacred a Piegan village in Montana. The uproar over this event doomed a transfer measure which seemed near passage as part of the army appropriation bill. After its defeat, the issue of transfer remained buried for several more years. Nonetheless, the War Department continued to control the military response to those Indians not on their assigned reservations. During Grant's eight years as president, the War Department followed General Sherman's principle of "peace within, war without" and undertook over two hundred military actions against the Indians.

This extensive war making compromised, but did not terminate, the efforts to establish peace and progress on the reservations. Indeed, a peculiar success by default fell to Grant's limited experiment with Quaker agents. On July 15, 1870, Congress passed a bill forbidding military personnel to hold civil office. This law represented an attempt by some members of Congress to reestablish the patronage and plunder which the Indian agencies had provided before Grant's reforms. The president, upset by these political maneuvers, followed the Board of Indian Commissioners' recommendation that the vacated agencies be awarded to other Christian denominations on terms similar to those held by the Society of Friends. Grant in this matter maintained his reform impulse but at the expense of army dominance of the Office of Indian Affairs. What had begun as a small religious experiment tacked on to a military approach to Indian affairs had expanded by mid-1870 to include all Indian agencies, numerous Protestant groups, and the Roman Catholic Church.

Before these developments, the original selection of the Quakers to serve as Indian agents captured much public attention. On May 1, 1869, the *New York Times* ran an editorial entitled "Broad-Brim and Breech-Clout" which applauded Grant's attempt to "Quakerize" the hostile Indians. Six days before, the same paper had expressed the wish that the Friends would create "a peaceful and cheap administration of Indian Affairs." This potential economic savings also impressed the *Rocky Mountain News* of Denver, Colorado, which noted, on May 5: "There are no shrewder business men than the broad brimmed sect furnishes." The editorial concluded: "Everyone but the Indian agents and those who share their plunder must of course wish the Quakers success."

Yet, before Grant expanded what became known as his "Quaker Policy" to all the major Christian churches, a few people questioned his choice. To these inquiries, Quaker leaders willingly and diplomatically responded. Benjamin Hallowell, secretary of the Baltimore area committee on Indian concerns of one branch of the Society of Friends, wrote a lengthy statement for the *Baltimore American* of June 21, 1869, in which he undertook to clarify the president's intent:

It is believed that President Grant, in looking to the Friends for some assistance in the improvement in [*sic*] the Indians, which he so much desired, was not led thereto by any belief in the superiority of *theirs* over *other* religious organizations, or that the right of membership in that Society would impart any qualification for an Indian agency; but that it was because the entire record of the Society of Friends towards the Indians, from the time of William Penn to the present day, was an unbroken one of kindness, justice, and brotherly friendship, which is traditionally known to the different tribes of Indians at this time.

President Grant's sagacity led him to see that *these traditional facts* will give the Society of Friends a prestige with the Indians, which, if properly used, might tend to restore that confidence in the National Government, which has been so sorrowfully impaired by the mal-administration of Indian affairs.[4]

Grant's first public statement on his new Indian policy did not undercut Hallowell's explanation. In his first annual message to Congress, in December of 1869, the president emphasized the need for reform in Indian affairs. In reference to the Quaker experiment, he noted the Friends' pacifism and reputation for "strict integrity and fair dealings." As to the *"traditional facts"* of Hallowell, Grant pointed to the "well known" peaceful settlement of Pennsylvania, which he compared favorably to the Indian wars that plagued the other colonies.[5] Grant's brief statement did not indicate whether he accepted the Quaker claim of an ongoing friendship with all Indians. Nevertheless, the president accepted the Friends as a people uniquely qualified to work among the Indians and based their qualification, as the Friends did themselves, upon the tradition of colonial Pennsylvania's "Long Peace."

Ironically for Friends, as well as for many other Americans, this tradition had a distinctly popular representation. Ever since its first public showing in London in 1775, Benjamin West's painting *Penn's Treaty with the Indians* had gained wide recognition and application. West's "historical" representation of the elderly Penn beneath the great elm — his hand outstretched, the Indians intent on his words — became a familiar image and a typical design on items in Quaker and non-Quaker homes on both sides of the Atlantic. By the 1850s, the treaty motif appeared on candle screens, lamp shades, trays, bed curtains, bed quilts, iron plates, cast-iron stoves, and even whiskey glasses. One English china maker who sold primarily to the American market used a representation of the treaty scene as his only pattern from 1830 to 1859.

West's image had its greatest distribution in printed reproductions, however. Engravings for books and for domestic display started appearing in the 1780s, and by the mid-nineteenth century, a copy of West's painting graced most English Quaker homes. Edward Hicks, a Friend and a respected American artist, included a treaty scene inspired by West in the background of most of his renditions of the *Peaceable Kingdom*. He produced these "primitive" paintings in Bucks County, Pennsylvania, between 1820 and 1849. After its founding in 1824, for its first gift the Historical Society of Pennsylvania presented a medal based on the treaty scene to its membership. The Philadelphia *Public Ledger* sent a copy of the painting to every subscriber as a New Year's greeting for 1857. The *Press* of Philadelphia used a similar greeting sheet in 1864. That same year, West's original painting went on display in Philadelphia as an exhibit to raise funds for medical aid to soldiers wounded in the Civil War.

During the Grant administration, Quaker committees wrote to some Indian leaders on stationery which displayed the treaty scene and Quaker visitors gave reproductions of *Penn's Treaty* to various Indian groups. After Samuel M. Janney took charge of the Northern Superintendency, he hung a copy in his Omaha office.[6]

The fact that Friends distributed, displayed, and even dined off representations of *Penn's Treaty with the Indians* revealed that what Benjamin West had created was either an unofficial seal for the Society of Friends or an emblem for a Quaker saint. By the 1820s, Quaker scholars had noted West's historical inaccuracies in buildings and dress in the picture, but these scholars still believed in the Great Treaty and tried to find original copies of the document. This search underscored Friends' concern for the validity of an event which had come to symbolize the Quaker movement. The all-important document did not reappear, but indirect evidence and oral tradition hinted at its existence.

When the small pacifist denomination accepted President Grant's invitation to serve as Indian agents, the Quaker movement had undergone over two centuries of sectarian development. A major schism divided the Society in the late 1820s, but both the Orthodox and Hicksite branches maintained Friends' interest in race relations.[7] Yet, despite the popular image of Penn's Great Treaty, Quaker work in race relations predominantly had focused on the plight of black Americans. Thus it was the Society's antislavery activity and aid to the freedmen which provided the major effective legacy for the work at the Indian agencies, rather than its earlier, modest efforts among a few native groups.

The beginning of the Quaker movement often is dated at 1652, thirty years before William Penn began his "Holy Experiment" in Pennsylvania. In that year, George Fox, the founder of the Society of Friends, climbed Pendle Hill in northern England and experienced a clear vision of a great people waiting to be gathered for the Lord. In the years following his revelation, Fox and his gathered group preached a simplified, fundamental Christianity which emphasized the power of the Lord's spirit within the individual. Friends regarded themselves as a revival of primitive Christian faith and called themselves "Children of the Light" and "Publishers of the Truth." At this time, the 1650s, the emphasis on spiritual religion in many puritan books and preachings stirred the thousands who eventually joined the Quaker movement. Quakers shared with other radical puritan groups a variety of customs and witnesses. They used simple speech, "thee" and "thou", and wore plain clothing. In both cases, they wished to break down the proud rather than to exalt the humble. Quakers also refused formal, customary recognition of authority and so would not remove their hats in court or have their spiritually inspired honesty questioned by the taking of oaths.[8]

In its first decade, the Society of Friends established two denominationally definitive concepts. The first, the "Inner Light," expressed the authority of spiritual revelation as it applied to every individual. Friends believed that a leading could come directly from God just as it had to the Hebrew prophets. The silent meeting, therefore, became an event in which one waited upon the Light. The second concept, the "Peace Testimony," established the Society of Friends as a pacifist movement and was an important corollary to the Inner Light, as it could be revealed to men corporately. Friends came to believe that in the grand crusade against sin and evil which they called the "Lamb's War," only spiritual weapons were consistent with the leadings of the spirit. The declaration of January, 1661, against taking up arms, either on behalf of an earthly kingdom or to bring on the kingdom of Christ, gave full form to the Quaker peace testimony.[9]

Inherent in both the Inner Light and the Peace Testimony was an egalitarianism which professed the spiritual unity of the human family. Quaker men and women felt free, therefore, to preach their "truth" to all people regardless of language, race, or culture. The first generation of Quakers never despaired that any human being could experience the Inner Light. They carried their message to Russia, Algiers, and Malta and tried to correspond with the emperor of China and

the legendary Prester John. Soon preachers arrived in the
New World to enlighten its inhabitants. In 1657, two Quaker
preachers met with the Wampanoags on Martha's Vineyard.
These Indians had already produced some converts to the
Puritan faith through the efforts of the Thomas Mayhews,
junior and senior. Yet no Quaker converts came out of this
meeting. Other Quakers, including George Fox in 1672 and
1673, would preach to Indian groups up and down the east
coast of the Anglo-American colonies with similar results.[10]

The early membership of the Society of Friends came
from the English-speaking world, especially the lower-class
rural peoples of the British northwest. As a radical purifi-
cation of Christianity, Quakerism had no creed, no sacra-
ments, no liturgy, and no structural system of conversion.
For those not in the English puritan tradition, exposure to
Quaker preaching might produce sympathetic agreement
with its spiritual message, but no understanding of the pos-
sibilities for membership. In time Quakers even avoided direct, active proselytism, in order not to stand in the way of
the workings of the Inner Light.[11]

Gradually a system of religious organization evolved for
the Society of Friends. The members of a local meeting for
worship usually became a Monthly Meeting, which was so
called because it met once a month to discuss the business
of the meeting. A Quarterly Meeting, held every three
months, was made up then of various Monthly Meetings
within a region. The ultimate gathering of Friends within a
large area occurred at the annual Yearly Meeting. Originally,
only one Yearly Meeting took place, in London, but by 1700,
as Quakerism spread across the Atlantic, other Yearly Meetings were established in New England, Baltimore, Philadelphia, New York, and North Carolina. These Yearly Meetings
set up various committees whose reports, when approved at
the annual gatherings, served as the major voice on Quaker
religious views and social concerns. Correspondence between
the various Yearly Meetings helped maintain a somewhat
united sense of fellowship, but no formal organization existed
beyond the Yearly Meeting. On all levels, from a small committee of a Monthly Meeting to the large assembly of a

Yearly Meeting, authority was based on consensus and agreement, not on formal structures or personal leadership. All meetings strove to follow the leadings of the Inner Light as shared by all members. So Quaker leaders might guide, but could not dictate, the opinions and actions of any meeting. In fact, meetings did not vote to resolve issues. A simple majority could not rule; instead full consensus, with lengthy, sometimes prayerful discussions, determined the views of a Quaker meeting.[12]

These organizational principles at times could lead to introspection and inaction instead of social concern and active benevolence. In the case of Quaker relations with American Indians, William Penn's policies of fair treatment and honest dealings gave way to neglect by the Pennsylvania meetings. Rapid settlement by Europeans, many of whom were not Quakers, opened the way for land swindles, some of them carried out by Penn's own sons. The Long Peace, begun by Penn in the 1680s, finally ended after the outbreak of the French and Indian War in 1754. A group of Quakers then began an effort to reestablish friendship with the Indians of Pennsylvania, but they found that few natives now lived in the regions of Quaker settlement. Not until the 1790s did the occasional visits and preachings of individual Friends give way to an organized program of missions, primarily to the Senecas, who lived in upper New York state, and to the Shawnees, who moved from Indiana to western Ohio and then out to Kansas. These missions were the undertaking of a few Yearly Meetings and were modest in scope, with the emphasis on practical schooling and demonstration farming. The grander social concern which seemed to engage the interest and effort of many more Friends involved the emancipation of black slaves. Yet here also, Friends questioned the proper action to take and most did not join the radical abolitionists when they came to the fore in the 1830s.

The Civil War and emancipation through a constitutional amendment ended the controversy over radical abolition. In the aftermath of war, the Quakers enthusiastically attempted to bring aid and education to the freedmen in the South. All the American Yearly Meetings of both branches

entered this crusade by sending clothing, seed, farm implements, and teachers. But soon warfare between federal
troops and western Indians became another cause for Quaker
concern. In its annual report of 1867, the Indian committee
of the Hicksite Baltimore Yearly Meeting feared that affairs
had reached the point where the western Indian had but two
alternatives, "swift extermination by the sword and famine,
or preservation by gradual concentration on territorial re-
serves and civilization." Some non-Quakers who had been
abolitionists before the Civil War had come to a similar conclusion out of their own humanitarian concerns. For example,
Lydia Maria Child published in early 1868 *An Appeal for the
Indians,* which called upon congressmen, ministers, missionaries, and Quakers to see that justice was done for that
"much-abused race." As had been the case with abolitionism
before the Civil War, both branches of the Society of Friends
followed an independent but somewhat parallel path to that
of the humanitarian reformers. A few individuals, such as
Alfred Love of Philadelphia and Samuel Tappan of New
York, associated with the new reform effort in Indian affairs
along with non-Quakers like Peter Cooper and Henry Ward
Beecher.[13] Yet the Indian committees of the various Yearly
Meetings did not form a united organization with these humanitarian reformers. Most Quakers kept to their separate
ways.

In 1868, the Baltimore Hicksites' Indian committee reported that it had given "solicitude and care" to the Senecas
on the Cattaraugus and Allegany reservations in western
New York. The committee also said that it kept "vigilant" in
current events among western Indians through personal correspondence and newspaper articles. Members of the committee visited the secretary of the interior and talked with
congressmen who had some supervision over Indian affairs.
These concerned Friends carefully read the reports of the
departments of Interior and War. In addition, Baltimore
joined with the five other Hicksite Yearly Meetings to send
aid such as blankets, clothing, seeds, needles, and $253.50 to
western Indians, especially the Cheyennes and Arapahos.
The committee's report concluded on an anticipatory note:

"Although no opening for active usefulness towards the Indians of that [western] country appears at present to exist, yet the duty certainly rests upon us, and we feel its weight, to be vigilant in observing the course of events, and when an opening presents, no matter where, in which we can see a probability of beneficial labor, to be prepared immediately to enter upon the important engagement."[14]

Apparently all six Hicksite Yearly Meetings felt the "weight" of duty which Friends as a group had inherited through their Peace Testimony and the popular image of William Penn's "Great Treaty." In the fall of 1867, aware of the efforts of the government's Peace Commission toward the Plains Indians, the Hicksite Yearly Meetings of Baltimore, Philadelphia, New York, Genesee, Ohio, and Indiana sent delegates to a conference on Indian concerns in Baltimore. A report that some prominent officials in the federal government had indicated that Friends should be entrusted with the care and "civilization" of the Indians prompted a memorial from the conference which was sent to Washington. In this document, the Hicksite Friends advocated four points for changing Indian policy. The first three recommendations dwelt on justice and protection for all Indians, the righting of old wrongs, the restoration of peace, and the appointment of agents and employees "of high character and strict morality." The fourth point presented a plan for the Indians' advancement:

Assign to the Indian a number of fertile tracts of well-watered country, as *permanent reservations, to be solemnly secured to them forever.* . . . . There, supply them well with seeds, stocks, farming implements, and manufacturing tools, and place among them, on these reservations, suitable, peaceful, enlightened, and conscientious persons to instruct them in agriculture, manufactures, the mechanic arts, and household duties, as well as in all the necessary school learning, and protect them from the intrusion of all others. . . . This is the present condition of the Indians in Western New York . . . who, but comparatively a few years ago, gave no more promise of improvement. . . than do now the various tribes west of the Mississippi River.[15]

In addition to the example of the Senecas, the Hicksite Friends could have mentioned their more extensive work with the freedmen, where Quakers also had emphasized farming and practical education.

Among the Hicksites, eastern Friends, such as Samuel Janney and Benjamin Hallowell of the Baltimore Yearly Meeting, led the way in the organization of cooperative efforts in Indian affairs. In 1867 the Orthodox Iowa Yearly Meeting, under the leadership of Enoch Hoag, Brinton Darlington, and Lawrie Tatum, had urged the formation of a joint Committee on Indian Concerns for all the Orthodox Yearly Meetings. Eventually, the Indiana, Western, and Ohio Yearly Meetings actively cooperated. Baltimore, New York, and New England then showed some interest. The leadership of the Western Orthodox Yearly Meetings came about, in part, because members of the Philadelphia Yearly Meeting could participate only as concerned individuals, not as official delegates. A new wave of theologically determined schisms had started to split up several Orthodox Yearly Meetings in the 1840s. As a way to avoid the perplexing decision of which side to recognize after these divisions, the Philadelphia Yearly Meeting in 1854 withdrew from all official correspondence with the other Yearly Meetings. Without an official delegation from Philadelphia, representatives of the seven Orthodox Yearly Meetings connected with the Committee on Indian Concerns held a conference in Baltimore in January, 1869. In a memorial from this conference to the federal government, the Quaker delegates advocated an independent status for the Office of Indian Affairs instead of a transfer from the Interior to the War Department. As for the future treatment of the Indians themselves, these Friends suggested: "Let the effort be made in good faith to promote their education, their industry, their morality. Invite the assistance of the philanthropic and Christian effort which has been so valuable an aid in the elevation of the freedmen, and render it possible for justice and good example to restore that confidence which has been lost by injustice and cruelty."[16]

The Orthodox delegates went in a body to Washington and presented their case to various officials influential in Indian affairs. On January 25, an audience was held with President-elect Grant. On the following day, a group of Philadelphia Friends led by Thomas Wistar also discussed Indian concerns with Grant. Although both groups were made up of Orthodox Quakers and neither, at least in writing, had suggested the appointment of Quaker Indian agents, the letter which Ely S. Parker wrote on behalf of Grant nearly three weeks later went to both Hicksite and Orthodox leaders. Parker, if not Grant himself, would have remembered the two branches of the Society of Friends because of his Seneca peoples' long association with both. The Quakers may have volunteered their services as Indian agents during their conversations with Grant, or the idea may have occurred to the president-elect and his Seneca aide afterwards.

Whatever the reason, the launching of Grant's "Quaker Policy" caused each major branch of the Society of Friends to begin the first concerted, corporate effort, among nearly all its Yearly Meetings, to benefit the Indians. In effect, the Friends' acceptance of their own legendary reputation in relations with American Indians forced both Hicksite and Orthodox Quakers to accept President Grant's invitation and to start the largest undertaking in Indian affairs in the history of their Society.

The Hicksites and the Northern Superintendency

After the Civil War, the membership of the two major branches of the Society of Friends totaled approximately one hundred twenty thousand to one hundred forty thousand people. Perhaps eighty to ninety thousand of these Quakers were Orthodox, and forty to fifty thousand, Hicksite. Compared to the great national Protestant denominations, such as the Methodists or the Baptists, the Friends were a small sect with its membership concentrated in the northeast and midwest. Over the two centuries of the Society's development, Quakers had retained many of their nonconformist characteristics. "Thee" and "thou" remained standards of Quaker speech; silent worship was still a major part of Quaker meetings; and the Inner Light, social benevolence, and the Peace Testimony remained keynotes of Quaker conduct. Even though the broad-brim hat and black cloth coat of "plain dress" generally had disappeared, Friends still wore what they considered "simple" attire. A few developments, beyond a change in sectarian clothing style, had begun to blur the lines which separated the Quakers from other Protestant groups. Among the Orthodox, revival meetings in Indiana and other midwestern states heralded the eventual establishment of a paid clergy for some Quaker meetings.

Conservative eastern Friends feared that these revivals meant eventual "amalgamation" with the Methodists, and indeed, among the Hicksites, another form of amalgamation, marriage outside their Society, no longer brought automatic disownment.[17] Still, in 1869, for the popular press and for the Quakers themselves, the Society of Friends remained a distinctive religious group which had been offered a role in President Grant's reform of Indian affairs. The Quakers brought to their new assignment a mostly legendary reputation for good will and good works among native Americans, and a program for the education and civilization of the Indians which conformed to the mainstream of humanitarian social benevolence. Many humanitarian reformers of the day, such as those in Peter Cooper's private, nongovernmental United States Indian Commission, had ideas for the "advancement" of the Indians similar to those advocated by the Quakers.

In the Hicksite *Friends' Intelligencer* of October 19, 1867, Samuel M. Janney had written a front-page article on Indian affairs. Consistent with the Peace Testimony, Janney lamented the "waste of life" in the warfare on the Plains, yet he also noted the pressures created by white settlement. Janney recognized that "to restrain the movements and prevent the aggressions of a population like that on our Western frontiers — so eager, so adventurous, so grasping, — is probably beyond the powers of any government." He believed that the Indians must be removed from the path of settlement and placed on lands "adapted for grazing and tillage." They must give up the hunt and adopt "habits of civilized life." Janney also observed: "It is believed by many that they [the Plains Indians] ought to, as soon as possible, abandon their tribal governments, and their mode of holding property in common, that their lands should be divided among the families, and held in fee simple, and a Republican form of government established among them."

Janney wished to strip away the savage, communal life and transform the Indian into a "civilized," independent farmer. Orthodox Friends held views similar to his. A letter in the Orthodox *Friends' Review* of February 13, 1869, claimed that "the public mind seems to be settling in the conviction that, as a measure of humanity the tribal organization of the Indians must be broken up; they must own the land in severalty, perhaps in trust, in order to prevent their parting with it for liquor; and that their children must be educated."

President Grant's invitation gave both branches of the Society of Friends an opportunity to carry out the process of "civilization" among the Indians. The Hicksite Committee on Indian Concerns of the Baltimore Yearly Meeting met on March 6, 1869, to consider Ely Parker's letter concerning Grant's proposal. Members of the committee included Benjamin Hallowell, who had received the letter, and Samuel M. Janney. The committee first considered whether Quakers could accept government appointments. The religion's ban on office holding had faded since the time of the American Revolution, and these Baltimore Friends, no doubt pleased by Grant's special recognition, pressed on to consider what type of Quaker could serve as an Indian agent. The members felt that important qualities included a prayerful heart, faith in the power and wisdom of God, tact in managing people, personal energy and industry, plus knowledge of farming, gardening, the construction of buildings, and the management of schools. Most important, these individuals must have strict integrity and reliability in financial matters. To the embodiment of all these Quakerly qualities, the government would grant a four-year appointment with a modest annual salary of $1,500. Aware that their entire branch of the Society should cooperate in this matter, the Baltimore committee composed a letter to the five other Hicksite Yearly Meetings asking them to send delegates to a meeting in Baltimore on April 17.[18]

Before this April meeting, the Baltimore Friends attempted to settle two important issues raised by Grant's invitation. The first concerned the relationship between the Hicksite effort and the work of the Orthodox Friends. On March 25, the Baltimore Indian committee gathered to compose a letter to leaders of the Orthodox branch. This remarkable document asked if "some measure cannot be devised in the wisdom of truth, by which we may be united as a Band of Brothers, to act together to aid the Government in this important concern." The letter continued:

In all practical concerns of life — in opposition to War, oaths, Slavery, and every species of oppression, injustice, and cruelty; alive to whatever affects the interests and welfare of humanity; — *we feel that we are all, as of one mind, and one heart,* and can thus with eminent propriety and strength, cooperate in the good work of endeavoring to raise our Red Brethren from the depth of misery, wretchedness, and impending extermination, to which they have been so sorrowfully sunk by the mal-administration of our Indian affairs.

Although the Quakers' work as Indian agents would create some examples of informal cooperation between the two branches, no Orthodox Friend responded to the Baltimore letter. One recipient, Thomas Wistar of Philadelphia, entirely ignored the letter in his personal journal.[19]

The second issue confronted by members of the Baltimore committee concerned the question of which Indians, under what organization, were to be overseen by the Hicksite Yearly Meetings. On April 5, 1869, Samuel Janney and Benjamin Hallowell met with President Grant and recommended that an entire superintendency be placed under the control of the Hicksites. Such control, the two men believed, would create greater cooperation and efficiency because Friends would appoint from among Friends the employees, such as farmers, clerks, and teachers, at all the agencies of the superintendency. In addition, the civilizing Christian example of a community of Quakers would be maintained at each agency. Grant approved of this plan and agreed to give the Hicksite Friends administration over the Northern Superintendency, which encompassed the native residents of Nebraska. He gave the Orthodox Friends the Central Superintendency, which embraced the Indians of Kansas and the Indian Territory, with the exception of the Five Civilized Tribes. In the Northern Superintendency, Grant wished to retain Superintendent H. B. Denman, but the Hicksites threatened not to participate unless they controlled the entire administration. After a brief delay, Grant yielded.[20]

Having won full responsibility for the operation of the Northern Superintendency, the convention of Hicksite delegates which met in Baltimore on April 17 considered the names of nominees from the various Yearly Meetings to recommend as Indian agents to the president and the Senate. For the vital office of superintendent, the convention had two excellent but aged leaders to consider, Benjamin Hallowell and Samuel Janney. Hallowell, at age seventy, had already retired from a long and successful career as a teacher and educator. In 1824, after leaving his position at the Quaker's Westown School in Pennsylvania, he had established a boy's school in Alexandria, Virginia, where his first students included Samuel Janney (only two years his junior) and Robert E. Lee. In 1845 Hallowell had helped found the Friends' Central School of Baltimore, and in 1859 he became president of Maryland Agricultural College. As for Samuel Janney, by 1869 he was probably the best scholar of Quakers in America. Beginning in the 1850s, Janney had published a series of Quaker histories and biographies. These books examined, among other topics, the lives of George Fox and William Penn and the causes of the Hicksite schism. A resident of Loudon County in northern Virginia, Janney was also a minister, teacher, and activist. He had written numerous letters and tracts against slavery in the 1820s and 1840s. The denial of the humanity of the black slaves greatly troubled Janney, and he eventually refused to support the colonization of freed slaves in Africa because he believed that slaves, once freed, could become productive citizens in the South. Slavery, Janney argued, debased the blacks and barred their progress toward civilized, Christian behavior. After the Civil War, Janney saw traditional culture as a similar bar to the Indians' progress.

The convention in Baltimore offered the position of superintendent to Samuel Janney. At the advanced age of sixty-eight, Janney hesitated to move himself and his family to Nebraska. After some sleepless nights and with the persuasion of his peers, he accepted the post. As for Benjamin Hallowell, his residency in Montgomery County, Maryland, allowed him to visit government officials in nearby Washington, D.C., as an unofficial intermediary for the Hicksites. He and Samuel Janney maintained a regular correspondence on such government matters as might affect the Hicksite administration of the Northern Superintendency. Later on in the 1870s, Benjamin Rush Roberts, who was also a member of Baltimore Yearly Meeting, seemed to assume this unofficial role of intermediary for Janney's successor, Barclay White.[21]

The approval of Samuel Janney's appointment as superintendent faced no opposition in Washington. Two of the six Hicksite nominees for agents, however, were rejected, because some senators did not wish to remove the present agents. Ely Parker, the new commissioner of Indian Affairs, insisted that all the Nebraska agents be Quakers, and with Grant's support, the Senate soon aquiesced. The convention of Hicksite delegates which had made the original nominations became the prototype for the body which would coordinate the Hicksite effort during the Peace Policy. The Central Executive Committee of the delegates selected by the Indian committees of the six Yearly Meetings (Illinois became the seventh Yearly Meeting in 1875) met at least once a year, most often in Philadelphia. At these meetings, reports were presented from the superintendent, the agents, and from Quaker groups who had visited the Nebraska reservations. Occasionally, petitions to the powers in Washington were written and then delivered to the nation's capital. During the year, the Indian committees of the Yearly Meetings had care and oversight of the various tribes: Philadelphia for the Otos, Iowas, and Sacs and Foxes; New York for the Winnebagos; Baltimore and Illinois for the Pawnees; Ohio and Genesee for the Santee Sioux; and Indiana for the Omahas. The Central Executive Committee normally deferred to these individual Yearly Meetings in the selection of new agents for the Indians under their care.

The Orthodox Friends organized their administration over the Central Superintendency along a similar pattern. The Associated Executive Committee of Friends on Indian Affairs held its annual meetings each August beginning in 1870. Its membership consisted of two representatives from each of the nine Orthodox Yearly Meetings. In order to circumvent the Philadelphia Yearly Meeting's bar on interaction with other meetings, concerned Friends in Philadelphia formed a private Indian Aid Association which then cooperated with the Associated Executive Committee. Midwestern Friends swept the first list of appointments, made at a gathering in Damascus, Ohio, in June, 1869. For superintendent, the Orthodox representatives chose Enoch Hoag, a self-educated Iowa farmer who had worked diligently for emancipation of the slaves and then had supported education programs for the freedmen. Iowa Quakers also gained appointments as agents at four of the eight reservations in the Central Superintendency. The other four appointees included one each from Kansas and Ohio and two from Indiana.

The thirteen native societies of the Central Superintendency numbered about nineteen thousand individuals and presented a diverse range of cultures. There were former eastern woodland groups such as Shawnees and Kickapoos and Plains raiders such as the Kiowas, Comanches, Cheyennes, and Arapahos. These latter tribes presented a stern challenge to the Peace Testimony of their Orthodox Quaker agents, especially during the Red River War of 1874-75. The Friends' agents found that they had to compromise their Society's pacifist ideal and, on occasion, call for federal troops when hostilities threatened. As for the goal of civilization and Christianization, the Orthodox Friends created no miraculous cultural transformations during their decade of service. One veteran of the work with the freedmen soon recognized that such social progress would be slow among the Indians. In a letter from the Sac and Fox agency in the Indian Territory, this Quaker teacher informed the readers of the *Friends' Review:*

I find this Indian civilization is a business in which 'we make haste slowly.' . . . I presume that some of our friends at home, when they learn that our whole year has been spent, and not a single convert to Christianity made, perhaps not a single Indian civilized, will conclude that the time has been wasted, and the funds which they have contributed, thrown away; and will point to our success among the freedmen of the south, contrasting it with that among the Indian tribes. The cases are not at all parallel, and will scarcely admit of any comparison whatever. In the former we found the ground prepared for the seed. There was a hungering and thirsting on the part of the freedmen for knowledge, and for the good news of the glad tidings of a crucified and risen Saviour. While in the latter we have the ground to clear from the rubbish of traditions, superstitions and prejudices, which have been collecting for ages.[22]

For the Quaker group whose efforts shall be the main focus of this study, these words could have served as both an accurate representation of the Hicksites' attitude and as a prophetic statement of their results in the Northern Superintendency. True to the egalitarianism of the Inner Light, the Hicksite administration would view the Indians of Nebraska as spiritual equals and not press for conversion to Quakerism. Instead, a generalized Christian education through Quakerly example and First Day (Sunday) schools tried to nurture the inherent spirituality of the Indians and point them toward the true religious path. In all other ways, however, the Hicksites would view the Indians as cultural inferiors, as wards under their care, who must assimilate the values of the white man in order to survive. Ultimately the Quakers assumed that "civilization" for the Indians did not imply a middle ground of acculturation where some white ways might be accepted. Instead the Quakers expected an eventual cultural conversion through assimilation. For Superintendent Samuel Janney and the first group of Hicksite agents, the key steps in the process of assimilation were the allotment of Indian lands, the establishment of farms, and the education of Indian children. These actions, in turn, meant the attempted breakup of Indian social and political organization.

To begin their efforts at assimilation, Janney and the six Hicksite agents arrived in Nebraska during the early summer of 1869. The new superintendent set up his office in Omaha, Nebraska's major city on the Missouri River. Janney could travel north or south on the river, and he had an east-west transportation link via the Union Pacific Railroad.

After his arrival, Janney found that many influential citizens of the city approved of the new Quaker administration. The *Omaha Daily Herald*, which supported Grant and his Peace Policy, welcomed the Quakers as a positive influence which would secure the "lives and property of our people, uninterrupted progress to our settlements, and safety to the Union Pacific Railway." Janney also discovered that Omaha's business community greatly appreciated the location of his office in their city because of the purchase of treaty goods and other Indian trade items from local merchants and because of the deposit of administrative and treaty funds in local banks.[23]

Janney's chief clerk, Thomas Saunders, a holdover from the previous superintendent, utilized these business connections to acquire a new home for his new employer. Janney despaired of finding a suitable house for his family in Omaha, so Saunders cleverly suggested to local businessmen that if Superintendent Janney could not find housing in Omaha, he would move his office and lodgings across the river to Council Bluffs in Iowa. Several businessmen responded to Saunders's threat by offering to build a suitable, nine-room house, well located in the city, and charge Janney only fifty dollars rent per month. Janney accepted this offer and located not only his family but also his office in the new house. With a government allowance of thirty-five dollars a month for office space, Janney had reduced his personal rent to fifteen dollars.[24]

Thomas Saunders proved to be an important aid to the new superintendent's work in other ways as well during the transition period between administrations. Although Janney desired an all-Quaker staff, he wisely retained Saunders, a non-Quaker, because of the chief clerk's experience and knowledge of the operations of the Northern Superintendency. Some Friends objected because they considered Saunders tainted by his participation in the previous regime. When the chief clerk resigned in September, 1869, because of family matters, Janney assigned his daughter-in-law, Eliza, to fill the position. Other Janney relatives also received appointments in the superintendency. A brother, Asa Janney, a former mill manager from Richmond, Virginia, was agent to the Santee Sioux. Asa, in turn, had three members of his family living at the agency. On the other reservations a similar pattern emerged, with Quaker employees and their families attempting to set a Christian example among Nebraska's Indians through the establishment of Quaker communities. At the Pawnee agency, eight Friends took up jobs ranging from farmer and blacksmith to schoolteacher and engineer. Sixteen white Nebraskans kept less lucrative positions, such as cook, seamstress, and farm laborer. At the Winnebago agency, six of the eleven employees were Quakers, with four Indians and a Canadian blacksmith holding the other jobs. Four of the five employees at the Omaha agency were Friends, as were two of the five at Great Nemaha.[25]

In the duties assigned Quaker men and women at each agency, the Hicksites adhered to social norms for female and male occupations. The men worked as blacksmiths, farmers, and traders, whereas the Quaker women served as schoolteachers, matrons, and, occasionally, clerks. The matrons had the responsibility of instructing Indian girls in the "civilized" female skills of sewing, food preparation, and general housekeeping. The male counterpart to the matron, the agency farmer, demonstrated to the Indian boys, and some men, "progressive" agricultural techniques. Both the matron and the farmer wanted to end female domination of native agriculture and have Indian men work in the fields while Indian women left the fields to work in the home.

Among their own membership, Quakers had always recognized the spiritual equality of the sexes. Indeed, from its earliest years the Society of Friends had allowed men and women to serve as ministers. Although some individual Quakers, such as Lucretia Mott of Philadelphia, advocated women's rights, Friends in general did not extend their ideas of sexual equality much beyond the religious realm. At its first meeting, ten of the twenty-four members of the Central Executive Committee which oversaw the Hicksites' efforts in Indian affairs were women. Yet, neither this committee nor the Indian committees of the various Yearly Meetings ever nominated a female Quaker for a major administrative position, such as agent or superintendent. This fact demonstrated how well Hicksite Friends accepted the predominant social attitudes on the roles of men and women.[26]

Despite this conformity to social norms, Quaker control of jobs in the Indian service eventually created resentment among Nebraska's white citizens. In addition, the Quakers found that many local whites not only desired the removal of the Quakers from the Indian service, but also desired the removal of all the natives from Nebraska. In 1871, despite the testimony of Samuel Janney, both houses of the state legislature passed resolutions calling on the federal government to remove all the Indians. The federal government would not carry out the state's request, but other trials, controversies, and two tribal removals confronted the Friends during their administration of the Nebraska agencies.

In 1869, Friends had just begun their arduous work. The six agents had seven different Indian tribes to administer, each with a distinct history and culture. For example, the two smallest tribes, the Iowas and the Sacs and Foxes of the Missouri, lived on the Great Nemaha reservation in southeastern Nebraska, to which they had moved in 1837. They numbered 228 and 90, respectively, and spoke mutually unintelligible languages. Their agent, Thomas Lightfoot of Pennsylvania, found the Indians "in a pitiable condition. Drunkenness, sloth and disease were decimating their numbers, while the worst class of white men were exploiting them and their misfortunes." Lightfoot's wife, Mary, a former abolitionist, established a mission school, while her husband attempted to promote agriculture and civilized ways. The Iowas proved themselves cooperative; the Sacs and Foxes, recalcitrant.[27]

Two other native societies, the Santee Sioux and Winnebagos, had undergone a series of disastrous removals from their homelands in Minnesota and Wisconsin. They both seemed somewhat receptive to Quaker plans for education, farming, and "civilization," perhaps because of the loss of land and lives which each society had experienced. Samuel Janney's brother served as the agent to the Santees, whereas

Howard White of New Jersey and the Philadelphia Yearly Meeting worked among the Winnebagos. White's father, Barclay, would replace Samuel Janney as superintendent in the fall of 1871.

The three remaining tribes — the Pawnees, the Omahas, and the Otos and Missourias — shall be examined closely in this study. These native societies considered as their homeland much of the region which had become the state of Nebraska. In their case, the establishment of reservations had been not a removal but a reduction of traditional village sites and hunting grounds. By the end of the Quakers' work, two of the three societies, the Pawnees and the Otos, had left Nebraska for the Indian Territory — in part, to escape their Quaker agents. The Omahas, on the other hand, worked out an accommodation to the plans of their Quaker administrators, but not the full assimilation to white ways which the Hicksite Friends desired.

None of the Nebraska natives, including the largest tribe, the warlike Pawnees, had fought against federal troops after the Civil War. But the absence of war with the United States did not mean that these Indians had a peaceful, placid existence. The 1860s and 1870s were a time of desperation for most of the native peoples of the Great Plains. The Nebraska Indians were plagued by the decline of the buffalo, the outbreak of epidemic diseases, the devastations of grasshoppers and droughts, and the depredations of red and white neighbors. Neither the Indians themselves nor their Quaker agents could effectively confront all these disasters. The Quakers' good intentions were not enough; and their program of assimilation, combined with the bungling of some agents, added more problems for the Nebraska natives.

On a nearly day-to-day basis, the record of the Quakers' work among the Nebraska Indians demonstrated that as honest Christian agents they did not abuse the native peoples with whom they worked. But these agents also did not appreciate the Indians' cultural traditions, and they did not understand the full range of problems which confronted these native societies. The Quakers believed in too simple a solution for the "Indian problem" — civilization and Christianization. In short, they hoped to turn the Indians into white men, and they often assumed that the establishment of single-family farms was an important first step. Soon after the Quakers gave up their work in Nebraska, Congress passed the Dawes Act of 1887, which called for the general allotment of all Indian lands. The Quakers applauded this act because it outlined a process for the division of reservations into individual Indian farmsteads. The Dawes Act severely eroded Indian landholdings and did not create the cultural transformation which the Quakers in the 1870s had so ardently advocated. If the Friends had been able to learn from the failures and frustrations which characterized their work among Nebraska's Indians, they could have understood why the Dawes Act would prove to be so misguided. Unfortunately, the Quakers viewed native culture in negative terms and continued to expect that the "right" policy, such as the Dawes Act, would bring on full assimilation. Yet the loss of communal lands would not end cultural identity. The American Indian would not vanish, and the Quakers, who did not learn from their experiences in Nebraska, only proved that they could be false friends to the native peoples of the United States.

CHAPTER TWO

War of
Attrition

When the Quakers arrived among the Pawnees in the late 1860s, they found a people trapped in a desperate war of attrition which had lasted for at least four decades. The major, but by no means the exclusive, enemy in this war was the Teton (or Western) Sioux, especially the Oglalas and Brulés. The expansion of the Teton Sioux across the northern and north-central Plains had been a major development on the Indian side of that frontier throughout the previous half-century.[1] The Pawnees and other village peoples on the Plains, such as the Mandans, Arikaras, Otos, and Omahas, had to confront their Sioux enemy on the buffalo ranges and sometimes on their own village lands. In these battles the Sioux often triumphed through their superior numbers. By the late 1830s, the Pawnees had been driven from the buffalo range along the North Platte, but their hunts along the South Platte and Republican rivers still attracted Sioux war parties. The fact that the Sioux and Pawnees fought over a declining resource, the buffalo, only served to intensify the desperation of their war. In addition, the Sioux recognized that the Pawnees' villages held many other resources, such as horses and food. So war parties also raided the villages while the Pawnees were away on the buffalo hunts. They burned the lodges and looted the cache pits where food was stored. When the Pawnees returned, Sioux raiders would sweep down to steal horses or kill the women as they worked in the fields.

Both the Sioux and the Pawnees viewed warfare and horse stealing as prestigious activities for their young men. Such cultural values prolonged hostilities and may explain why the Sioux seemed especially determined, beyond the acquisition of resources, to destroy the Pawnees. The Sioux had found an obstinate and worthy opponent, which in the serious "game" of warfare among the Plains Indians meant numerous opportunities to take glory, loot, and lives. This same motivation also explains why the Pawnees' young men, as they continued to lose their war with the Teton Sioux, launched horse raids against powerful southern Plains groups like the Cheyennes and Comanches. These forays departed the villages on foot and could be easily trapped on the prairies if discovered. In 1854, an overwhelming force of Cheyennes and Kiowas surrounded such an expedition of 113 Pawnees, who died almost to a man.

Other, nonhuman, enemies, such as the exotic diseases of Europe, plagued the Pawnees as well. In the mid-eighteenth century the four bands of the Pawnees numbered an estimated 20,000 people. Then in 1750, smallpox and measles reduced one of the bands. A second epidemic of the same diseases in the 1790s infected all four bands, and perhaps as many as one-half of the Pawnees died. In the 1830s, just as the war with the Sioux began, smallpox recurred, first in 1832, then again in 1838, when 2,500 Pawnees died. By 1850 a government census counted 6,244 Pawnees. Increased contact with whites made syphilis, dysentery, and tuberculosis nearly endemic. Influenza, smallpox, and cholera caused irregular devastations. In addition, war with the Sioux disrupted the Pawnees' social economy. Buffalo hunts had become an irregular source of food. Agriculture became essential to maintain nutrition, but any crop failures meant starvation. The population figures continued to slide downward. By 1869, there were fewer than 2,400 Pawnees.[2]

In the face of devastation from warfare, disease, and starvation, the Pawnees clung tenaciously to basic cultural patterns. Hunting and horticulture continued in their seasonal cycles, supported by religious rituals. After the last frost in late April or early May, the Pawnee women planted their

corn, squash, pumpkins, beans, and melons in the loose soil
of the river bottoms. The crops were hoed twice in June, after
the ceremony of the Young Mother Corn and before the departure of the summer buffalo hunt. In early September, the
bands returned to their villages for the harvest and the year's
most elaborate series of ceremonies. By mid-November, the
Pawnees had left on the winter hunt, hoping to acquire a
supply of meat before the first severe weather, after which
they moved from creek bottom to creek bottom to camp. In
early March the bands returned to their permanent earthlodge villages in time for the beginning of the ceremonial
year.[3]

The Pawnee earthlodges and the villages to which they
belonged were the linchpin of Pawnee cultural identity. The
lodge and village defined and symbolized the Pawnees' world.
Neither could be easily abandoned despite the desires of the
federal government or Quaker agents. The complex earthlodges testified to the Pawnees' architectural sophistication.
They measured fifty to sixty feet in diameter with a clearance
of twelve feet toward the center. Built around a series of
wooden posts, the lodges were covered with willow webbing,
prairie grass, and a final layer of sod, and were normally
shared by two large families. The earthlodge meant much
more than home, because the Pawnees, a people devoted to
star worship and astronomy, tied their astral cosmology into
the structure of their buildings. Inside the earthlodge the
floor represented the plain of the earth; the roof, the sky
above; and the smoke hole was the zenith, the abode of the
center, Tirawa. The willow-branch webbing of the roof por-
trayed the stars; the grass, clouds; and the layer of sod signified Mother Earth — the dwelling and final resting place
of all.[4]

The Pawnees built the stars not only into their houses
but also into the organization of their villages. For example,
among the Skidi band, until the decline of population caused
considerable consolidation, each village possessed a sacred
star bundle. These bundles demonstrated the direct link between the villages and the astral gods and so religiously
justified the social grouping. Each bundle contained objects

of immense religious significance, such as two ears of maize which represented the mother of the people. The member of any village related his descent to a common ancestor and married only within his community. Priests of each village controlled the bundles for their use in sacred ceremonies. The village chiefs were responsible for the bundles as physical objects, an obligation which paralleled the chiefs' responsibilities for the safety and welfare of the village itself.

The chiefs held effective power mostly at the village level because the Pawnees were not a unified tribe, but a confederation of villages which affiliated with four different bands and two major divisions. One division, the South bands, consisted of the Kitkehaxkis, the Chauis, and the Pitahawiratas. The other division, the Skidi band, had probably established itself in the early sixteenth century along the Loup River in the same general area as the Pawnees' mid-nineteenth-century reservation. The Skidis considered themselves closer relatives to the Arikaras than to the South bands; and the South bands, in turn, considered the Wichitas closer relatives than the Skidis. The South bands moved to the Loup later than the Skidis; but each division claimed a traditional dominance over the other, and neither accepted a fully peaceful confederation until the early 1800s. By the mid-nineteenth-century, in the face of Sioux expansion and other challenges, the Pawnees had become a more unified society with a political structure based on consensus among the chiefs of the four bands.[5]

Pressures from Sioux raiders also may have influenced the Pawnees' relations with the government of the United States. In 1833, Pawnee chiefs met with United States commissioners and signed a treaty which terminated the Pawnees' right to lands south of the Platte, but left this area as a hunting ground for the Pawnees and "other friendly Indians." The four bands gained $4,600 worth of goods given annually for twelve years and $500 worth of agricultural implements for five years. As soon as they settled north of the Platte, they would receive teachers, farmers, blacksmiths, livestock, a corn mill, and twenty-five guns per village. In addition, the United States agreed to appoint an arbiter in any future disputes that the Pawnees had with other native societies.

The promise of guns and arbitration may have convinced the Pawnees that they had acquired an effective ally against the Sioux. The four bands soon learned, however, that such was not the case. Sioux raids continued and, not wishing to move closer to the Oglalas and Brulés, the Pawnees did not fulfill the requirements of the 1833 treaty by relocating their villages north of the Platte. Yet the Pawnees did not turn on their ineffective white allies. Aside from the usual mistaken killings and panicked provocations on the part of settlers and soldiers, the Pawnees never experienced what, even in the vague terminology of Indian-white relations, could be called a "war" with the Americans. For later white groups who traveled the overland trails on their way to Oregon and California, the Pawnees became threatening, though still friendly, figures. Occasionally minor thievery and horse stealing occurred, but more often the Pawnee visits with the wagon trains were in order to fulfill a desire for coffee and sugar by means which the whites saw as begging.[6]

The first whites to establish a mission among the Pawnees were two Presbyterians sent in 1834 by the American Board of Commissioners for Foreign Missions. Eventually those missionaries persuaded some Pawnees in the early 1840s to build two villages on the north side of the Loup Fork twenty miles above its junction with the Platte. In this location, a portion of the bands gained limited exposure to white American methods of education and agriculture under the provisions of the 1833 treaty. But the problems of warfare persisted. In the spring and early summer of 1843, three parties of Pawnees went out to steal horses and lost eighty to ninety men. On June 27 of that year, the Sioux attacked the new village of the South bands. Missionary Samuel Allis described the battle:

It was judged that 300 Sioux attacked the village about six oclk. [*sic*] in the morning (mostly on horses). As soon as the Pawnees were appraised of their being near, they went out about 1½ ms. to meet them but after a short conflict were driven back to their village and the enemy commenced fireing their lodges, & fighting for horses, (that were shut up in their pens.) And as the women and children fled from their lodges that were on fire, the Sioux would shoot them down, many of them consequently fell victims to the savage destroyer. The enemy was so numerous they formed a line from the bluff to the river, which is over a mile. A party would rush from the bluff to the village fight until they got some horses, and then rush back to the bluff with stolen horses, while others were fighting, the *bloody* conflict continued, four or five hours until their horses were all stolen. There were 68 killed, and upwards of 20 wounded, and from 41 lodges, 20 of the largest was burnt, and 200 horses stolen.[7]

After this disaster, the Pawnees became contemptuous of the ineffective protection of the United States government. They showed whites the combs, spoons, forks, pins, and knives given as treaty goods and said, "See what our Great Father sends us to fight the Sioux with." Instead of such items, the Pawnees asked for "plenty of guns" and even cannons. The government did not respond and the Pawnees had little protection during the winter hunt of 1843-44. On the buffalo ranges, the Sioux repeatedly attacked the Skidis and Pitahawiratas. These bands brought back little meat in the spring. Allis's missionary colleague, John Dunbar, believed that of the three thousand Pawnees on the Loup Fork, "one third of them had, neighter [*sic*] a kernel of corn nor a mouthful of meat in the world." In the face of such suffering, Dunbar and Allis continued their efforts until Sioux raids and burnings in the summer of 1846 forced them to abandon their mission. Dunbar concluded: "We have hung round the Pawnees for a long time, and endeavored to do them good. The idea of giving them up is painful to us; but their prospects are dark, and as we turn away from them, we commend them to Him who has the hearts of all men in his hands." In 1847, the Pawnees returned from their summer hunt to find their village on the Loup destroyed by yet another Sioux raid. Twenty-three Pawnees had already died that year in two Sioux attacks. Rather than face more destruction, the four bands left the Loup Fork and moved back south of the Platte.[8]

Abandoned by missionaries and bound by a treaty that no longer gave financial aid and never had given protection, the Pawnees continued to resist what the agent at Council Bluffs called "a war of extermination"carried on by an estimated twenty-five thousand Sioux. In the new villages 150 miles south of the Loup Fork, guards protected the women, not only as they worked in the fields, but also as they traveled to and from them. Visitors reported sentinels posted all through the night on top of the lodges.

The fierce competition over a declining natural resource, the buffaloes, brought other tribes into the war zone on the prairies. In the summer of 1853, one thousand Cheyennes, Sioux, Arapahoes, Comanches, and Kiowas attacked four hundred Potawatomis, Otos, Pawnees, and Iowas. In the fall, the Sioux and the Cheyennes drove the buffaloes from where the Pawnees hunted by setting the grass on fire. That winter, an army captain issued rations to the Pawnees after he found them in a starving condition.

Regardless of their plight, the United States government considered the Pawnees to be settled on lands no longer their own and in a location which might disturb wagon trains on the way to Oregon. For these reasons, the United States attempted to establish a new treaty with the Pawnees. Commissioner James W. Denver accomplished this task on September 24, 1857, when sixteen chiefs, four from each band, signed a document much more extensive than the agreement of twenty-four years before. The "confederate bands of the Pawnees" relinquished "right, title, and interest" to all lands owned or claimed previously by them except for a tract of land on the Loup Fork which measured thirty miles from east to west and fifteen from north to south. In return for accepting this reservation, the U.S. government promised to pay $40,000 per annum for five years, and thereafter, $30,000 as a perpetual annuity, one-half of which would be in goods and articles. Aside from the now familiar promises to establish schools, supply tools, hire laborers, and build a mill, the United States agreed "to protect the Pawnees in the possession of their new homes" and retained the right to build military posts on the reservation.

Once more, the Pawnees undertook the difficult process of removing their villages and reconstructing their massive, complex earthlodges. By 1859, they had settled on their new reservation; but beyond such relocations, the full extent to which white influences or Sioux depredations had modified the patterns of Pawnee life remained difficult to determine. Certainly change had occurred. In one significant area, agriculture, the Pawnee women, on their return to the Loup Fork, began to use upland fields plowed and abandoned by Mormons who had trekked through the area on their way to Utah. These hundreds of acres became the primary area of Pawnee cultivation. Located nearer the villages than the traditional river-bottom plots, the Mormon fields afforded the women better protection from Sioux raiders. The method of cultivation did not change, only the location. However, this upland location exposed the Pawnees' hoe agriculture to the cycles of drought and grasshopper plagues which began on the Central Plains in the mid-1860s.[9] Crop failures joined hunting failures in the Pawnees' spiral of decline.

In addition, the United States' promise of protection proved of little value on the Loup Fork. In the summer of 1860, even with a company of U.S. soldiers on the reservation, the Sioux destroyed sixty Pawnee lodges. Early in 1861, with the Pawnees off in their winter camps, the Sioux virtually occupied the reservation. That fall they burned the prairies to prevent a successful Pawnee hunt, and by January many Pawnees had no food. In 1863, 1864, and 1865 the Pawnees' agent requested one hundred to two hundred rifles for defense against the Sioux. In the past, Washington officials had ignored requests to arm the warlike Pawnees even as a means to protect them from the warlike Sioux. But with the Civil War underway, and the small U.S. army in the west fighting its own losing war against the Teton Sioux and Northern Cheyennes, Gen. S. R. Curtis decided to organize a company of Pawnees under white officers. Armed and paid by the government and under the command of Maj. Frank North, the first group of seventy-seven "Pawnee Scouts" rode beside U.S. troops in 1864. A larger, reorganized group of one hundred scouts enlisted in 1865. They served as outriders for the white troops but also fought as a unit in their own Indian style. Yet what to the Pawnees may have appeared to be a military alliance with the United States did not drive the Sioux from the buffalo ranges. In 1867 the number of Pawnee Scouts was increased to two hundred and given responsibility to guard the route of the Union Pacific Railroad. In gratitude, the railway company allowed the Pawnees to ride free on the line. Soon the Pawnees began to make regular visits to the city of Omaha. After the Quakers arrived, this easy mobility via the railroad was discouraged and Pawnee service in the U.S. Army was suspended.

In August of 1868, the year before the Quakers' arrival, the cycle of calamities among the Pawnees continued. Charles H. Whaley, the Pawnees' sixth agent in eight years, reported that the hunters had found plenty of buffalo on the plains, but Sioux hostilities had prevented any success. The Sioux did not attack directly but instead waited until the Pawnees had scattered in their chase of a herd and then battled small groups or raided the unprotected camp. The Pawnees would rush back to the camp to defend their families and leave to spoil on the plains the buffaloes they had killed. Six Pawnees returned early in August to discover that on the third and fourth of that month, grasshoppers had eaten all their crops except a little corn. Whaley described this disaster: "They [the grasshoppers] covered the entire surface of the land, on some places two or three deep. They were upon all the vines and every blade of corn; upon the houses and upon the trees." In addition, Whaley reported that owing to the Sioux raids, he had difficulty inducing employees "to remain and perform their duties under this constant state of fear and alarm."[10]

Perhaps ignorant of such warnings, in the summer of 1869, Samuel Janney took over the superintendent's office in Omaha, and the Pawnees' new Quaker agent arrived at the reservation on the Loup Fork. The Baltimore Yearly Meeting's Indian committee had selected Jacob Troth, a forty-one-year-old farmer from Fairfax County, Virginia, to serve as the Pawnees' agent. As he took up his duties on June 1, Troth soon discovered that the twenty-four hundred Indians of his agency needed an emergency supplement to their food supply. Gen. Christopher Augur's decision not to allow a summer buffalo hunt, combined with the destruction of much of the Indians' corn by grasshoppers, forced Troth by the beginning of July to request a sixty-day ration of beef and flour at an estimated cost of nearly fourteen thousand dollars.

In previous years, the disruption of the Pawnees' semiannual hunts or the destruction of crops had brought on near starvation. The chiefs complained bitterly of Augur's order. The general defended his action on the grounds that he felt his soldiers, in their pursuit of the Sioux, might not distinguish between friendly and hostile Indians. On July 21, with meat in short supply, Troth allowed a group of Pawnees to travel twenty-three miles north of the reservation to bring back the carcasses of thirty-eight cattle drowned in a river crossing. The next evening news arrived that Augur had rescinded his order with the stipulation that each band must go out with an interpreter and display the U.S. flag. The Pawnees rushed off on the hunt with 240 hundred-pound sacks of flour supplied by their new agent. A visiting delegation of eastern Quakers who witnessed these events concluded that Troth was the "right man in the right place," if his health held up.[11]

The eastern delegation had arrived at the reservation in July. They noticed that out of fear of the Sioux, the Pawnees had crowded their "mud lodges" close together, and that horses remained penned next to the lodges at night. The delegation examined a cache pit and noted that the Pawnees cultivated the Mormon fields but did not occupy the abandoned Mormon buildings. The Quaker visitors optimistically estimated corn production at 80 to 100 bushels an acre. They visited "Big Eagle" of the Skidis (probably Le-cuts-la-sharo, Eagle Chief) and commented on his four wives, all sisters. The mud, manure, green pools of water, and general "filth" of the villages distressed the eastern Friends. The "overcrowded" and poorly ventilated earthlodges shared by twenty-five to fifty people also upset them. Yet the Hicksite delegation did not despair of their Society's new undertaking and strongly recommended that no Indians be removed from Nebraska.

On July 21, Benjamin Hallowell, one of the eastern visitors, spoke through an interpreter to a gathering of three chiefs and fifty warriors:

Brothers, the Great Spirit has filled our hearts with love for you, and induced us to leave our homes, which are a great way off, to come and see you. We are Quakers. Wm. Penn, a Quaker, made a treaty with the Indians to last as long as the sun, moon and stars should give their light. This has never been broken. We live near Washington, and know your Great Father. He loves you and will do what is right for you. He requested me to impress you with the necessity of obeying the laws of the United States, and that he will protect you by these laws, the same as if you were white. There shall be no difference made — they shall be the white man's laws and the Indian's laws. Indians in Ohio and New York States have since 1795 been under the care of Friends. We now take you and other Indians under our care. We know you wish to learn to live like white people. We will help you.[12]

Hallowell had overstated both the history of Quaker-Indian relations and the Pawnees' interest in taking up white ways. However, his statements on Indians and the law had an immediate implication. A month before Hallowell's speech, the body of a white farmer, Edward McMurty, had been found in a pond on an island in the Platte River. The corpse had three or four bullet holes in its left side, a wound on the wrist, and an arrow fifteen inches long embedded in the mouth. With scanty circumstantial evidence, a coroner's jury had decided that some Chauis who had been camping on the island were responsible for the murder. White settlers of the area threatened "undiscriminating warfare on *all* Indians" found off the reservation. The new Quaker agent and superintendent tried to persuade the Pawnee chiefs to deliver the guilty people to the U.S. marshal. Pitalesharo, a chief of the band whose members stood accused, informed the Quaker newcomers, "We do not allow our men to kill white men. We send our warriors out with white men to kill Sioux." In early July, the U.S. marshal came on the reservation to arrest eight Pawnees, not all of them Chauis. These men were in jail in Omaha when Benjamin Hallowell spoke of Quaker friendship toward the Indians and of equal protection under the law. Once more, Pitalesharo had an appropriate response: "I like the Father's talk very much, but I feel very bad about my boys at Omaha. I want you to do what you can for them."[13]

Responding to Pitalesharo's request, the Quakers helped mount an effective defense in what became the murder trial of Yellow Sun, a sixty-year-old Chaui, and three other Pawnees. A skilled lawyer, retained by the Quakers, represented the accused murderers through a series of hearings and trials which shifted from the federal to the state courts. The prosecuting attorney regularly failed to produce important witnesses or necessary records for the state trials. Postponement followed postponement until, in mid-June of 1871, the state district court released the four prisoners on $1,500 bail for each. Four Pawnee chiefs agreed to supply $5,000 of the bond from treaty annuities. The judge required Agent Troth and Superintendent Janney to pay the remaining $1,000. After nearly two years in jail, the Pawnee prisoners returned to the reservation, and the state courts never reopened the case.

The new Quaker administration in the Northern Superintendency had insisted on justice for the Pawnees over the trumped-up charge of murder. Unfortunately, no court of law, or any equivalent forum, could terminate Sioux hostilities toward the Pawnees. In August and September of 1869, a Sioux party of 150 under the leadership of the appropriately named Pawnee Killer came down from the Dakota Territory. They attacked and killed all eleven members of a white survey expedition on the Republican River. Then on September 21 the Sioux raided the Pawnee reservation, killed one herder within a mile of the agency buildings, and stole many horses. Some Pawnees joined the U.S. troops that pursued Pawnee Killer's band, but they recovered nothing.

Neither Jacob Troth nor Samuel Janney could control the actions of Sioux raiders, but they thought they could control all belligerent activities by the Pawnees. Rather naively, they hoped that if one side stopped hostilities, then the other could be persuaded to stop. A distinctly pacifist outlook motivated the two Quakers' efforts at a three-part program to (1) end Pawnee horse stealing; (2) dismantle the Pawnee Scouts; and (3) begin peace negotiations with the Oglalas and Brulés. These policies angered the Pawnees, disturbed some whites, and had no effect on the Sioux.

In fact, horse stealing by the Pawnees involved more than their war with the Sioux, because the Pawnees tended to steal their horses from Southern Plains tribes. The Sioux then stole the Pawnees' horses and occasionally the Pawnees tried to reacquire horses from the Sioux. If the Sioux stopped their raids, then the Pawnees might not need to carry out horse raids to the south; but Troth and Janney wanted the Pawnees to stop first, which meant a sharp decline in the Pawnee horse herds if the Sioux continued their raids. With no desire to give up the prestige and prosperity associated with their horses, the Pawnees chose to either ignore or mislead their Quaker administrators.

In January of 1870, two groups of Pawnees returned with over a hundred horses they had seized while on a visit to the Indian Territory. Superintendent Janney already had instructed Agent Troth to return the stolen horses that belonged to white settlers or to Indians at peace with the United States. The Pawnees resisted Troth's insistence that the horses be returned. He selected six men whom he considered the principals in the southern raids and had them imprisoned by General Augur at the Omaha barracks. Augur seemed reluctant to comply and kept his prisoners for less than two weeks. The Pawnees, after all, were allies of his white troops. Augur said the stolen horses might belong to the Southern Cheyennes and Arapahos. Some Pawnees said the Comanches had owned them. Troth wrote to the Orthodox Quaker agents in the Central Superintendency, but no Indians claimed the horses. Yet Troth insisted that the stolen herd be returned to Fort Harker (Kansas) where the unknown rightful owners could claim them. Pawnee leaders protested this decision and informed Troth that many of the contraband ponies had died over the winter or had been stolen by the Sioux. As a compromise, the Quaker agent allowed the Pawnees to return a reduced number, and the Pawnees no doubt culled the ponies they could afford to give up. They delivered the motley herd to Fort Harker that April.

Troth and Janney had attempted to countermand Pawnee horse raids, but they could not stop Sioux depredations. On May 19, 1870, a Sioux party killed a Pawnee woman, wounded a Pawnee man in the leg, and made off with many horses. The next day, in council with their agent, the Pawnees claimed that if the government would not require the Sioux to return the horses, as the Pawnees had done at Fort Harker, then the Pawnees would take their own revenge. Troth said he could not allow the Pawnees to retaliate, but he did accept a proposal that chiefs of each tribe hold a peace conference in Washington, D.C. Janney approved of this peace initiative. On June 22 the Quaker superintendent met with Red Cloud in Omaha. The Oglala chief and his party had just visited Washington and were returning home on the railroad. In response to Janney's suggestion of a peace treaty, Red Cloud claimed that the Sioux and Pawnees had once been at peace, but the Pawnees had turned against the Sioux, joined the white soldiers, and killed many of the best Sioux men. He could not stop now and make a treaty which in any event would require consulting with his people. After Red Cloud's rejection, Janney tried to contact Spotted Tail of the Brulés, but the agent at Whetstone replied that the Sioux in his area did not recognize one "chief." The agent promised to do all he could to help the Quakers' plan, but doubted a peace treaty would effectively restrain the Sioux.[14]

Although their peace overtures had failed, the Quakers still insisted on the disbanding of the Pawnee Scouts. In September of 1869, Janney had first complained about the "expediency of employing the Pawnees" in military service. His letter came after the agent at Whetstone had warned that a party of forty or fifty Sioux had started south for vengeance because of the Pawnees' role in the recent army campaign. By February of 1870, Janney and Troth had added new arguments against Major North's enlistment of Pawnees. The two Quakers believed that the scouts associated with bad whites, learned to drink and gamble, and thus became the least "tractable" of all the Pawnees. They claimed that the Pawnee chiefs wanted their young men to stay at home and till the soil; but instead, the scouts kept up the longstanding feud between the Sioux and the Pawnees. According to the Quakers, "respectable" white neighbors agreed with these views, but no petition of Indian or white origin accompanied the correspondence. Commissioner Parker was willing to cooperate in this part of the Quakers' plan for peace. By June of 1870, the War Department, at the request of the Office of Indian Affairs, had prohibited the enlistment of Pawnees "because of bad effects upon them."[15]

General Augur did not agree. He protested to Gen. John

Pope that eight to ten Pawnee guides were needed for his summer operations on the Kansas plains. The scouts, he claimed, were the only people available who knew the country. The president of the Union Pacific Railroad also complained. The Pawnee Scouts protected his rail line so well that he had even hired some as private guards along the road. The railroad president also denounced the Quakers' "Utopian notions of philanthropy" which he said had ended a program that deterred warfare and allowed some Pawnees to earn money for their families.

The absence of the Pawnee Scouts in the summer of 1870 did not cripple the Union Pacific, but it did not stop the Sioux either. On June 22, near the Pawnee village, federal troops joined by some of the Pawnee men briefly surrounded a Sioux party, killed one warrior, but also killed one Pawnee and wounded three others in the cross fire. Ironically, a military action with Pawnee support, equivalent to the use of the scouts, had prevented a successful Sioux raid. On the morning of October 6, the Sioux attacked again. This time two women died and one man suffered three gunshot wounds. Again the Pawnees joined the soldiers in pursuit. At a council after this raid, Janney heard denunciations of the Brulés and Oglalas. The chiefs asked why the Sioux were not sent to jail and forced to return stolen horses as had happened to the Pawnees. In a grand anger, they threatened to join other Indians in a war of extermination against the Sioux. Still wanting to avoid bloodshed, Janney again recommended that the two native peoples establish a treaty.

Renewed efforts to begin peace negotiations during the winter of 1870/71 again proved futile. The Santee Sioux offered their reservation as a site for the peace conference, but the Oglalas and Brulés did not respond. That summer two Pawnee schoolboys died in a June raid, and Spotted Tail's Brulés bragged to their agent that they had done the deed. Janney demanded that the Sioux murderers be arrested and tried, but nothing happened. In the meantime, the Pawnees continued their raids to the south. In his annual report, written for the Indian Bureau in early September of 1871, Troth optimistically stated: "The practice of sending out war parties for plunder and scalps has been abandoned by the Pawnees, and I require them to return all property . . . belonging to other parties." A month later Troth saw the folly of his statement. A large Pawnee party returned from the south and reported that the Cheyennes had killed two of its members. Troth explained to his superintendent that he had often approved visits by small groups to the Indian Territory when they expressed an interest in establishing friendships with old enemies. Apparently, the armed party which fought the Cheyennes had left for unfriendly purposes, but Troth hesitated to claim he had been intentionally deceived.[16]

By the summer of 1871, Jacob Troth and Samuel Janney had made no progress in establishing a peaceful existence for the Pawnees. With warfare and raiding still part of the Pawnees' daily lives, the Quaker plan to transform Pawnee society into a farm economy also did not progress. In these efforts the overbearing attitude exhibited in the Quakers' peace initiatives had to give way to compromise between the Quaker administrators and the Pawnee chiefs. Yet the threat of Sioux attacks remained a factor even in these negotiations. For example, the Pawnees would not agree to allot their lands and settle on individual farms. Superintendent Janney reported that the Pawnee chiefs opposed division of the land "under an apprehension that it would scatter them over a large area & expose them to danger from the depredations of the Sioux." Janney suggested, and Troth accepted, a plan of four villages, one for each band, with farms laid out around them. In December, Troth reported that the Skidis had selected their land and wanted to apply their annuities toward farming.

Although the Skidis would consistently express the most interest in taking up farming, statements by the leaders of the four bands showed that Sioux aggression influenced their views. In February of 1871, the chiefs anxiously asked for peace with Spotted Tail's Brulés so they could build houses and start farms. Such statements stimulated Quaker efforts towards peace, but produced few Pawnee farmers. Discussion rather than ground breakings continued into May, when the chiefs' council rejected allotment in severalty and insisted that the bands regulate the division of the lands. Apparently, the bands wished not only to control the proposed new villages, but also the surrounding farmland. Although Janney and Troth saw social progress in the chiefs' plan, it really amounted to a demand for the political status quo. Meanwhile, the chiefs regularly requested guns for their warriors in order to better defend themselves from the Sioux. Their pacifist Quaker administrators chose to ignore these requests.[17]

The recommendations of the Pawnee chiefs' council which were not ignored apparently involved trade-offs with the Quakers. The chiefs controlled distribution of annuity goods and the application of annuity funds acquired in the treaty of 1857. With the decline in hunting and agriculture, this power became a significant demonstration of the chiefs' hereditary leadership, but it also demonstrated their increased dependence on the federal government to maintain that leadership. In two years, however, Janney and Troth asked the council for only $2,000 in annuity funds to be used to help convert the agency mill from steam to water power. Troth had estimated the full cost of this project at $3,750. The chiefs approved the lesser request, perhaps unaware that Janney and Troth had discussed selling part of the reservation to make up the full cost.

Finally, in July and September of 1871, the two Quakers participated in major adjustments of the distribution of the Pawnees' annuity goods and funds. Disease had swept through the Pawnees in June, forcing the agency school to close so the teachers could attend to the sick. For two years the agency had relied on a doctor from nearby Columbus who charged outrageous rates. At Troth's urging, the Baltimore Indian committee had rushed through Washington channels Albert Thompson's nomination as agency physician. In July, the chiefs' council approved the application of $1,000 for medicines out of the annuity funds in order to support the new doctor's work. The council also resolved to spend $3,000 for payment of services rendered to the sixteen council chiefs, four from each band, as well as to six soldiers from each band. These twenty-four soldiers, or braves, did not sign council resolutions but held the right to speak in council. Janney complained to Commissioner Parker that the chiefs already distributed the annuity goods unfairly, ignoring the needs of poor and aged women. He said he would consent to the $3,000 payoff only if he, as superintendent, could distribute the treaty goods. The Pawnee chiefs apparently consented to this arrangement, and at the next council, in late September, they approved another Quaker plan to apply $3,000 toward the water power project, a survey of their lands, and the purchase of mowing machines and agricultural implements.[18] In two councils the chiefs and the Quakers had traded off for their various interests $7,000 out of the $15,000 annuity.

A concern for traditional responsibilities, rather than greed, as implied by the Quakers, probably motivated the demand of the chiefs and braves for $3,000 in annual income. Quaker officials and most white observers never fully understood the chief's role in Pawnee society. A traditional Pawnee chief served by consensus. He did not command by the implied violence of power. At the village level chiefs functioned as administrative officials. Their influence came from being, in effect, the head of an extended family. The village community centered on the chiefs with the subordinate braves, or soldiers, carrying out active, somewhat executive, roles. Wealth supported the hospitality and charity expected of these village leaders, but in each of the four bands the position of chief or brave was hereditary in certain families. To be a chief, however, required a proper personality. These men were expected to be patient, quiet, understanding, and dignified. They tended to be neither violent nor aggressive, and if they participated in battles, they usually planned and directed actions instead of plunging into the fight. A chief's main efforts — in harmony with the band's priests — went toward the maintenance of the Pawnee village life and its yearly cycle of seed-time, hunt, and harvest. Chiefs, above all, were defenders of the status quo.[19]

Quaker officials never recognized the parallels between Pawnee chiefs and Quaker leaders. For example, no head chief for all four bands of the Pawnees existed, just as no paramount leader existed in either branch of the Society of Friends. Traditional Friends, especially in Janney's Hicksite branch, rejected "hireling ministers." Each local Quaker meeting appointed clerks from its membership, just as each band and village had its chiefs. In making decisions elders and "weighty" Friends could have great influence, but the goal was the consensus of the meeting under the guidance of a presiding clerk. Coordinated actions by local meetings, as in a Yearly Meeting or in various committees, also operated through consensus — not unlike the Pawnee chiefs' council. In addition, the personality traits which marked a Pawnee chief would have been appreciated in a Quaker leader, especially the emphasis on quiet patience and the avoidance of personal violence.

After two years and four months as superintendent, Samuel Janney retired from his work in the fall of 1871. Janney had written at length before Grant's election about what policies the government should establish for the Indians. In his brief time as superintendent, this Hicksite leader had discovered that, at least in the case of the Pawnees, effective results did not follow from written ideals. Janney's replacement, Barclay White, a member of the Philadelphia Yearly Meeting's Indian committee, took up his duties immediately. White remained superintendent until the abolition of the position in 1876. A diligent and thorough administrator, White left an extensive record of his efforts among the Indians of Nebraska. The Pawnees would provide distinct frustrations for White, as they had for Janney.

In October of 1871, the new superintendent made his first visit to the Pawnee village, which he felt resembled from a distance "a cluster of hay stacks so old that their tops have settled down." At White's first council, the chiefs asked for 3,000 grains of corn, so they could see how they would divide up their $3,000. Pitalesharo showed the new Ar-tip-it ("grandfather") a medal he had received from President Buchanan. He then requested a medal from President Grant, because he approved of Grant's generosity. When asked about visits to friendly tribes in the Indian Territory, White said the government would protect the Pawnees if they carried a proper pass for the visit. At the mention of government protection, "a derisive laugh passed around the council." The chiefs sarcastically asked about protection from the Sioux and the arrest of those who had recently killed the Pawnee students. White could only say that he would write to Washington. "My situation was embarrassing," he reported. The chiefs also complained that they should distribute the annuity goods, but White insisted that if the chiefs and soldiers were to continue to receive $3,000 then he would personally oversee the distribution, as Superintendent Janney had done. White recalled that the old women expressed delight over the generous annuity portions they received at his first visit.[20]

For Barclay White, the distribution of treaty annuities became a standardized event which he described in his private journal. On his arrival at the Pawnee agency, the chiefs normally made a social call and inquired as to the welfare of the other native peoples under his supervision. A corps of employees, "a portion of whom are always Indians," would unpack the annuity goods, compare the contents with invoices, and then store them for inspection. Another group completed the quadruplicate copies of payrolls for the annuity funds. One or more councils held in the agency building preceded and sometimes followed the annuity payments. The council determined the day and place of payment. In the preliminary council meeting, the superintendent made some short remarks which Baptiste Bayhylle, a Skidi mixed-blood and agency translator, would then render into Pawnee. The pause for translation allowed White to consider his words and speak concisely. The primary chiefs of each band then made speeches in regular order. By tradition, the Chauis' leading chief, Pitalesharo (literally "chief of men"), spoke first, with animation and many gestures. Bayhylle again translated. Tirawahut-lasharo, Sky Chief of the Kitkehaxkis, often forcefully spoke in opposition to proposals of the Quakers. The third orator, Le-cuts-la-sharo, Eagle Chief of the Skidis, favored some Quaker programs but was not an eloquent speaker. "It was his practice to frequently visit the school house and watch with intensive interest the progress of a favorite son in acquiring the white man's education."

The aged chief of the Pitahawiratas, Ter-re-kaw-wah, spoke last before the three subordinate chiefs and the six soldiers from each band had the right to remark. A respectful orderliness characterized most of these assemblies.[21]

Barclay White and other observers often identified Pitalesharo as the primary chief of all the Pawnees. No such position existed. The South bands recognized a primary chief who served until death. The position rotated among the three bands and did not apply to the Skidis.[22] Extra prestige, but no paramount power, existed for this special chief because of the emphasis on consensus in councils. The Quakers' (and others') mistaken identification of a paramount chief caused them to give inappropriate weight to Pitalesharo's words and showed that white officials ignored the division between the Skidis and the South bands.

Nonetheless, as primary chief of the South bands, Pitalesharo, at nearly fifty years of age, still had an imposing physical presence. He stood over six feet in height, but his features were marred by a deeply pit-marked face — a reminder of the smallpox epidemic of 1838.[23] The error over his exact political position among the Pawnees arose in part out of the tradition of his speaking first to white officials at council meetings. In addition, Pitalesharo's mark consistently appeared at the top of all documents signed by the council. The marks of the other fifteen chiefs appeared below his with their names written out on the left side.

How Pitalesharo gained his position as first speaker and first signer is unclear, but Baptiste Bayhylle, the Pawnee agency interpreter, may have played an important role. Bayhylle, of mixed Spanish, French, and Skidi descent, had been admitted to the chiefs' council in the mid-1860s, after he became official interpreter at the agency. His story exemplified the influence and power which interpreters could acquire because of the essential role they often played in Indian-white relations. Although not a hereditary chief, Bayhylle was the uncle of the Skidi leader Lone Chief and as the only English-speaking member gave advice to the council, especially before a meeting with the agent. Bayhylle could suggest what the chiefs should say and in what order they should speak. He also witnessed and placed his mark on all council documents. Whether Bayhylle translated Pitalesharo's words to make him appear paramount or just allowed white listeners to draw their own conclusions remains a mystery. Quaker officials in the 1870s were no exception to the white rule of finding paramount chiefs whether they existed or not. Euro-Americans regularly sought out native American "kings," "sachems," and such. This illusion of native power eased negotiations, and may explain why Barclay White harbored his ignorance about Pitalesharo. Of this Euro-American predilection, Baptiste Bayhylle was well informed. In 1878, he would ask to be certified in writing by the commissioner of Indian affairs and the secretary of the interior as "Head Chief of the Pawnee Tribe of Indians."[24]

After hearing the chiefs' speeches and their translation, Barclay White could then distribute the treaty supplies and funds to the four bands. This payment produced a colorful, expressive event which visiting artists often sketched. The distribution normally started at nine in the morning and could take more than one day. The Pawnees arrived in what White considered "holiday" attire of scarlet, green gray, or white blankets. They came on foot, in farm wagons, or on horseback. The chiefs inspected the goods and signed in quadruplicate receipts which the agent, interpreter, and two army officers then certified. If military officers could not attend, then two citizens of the state served as witnesses. The annuity goods included shoes, hats, coats, vests, hardware items, and a variety of textiles (blankets, sheets, shawls, cotton flannel and woolen shirts, drilling thread, ticking, and calicoes). Distribution started with Pitalesharo and progressed through the chiefs of each band and the head of each family. Chiefs received the same share in goods and monies as the youngest of the Pawnees, even if the latter were only a day-old baby. Any fractional remainder was divided among the chiefs. White also noted that "not unfrequently a favorite child of tender years is enrolled as the head of a family of adults and receives their shares. If this is performed in a business-like manner the act is generally greeted with applause by the admiring relatives."[25]

1. *Barclay White on the front porch of the Northern Superintendency's office in Omaha, Nebraska. This nine-room building provided offices for the superintendent and lodging for his family. It was built in 1869 for Samuel M. Janney by a group of Omaha businessmen who feared that the superintendent's office might be moved to Council Bluffs, Iowa. The woman on the front porch is not identified. (Journal of Barclay White, 1:282. Courtesy of the Friends Historical Library, Swarthmore.)*

2

3

2. *Yellow Sun and three Pawnee prisoners after their release in 1871. These four Indians had first been tried for the murder of Edward McMurty in 1869. The photograph was probably made in a studio in Omaha in mid-June 1871. Back row left to right: Champion S. Chase, lawyer for the defense retained by the Quakers; Baptiste Bayhylle, interpreter and Skidi mixed-blood; Barclay White, superintendent; Henry M. Allis, white interpreter; Jacob M. Troth, agent. Front row left to right: Tie-ta-sha-cod-dic, Strikes Chief of Kitkehaxkis; Horse Driver, a Kitkehaxki and former prisoner; Yellow Sun, a Chaui and former prisoner; Little Wolf, a Pitahawirata and former prisoner; Blue Hawk, a Chaui and former prisoner; Tirawahut-lasharo, Sky Chief of Kitkehaxkis. (Journal of Barclay White, 1:301. Courtesy of the Friends Historical Library, Swarthmore.)*

4

3. *Pawnee earthlodge village, Genoa, Nebraska, 1875. In the background is the government's manual labor school. For the first five months of 1875, only the assimilationist faction of the Skidis remained on the Nebraska reservation. (Courtesy of the Nebraska State Historical Society.)*

4. *Ter-re-kaw-wah. A chief of the Pitahawiratas, he was a traditionalist who advocated removal to the Indian Territory. He appears to have been a good friend of the trader and former Presbyterian missionary Lester Platt. (Journal of Barclay White, 2:30. Courtesy of the Friends Historical Library, Swarthmore College.)*

5. *Le-cuts-la-sharo, Eagle Chief of the Skidis. The primary leader of the Skidis, he stayed behind in Nebraska until the assimilationist Skidis removed to the Indian Territory in June of 1875. (Courtesy of the Nebraska State Historical Society.)*

6. *La-ru-chuk-are-shar, Sun Chief of the Chauis. The nephew of Pitalesharo, he continued to be a leader among the South Bands in the Indian Territory. (Photograph by W. H. Jackson. Courtesy of the Nebraska State Historical Society.)*

7. *Pitalesharo, Man Chief of the Chauis. The primary chief of the South Bands, he held this position until his mysterious death in 1874 before the Pawnees' removal. The photography was taken in 1868 when Pitalesharo was in his late forties. He was over six feet tall, approximately the same height as well as about the same age as Barclay White, the Quaker superintendent. (Photograph by W. H. Jackson. Courtesy of the Nebraska State Historical Society.)*

8. *Little Pipe, traditionalist Oto chief and one leader of the Coyote faction. In the fall of 1873, he was part of the Oto delegation that met in Washington, D.C., with Commissioner of Indian Affairs Edward P. Smith. (Courtesy of the Nebraska State Historical Society.)*

9 **9.** *Arkeketah (or Stand-by).
Another leader among the Coyotes,
he also went to Washington in 1873
to talk to Commissioner Smith.
(Courtesy of the Nebraska State
Historical Society.)*

10. *Medicine Horse. He appears to
have been the primary leader
among the Coyotes. In May of 1881,
he and Little Pipe led this Oto
faction to the Indian Territory
without official government
approval. (Courtesy of the
Smithsonian Institution.)*

11. *Sketch of Oto village and
government agency buildings in
Nebraska. Both earthlodges and
bark lodges are depicted. This is
one panel of a larger undated
drawing done by Albert Green, the
first Quaker agent to the Otos.
(Courtesy of the Nebraska State
Historical Society.)*

10 **12.** *Omaha leaders, circa 1866. Right
to left: Louis Saunsousi, No Knife
(Ma ha ninga), and Joseph La
Flesche. La Flesche had been a
principal chief on the Council of
Seven Chiefs since 1853. He helped
establish the "village of the 'make
believe' white men" and organized
what later became the "young
men's party." By the mid-1860s,
"paper chiefs" appointed by the
agent began to replace the Council
of Seven as the effective governing
body of the tribe. No Knife became
a "paper chief"; La Flesche did
not. Louis Saunsousi served as an
official government interpreter.
Like La Flesche, he was the son of
a French trader and an Omaha
woman. (Courtesy of the Nebraska
State Historical Society.)*

11

12

13. *Omaha Indian village, 1871. The few frame houses are of modest size. Later Quaker observers noted* *the persistent use of tipis by the Omahas. (Courtesy of the Nebraska State Historical Society.)*

Despite such touching scenes, White viewed the annuity payments as a program which retarded Pawnee progress toward civilization. "One Pawnee after receiving his annuity money showed me with pride his cultivated finger nail which projected unbroken about two inches beyond the end of his finger, he could not have offered me stronger evidence of his *laziness*."[26] Superintendent White, in concert with his predecessor, Samuel Janney, and other eastern Friends, believed that the cure for such problems would come through effective education and the establishment of male agriculture. First, however, the image of the "savage" should be erased.

As White would later explain to a Philadelphia Quaker, "I have no unity with exhibitions of Indians as Indians." He regularly forbade the use of Pawnees in "Wild West" shows, whether directed by Sidney Barnett of Niagara Falls or by William F. Cody, the famous "Buffalo Bill." Such shows, White argued, supported the "savage" traditions of the Pawnees, and placed them in the hands of "un-Christian" sorts. A personal visit by Buffalo Bill to White's Omaha office in November of 1871 had apparently left no positive impression on the Quaker superintendent.[27]

Barclay White desired that Nebraska's Indians be presented in a favorable light. For this reason, he objected to the Union Pacific's practice of allowing Pawnees to ride on freight cars without charge in repayment for protection previously given the railroad by the Pawnee Scouts. These free rides allowed "vagrant members of the tribe" to "hang around the depots" and "produce an impression upon travelers . . . which is injurious to the character and standing of the whole Indian race." White preferred images of Indian "progress" and so suggested that twelve full-blooded schoolchildren from among the Indians in his Northern Superintendency be set up in a classroom at the Philadelphia Centennial Exposition in 1876. He had hoped to show that Indian children could be as neat, clean, and receptive to learning as whites of similar ages, but his suggestion was not followed.[28]

Some Pawnee children might welcome new ideas in the classroom, but the chiefs of the four bands were not so receptive to white concepts in their council meetings. On June 8, 1872, Agent Troth confronted this obstinate attitude when he tried to discuss the concept of God and the observance of the Sabbath. Troth told the assembled chiefs: "I thought this would be a good time to read and explain about God — You believe in the same God as we do. he is above all — our happiness and comfort depends on him — we ought all of us try and learn to do what pleases him." The Pawnees did indeed believe in one god, Tirawa, whom they saw as the source of both the four bands' prosperity and the chiefs' own prestige. With some irony and apparent pride, the Pawnee leaders tried to inform Agent Troth about their religious beliefs. Pitalesharo responded first to Troth's words: "What you say is good. we all know that God is governor of all. It is an old story with us that there used to be a very large race of persons that did not mind God[,] who to show them that he was ruler drowned them. We know it rest with God who makes us poor or rich."[29]

Tirawahut-lasharo (Sky Chief of the Kitkehaxkis) then addressed Troth and elaborated on his fellow chief's remarks: "We all understand that you are telling us the truth. God made us Indians and gave us these grounds to live on. As soon as our children get old enough to understand their Father tells them of God." Tirawahut-lasharo talked of feasts and ceremonies which pleased Tirawa. He emphasized: "I like this way [of life] and dont [*sic*] want to lose it. . . . Our old men are dead and we dont know God's day but it seems you must know the day. for that reason the white men are not poor."

Ter-re-kaw-wah, the elderly traditionalist of the Pita-hawiratas, thought: "It is a good thing to keep Sunday" because if God (Tirawa) "likes a person he makes him live a long while and be rich." But Ter-re-kaw-wah warned that his people would still hold their own religious ceremonies even if they occurred on "the day of Rest." Le-cuts-la-sharo (Eagle Chief of the Skidis) agreed: "We still have things that God gave us and want to keep them." Yet, this cooperative Skidi leader concluded, "it is good to have a certain day to rest. You know better than we for you have writings and we have none so [we] forget."

Pitalesharo, perhaps upset by Eagle Chief's conciliatory tone, remarked to the Quaker agent: "I have never forgotten what the old chiefs told me. We believe in God. to keep always those things he gave us. I am doing what we always do before we go on a Hunt. We are done talking about God I suppose." Relieved by the end of the religious discussion, Tirawahutlasharo nonetheless desired some practical results from the council. He informed Troth: "Now we are done talking about God — we would like you to hurry up the Annuity money or or [*sic*] something else before we go on the Hunt."

By the summer of 1872, after three years of Quaker supervision, the Pawnees had shown that they were not receptive to white concepts of progress or to Quaker ideas of religion. In the face of Sioux depredations, virulent diseases, and intermittent starvation, the chiefs of the four bands struggled to maintain consensus, unity, and cultural survival. Quaker observers, who never appreciated the traditional role of the chiefs, kept insisting that proper white administration could produce the desired social transformation. To this end, in June of 1872, two men and two women from Baltimore's Committee on the Indian Concern visited the reservation and decided that Jacob Troth and the matron of the agency's Manuel Labor School, Elvira Platt, should be replaced. The Baltimore committee told the secretary of the interior that Elvira Platt had been dismissed because she was "not efficient" and her treatment of other teachers and employees did not promote "harmony." The committee's letter neglected the significant fact that Platt was not a Quaker, but it did mention that female pupils between the ages of fourteen and sixteen had become sexually active. Such a development was normal in Pawnee eyes but shocked the Quakers. The committee claimed that Platt had allowed this "immorality" to continue "unchecked." This inattention could have proved "ruinous" to the school. No equivalent, full explanation of fellow Quaker Troth's removal came to Washington, but nonetheless the Baltimore Friends pressed ahead with his replacement. They examined thirteen applications for the position of agent and chose William Burgess, who for fourteen years had served as headmaster of the Millville (Pennsylvania) High School. After his approval by the U.S. Senate, Burgess appointed his wife, Mary, to replace Elvira Platt.[30]

These dismissals and replacements had little effect on the Pawnees, but they created a strong response among the whites who lived near the reservation. Their complaints about the Baltimore committee's decision, plus a petition against the new Hicksite agent, produced a detailed government investigation of the Pawnee agency. This investigation revealed little about the Pawnees and their condition, but uncovered a great deal about the relationship between the Nebraska settlers and the Quakers. Each side of this relationship held distinctly different views about the purpose behind the operation of an Indian agency. As one might expect, the Quakers wanted the agency to benefit the Pawnees; the settlers wanted to benefit themselves.

For neighboring farmers, the benefits of the Pawnee agency were, at least, threefold. First, merchants and farmers could sell stock, seed, finished lumber, implements, and other goods to the agency. Superintendent Janney and Commissioner Ely Parker had allowed local, open-market purchases by the Winnebago and Pawnee agents since early 1871. These small-scale purchases came to local interests more readily than the larger annual treaty purchases, which often went to huge eastern suppliers. Second, many farmers in the surrounding counties relied on the agency's mill to grind their grain, and they often complained when the mill was not in operation. Third, these farmers had also come to view the Pawnee reservation as a source of free timber and, occasionally, free land. A new agent might adversely affect all of these benefits.

In August of 1872, President Grant and Barclay White received a series of five petitions protesting the Baltimore Indian committee's decision to remove Agent Troth. The wording on some of the petitions duplicated that on others. All agreed that Troth was "honest, energetic, capable and efficient," and that he worked for the best interests of the Pawnees and the U.S. government. The petition from Platte County was signed by 194 people; 92 signatures from Hall County defended the agent; and 73 residents of Boone and

Madison counties agreed. The petitions called Troth's administration a success, and concluded that the effort to remove him was "solely of a personal nature."[31]

Officials in Washington did not respond to these five petitions, but seven months later, when still another petition with only twenty-seven signatures arrived, the secretary of the interior responded promptly. This new petition, dated March 29, 1873, called for the removal of Agent William Burgess and the abolition of the Quaker Policy at the Pawnee agency. These petitioners, who were from Platte County, bluntly claimed that the Pawnee agency existed for the economic benefit of Quaker interlopers and not for the betterment of the Pawnees or the enrichment of neighboring Nebraskans. They announced, "To the Quakers belong the Spoils," and then proceeded to specify their charges. Thousands of dollars appropriated by the government had been squandered on a flour mill, milldam, and race, whereas all daily needs of flour could be purchased in Columbus, Nebraska — twenty miles away. Additional thousands had been wasted on agricultural machinery and implements which became "the common property of all Quakers in Platte County" and were either broken or destroyed in prairie fires. Farm wagons purchased for the Indians had been bought by Quaker employees for nominal sums and sold to settlers for private gain. The contract for the weekly beef supply at the Manual Labor School went to "a brother Quaker" with no advertisements as provided by law. The agency's Quaker miller drew a large salary but spent his time cultivating his own large farm. The same man, for his own use, cut and hauled wood on the reservation over the protests of the Pawnee chiefs. Other settlers had been refused wood on any terms. In addition, the miller's son, age thirteen, served as agency engineer for a salary of $1,200 a year although "he was entirely ignorant of his duties." The petition concluded that the Indians had starved during the past winter "while the degenerate descendants of noble Penn — protected, fostered and encouraged by the American Government — have proved recreant to every trust reposed in them."[32]

The secretary of the interior appointed Judge William J.

Haddock of Iowa City, Iowa, to investigate. He arrived at the Pawnee agency before the anti-Quaker petition was a month old and took several days of testimony from nearly one-half of the petition's signatories. Other local residents who wished to denounce the Quaker Policy also appeared. Sixteen people, mostly Friends, supported the existing administration. These witnesses, along with numerous onlookers, crowded into the hearing room, but, significantly, no Pawnees seem to have been present.[33] Apparently Haddock did not consider the Pawnees to be directly part of the controversy and so neglected to call Pawnee witnesses. No one questioned their omission from the proceedings.

During these hearings, the local Nebraskans expressed their resentment over the hiring of Quaker outsiders as employees at the Pawnee agency.[34] Three of the anti-Quaker witnesses had either previously worked at the agency or felt they had better qualifications than the present employees. Most of the other witnesses may have shared this complaint, as they were either farmers or farm laborers from near the reservation.

In response, Barclay White, Jacob Troth, and William Burgess felt free to cross-examine the petition's supporters. Most admitted they had signed the petition while visiting D. A. Willard's store. Willard, formerly the agency trader, claimed that he had not read the petition before signing it. The Quakers felt that the ex-trader had taken a leading role, so their cross-examination attempted to discredit Willard as any friend of the Pawnees. The thirty-two-year-old merchant admitted to buying annuity goods from the Pawnees at his off-reservation store for the lowest possible prices. Willard candidly stated: "I came out here to do as well as I could trading and make all the money I could." Willard even agreed that his method of trade might be a principal cause of Pawnee poverty.

Others, when questioned by the Quakers, admitted that they did not know Agent Burgess or were unfamiliar with many points of the petition. Yet these witnesses still had their own specific complaints. The Quakers in rebuttal pointed to their responsible administration of the agency.

The Baltimore Indian committee sent visitors, gave advice, and had even decided to remove Agent Troth, a man whom hundreds of the best citizens of adjoining counties had defended, including the author of the anti-Quaker petition, W. B. Dale. Barclay White hinted that Dale wanted to be the new Pawnee agent.

Judge Haddock did not limit his investigation to the extensive, somewhat jumbled testimonies made before him. He observed the daily operations of the agency and its schools. He also privately inquired as to the character of each witness who appeared before him. Haddock surmised that all were reliable and credible and that each had stated what he honestly believed to be the facts. In general, Haddock's report to the secretary of the interior exonerated the Quakers. The Pawnees' poverty he attributed to Sioux depredations and not Quaker incompetence. Haddock did agree with the Baltimore delegation of the previous year in its assessment of Jacob Troth's abilities. The power conversion of the mill had not been done under skilled supervision with skilled plans. Of the $9,000 spent, only $1,500 in new machinery for the mill proper remained usable if power could be supplied. Haddock noted Troth's honesty and popularity among the settlers but concluded "that agent Jacob M. Troth in the matters pertaining to the flouring mill, the agricultural department and other interests did not manifest sufficient judgment and ability for the position he occupied." As for William Burgess, the new agent had only served a short time, and so was not justly chargeable with any mismanagement. Haddock declared: "As far as can be now seen, he will make a good officer, at least nothing to the contrary appears in the testimony."[35]

Judge Haddock took great pains to present the opinions which produced the anti-Quaker petition. Many of the Nebraskans, he discovered, "have a strong antipathy to the Quakers. This feeling to some extent is reciprocated." Haddock found other attitudes about the Quakers which had not been clear in the testimony:

Some of the petitioners and many of the inhabitants adjacent to the Reservation believe that the Quakers are clannish and bigoted and manifest a sort of self assertion and self satisfied air that pervades the whole Hicksite mass which to them is perfectly exasperating. They also consider that the Quakers have not sufficient knowledge of western life and business and particularly of the Indians to make the most or anything creditable of their opportunities.

To the Nebraskans, the Quakers remained outsiders. This opinion included the four or five Quaker farmers who lived off the reservation. The Nebraskans considered plans to civilize the Pawnees as "fine spun, impracticable theories" created "at Quaker meetings in Eastern cities." The eastern delegations of Friends who visited the agency left a negative impression on the locals, who noted that, besides having "no knowledge whatever of the matters of which they are expected to report," some of their members were "ancient ladies."

Haddock merely reported, with some sympathy, the views of the local settlers. He did not dig for the motivation behind the petition. The agency's neighbors denounced the Quakers' abilities in Indian affairs, but the Nebraskans' own testimony revealed little knowledge of the agency's operation or of the Pawnees. Only former employees, who had good cause to resent the Quakers' arrival, demonstrated such knowledge. The other petitioners resented the salaries given Quaker employees. Farmers hit by drought and grasshopper plagues would understandably feel a certain economic jealousy about "outsiders" with federal incomes. Some Nebraskans considered such salaries to be easy money not based on hard work, and so denounced the Quakers as lazy, inefficient, and impractical. Haddock noted in his report that the local settlers "consider that the character of the Quakers is more modified by the indolence of the Indians than the Indian character is stimulated by Quaker industry."

The local view of indolent Indians and lazy Quakers revealed an important factor which underlay the whole controversy. Many of these Nebraskans had probably chosen their homesteads because of the presence of old neighbors and kin from previous settlements before the move west. Indeed, they might have come west with such a group in order to settle together.[36] Such familiarity bred a strong sense of community and explains why both Quakers and Pawnees were perceived as outsiders. For this reason, the real issue was not whether Quakers should control the Pawnee agency, but whether local Nebraskans as opposed to Quakers and Pawnees would gain economic benefits from the agency. This question as to whether the local community or "outsiders" should control government programs became a familiar argument in the twentieth century after the development of major federal spending programs. Yet here, in the early 1870s on the farmers' frontier, was the same controversy. For local Nebraskans, the arrival of the Quakers meant that employment at the Pawnee agency was one economic benefit apparently lost. In addition, the closing of the flour mill in 1871 meant no convenient milling for neighboring farmers, whereas plans to reopen the mill threatened millers in Columbus. With these economic tensions present, William Burgess arrived in January of 1873 and blundered when he changed the beef contract at the Manual Labor School from John Lawson, a local supplier, to William Coffin, a fellow Quaker.

Clearly, the local Nebraskans resented the appointment of Burgess because he reminded them that outsiders controlled the Pawnee agency. Jacob Troth, on the other hand, had defused some of this resentment by becoming active in local political affairs. In September of 1872, Troth was elected secretary of the Platte County Republican Convention and was sent to the state convention as one of the county's delegates. He also had served as president of the Platte County Agricultural Society. The flood of petitions protesting his removal as agent testified to Troth's acceptance as a leading local figure. Nonetheless, two other leaders in the county's Republican Party — the trader, D. A. Willard, and the beef contractor, John Lawson — both became active in the effort to remove Agent Burgess. These men may well have agreed with the letter in the *Platte Journal* which implied that local supporters of President U. S. Grant had begun the petition against Agent Burgess and that such good Republicans "expected to participate in the fight for position if the friends [*sic*] are removed."[37]

The loss of his supply contract for the Pawnee agency may explain why John Lawson, a disgruntled Republican, wished to see William Burgess displaced. But for the local farmers who came to testify against the Quakers, another economic issue perhaps better explains their opposition. These settlers were greatly angered by the effort on the part of Jacob Troth and Barclay White to stop the cutting of timber on the Pawnee reservation.

In October of 1872, some Pawnees in a council meeting with Agent Troth had complained that white neighbors regularly took timber off the southern part of the reservation. Troth told the Pawnee chiefs to investigate, and on November 8 they reported that whites had cut a large number of trees, loaded them on wagons, and taken the stolen wood south. The next morning Troth rode with the chiefs to the banks of the Loup Fork. The settlers had cut swaths through the trees on each side of the river as well as on islands in the stream. A well-defined wagon trail led south to houses and farms on the way to Clarksville. Troth followed the trail and stopped at nearly every house along the route. All had timber. Those farmers who talked said they got their wood from along the thirty miles of the Loup Fork which ran through the Pawnee reservation. On his way south, Troth met four wagons headed toward the reservation to cut the Pawnees' timber. The drivers explained that they had nowhere else to get wood. Besides, they had heard that the Indians had sold their land to the federal government. Wasn't the presence of surveyors proof of the sale?

The settlers' disingenuous response exercised a convenient lapse of logic. Surveys occurred before land sales, not after. The one in progress on the southern part of the reservation involved fifty thousand acres (all south of the Loup Fork). Jacob Troth and Barclay White wanted the funds from this sale applied to the task of settling the Pawnees on individual farms, which meant building houses and purchasing seed, stock, and implements. Congress had accepted the Quaker plan and on July 15 a Pawnee council reluctantly approved it as well. The Pawnee chiefs may have reasoned that the money acquired could at least help feed the four bands instead of turning them into farmers. In late October, the surveying team arrived and noted that white farms along the reservation's eastern boundary extended onto the Pawnees' land. In November, Troth uncovered the large-scale timber thievery.[38]

In his report to Barclay White, Troth recommended that the culprits not be brought before the U.S. district court. The Quaker agent estimated that he could prosecute some one hundred cases, but he felt that the Pawnees would gain nothing because convictions would be difficult. Troth suggested instead that the farmers pay for the timber as a post facto purchase. By late November, confrontations between the Pawnees and the timber thieves had led to assaults and threats of bloodshed. During December and January, Barclay White began to follow Troth's advice.

As superintendent, White appointed commissioners in the towns of Lone Tree, Clarksville, and Silver Creek, all south of the reservation. These appointees canvassed the local area for the names of those who had taken timber off the reservation. White then visited each town and met with a total of 142 people, who acknowledged taking 443 loads. These citizens settled for a payment of sixty-two and a half cents per load, which was certainly a bargain compared to the estimated price of one dollar a load and five dollars a cord at which others sold wood in the area. Only 2 people, who claimed to have taken 5 loads total, refused to pay. White gave their names to the U.S. marshal and also placed advertisements in the local newspapers warning that future trespassers on the Pawnee reservation would be reported to the grand jury of the U.S. district court.

White discovered that men of all classes and professions, including some of the best citizens of the county, had cut timber on the reservation. One man said he had never been called a thief before and then paid for what he took. Another explained that he had to take the Pawnees' wood because his own neighbors, some at gunpoint, took timber off his farm. Apparently, neighboring whites viewed the reservation timber as yet another resource for purely local benefit. The Quaker superintendent's vigorous public effort to end the expropriation of this resource probably fueled the discontent which led to the anti-Quaker petition of March, 1873. In addition, William Burgess, perhaps out of ignorance, allowed the agency's engineer, Barclay Jones, to cut reservation timber for his personal use. The Pawnee council had complained of Jones's actions in November. Agent Troth had made his engineer stop, but with Burgess's arrival in January, Jones sought and received the new agent's permission to start cutting again. Jones hauled this timber to his private farm off the reservation. Upset by what appeared to be a double standard for timber use, local farmers noted the Quaker engineer's actions in the March petition.

Barclay White's efforts against the timber thieves not only stirred up local antagonism against the Quakers, but also failed to stop the loss of the Pawnees' timber. In his journal, White noted that local settlers continued to cut wood on the Pawnee reservation until the four bands had completely left the state. As for the Pawnees, they not only had to confront white neighbors in competition for one important resource, timber, but they also continued to confront the Sioux over another increasingly scarce resource, the buffalo. When Barclay White asked a Pawnee council in February of 1873 what they wished to do with more than two hundred dollars he had received from the timber thieves, the chiefs replied that they needed food right away because the Sioux had driven them off their western hunting grounds. As Quakers and local whites squabbled over who should control the Pawnee agency, the Teton Sioux had ridden down from the Dakota Territory to renew their war against the four bands.

CHAPTER THREE

Exodus

No policies advocated by the federal government or by the Quakers had affected the Sioux's relentless raids against the Pawnees. The four bands had signed two major treaties with the United States, in 1833 and 1857. The protection promised in each treaty had not materialized because the U.S. government had been insincere in its promise to protect one warlike Plains society from another. The United States had signed both treaties primarily to move the Pawnees out of the path of white settlement. With the arrival of the Quakers, a minor military alliance with the United States, in the guise of the Pawnee Scouts, was terminated. The Quakers' own efforts to establish a peace treaty between the Sioux and the Pawnees proved fruitless. In addition, during its first four years, the military side of the Peace Policy had not kept the Teton Sioux confined on their great reservation to the north. Indeed, the U.S. Army had yet to wage a successful military campaign against these western Sioux. By the end of the 1870s, battlefield victories resulted in containment of the Oglalas and Brulés, but this development came too late for the Pawnees. After more than forty years of warfare, the Pawnee chiefs made the desperate decision to abandon their homeland in Nebraska in order to preserve their traditional way of life. Although it was nearly a Hobson's choice, this decision threatened to shatter the consensus which held together the South bands and the Skidis.

The Sioux began a series of raids in late November of 1872, at the start of the Pawnees' winter hunt. They stole a large number of horses. In early December, Red Cloud's Oglalas took fifty ponies during one week. Some Pawnees pursued the Oglalas to near Fort Laramie but failed to recapture their horses. Despite such raids, over fifteen hundred Pawnees, nearly two-thirds of their entire population, tried to continue their hunt along the Republican River. In late December, General Ord, the commander of the Department of the Platte, warned Barclay White that a large party of Brulés under No Belly's leadership had started toward the Pawnee encampment. Apparently reluctant to appeal directly for army aid, White wrote to Indian Commissioner Walker for advice on how to protect the Pawnees. No directions from Washington followed, but fortunately the Brulés did not attack. Rather they chose to steal over a hundred horses while the Pawnee men were out on a surround. Greatly discouraged by the constant horse stealing, the Pawnees returned early to their reservation villages. Many, forced to walk, packed what goods they could on their backs. They left much behind.

At a council with Barclay White in late January, Lasharoturi, a chief of the Pitahawiratas, told of the disastrous winter hunt and demanded that two hundred soldiers aid the Pawnee warriors in recapturing their horses. White said he would not ask for soldiers. He emphasized that the Pawnees must not fight the Sioux even though one man had been killed. In his report to the commissioner of Indian Affairs, White did ask for help in recovering the horses, but he also said that the Pawnee buffalo hunts should end in order to stop the Sioux raids. In place of buffalo meat, the Quaker Superintendent suggested a beef ration.

Whether beef or buffalo, the Pawnees desperately needed meat during the winter of 1873. By late February, agent Burgess reported the people destitute. A month later, the chiefs' council requested supplies be purchased with $3,000 from treaty funds held in the U.S. Treasury. Burgess supported this petition. He believed the new supplies, along with stores from the cache pits, would get the Pawnees through to spring. Neighboring settlers noted the Pawnees' poverty and commented on it during Judge Haddock's investigation. Still, Barclay White pressed his case for the end of the semiannual buffalo hunts. He told Washington officials that two problems retarded Pawnee progress — Sioux raids and buffalo hunts. White wanted the Pawnees to abandon their hunts in return for twenty thousand pounds of beef on the hoof delivered each week for four years. The Pawnees, however, showed little inclination to support White's plan. In council, Pitale-sharo complained of the slaughter caused by white hunters. The Chaui chief bluntly stated: "Those Buffaloes are mine. Our fathers owned both land and the animals feeding on it. We sold the land to the whites, but reserved the Buffalo."[1]

As White later explained to a new commissioner of Indian Affairs, Pawnee leaders refused to admit that the Treaty of 1857 annulled their right to hunt along the western flow of the Republican River. Instead, they insisted that the Paw-nees retained the hunting privileges granted by the Treaty of 1833. Frustrated by such views, Barclay White acquiesced to the Pawnees' preparations for another summer hunt. Fac-ing the inevitable, the Quaker superintendent tried to find a reason for the renewed Sioux raids as well as a way to protect the Pawnees. As with the requests for soldiers or statements on treaty rights, White tended to discount the Pawnees' own explanations, which centered on the murder of three Brulés that past November.

Two Chauis had reported to William Burgess in early January that the Brulés held the Pawnees responsible for the murder in Nebraska of Whistler, Fat Badger, and Hand Smeller. Barclay White had reported the deaths of the three Brulé chiefs to the commissioner of Indian Affairs. He had blamed local whites for the murders. So, at first, he dismissed the Chauis' report in January. The Quaker superintendent added the illogical argument that Whistler's band, the sum-mer before his death, had hunted near the Pawnees on the buffalo range with no incidents. Later, White would give some credibility to the Chauis' explanation, but he seemed to feel the primary responsibility for the renewed hostilities lay with administrative shortcomings. For the peaceful sum-mer hunt of 1872, White and Jacob Troth had hired John B.

Omohundro ("Texas Jack") to accompany the Pawnees and to stop white hunters or Sioux warriors from interfering. Before the disastrous winter hunt of 1872 / 73, White had asked for two white "overseers"; but when no reply came from Washington, the Pawnees were allowed to leave unaccompanied. Now, in late May of 1873, White, in full agreement with General Ord, asked permission from Washington to appoint one or two reliable white men to accompany the Pawnees on their summer hunt.[2] In the midst of a renewed war, the pacifist superintendent thought he had found the safest solution short of calling out the troops.

Agent Burgess moved as cautiously as his fellow Quaker. In early June, rumors that buffaloes were grazing near Fort Kearney brought a request that sixty young men be allowed to undertake a short hunt for much-needed meat before the traditional July expedition. Burgess withheld his consent because no permission to employ a white overseer had come from Washington. Barclay White wrote again to the new commissioner of Indian Affairs, Edward P. Smith, suggesting that the necessary white "caretakers" receive $100 a month for accompanying the Pawnees. Permission eventually arrived from Washington, and Burgess appointed John W. Williamson, a non-Quaker Nebraskan who had occasionally worked as a farmhand on the reservation.

The Pawnees needed a successful hunt. Grasshoppers and bugs had ravaged the reservation's summer crops of oats and potatoes. Desperate for food, some Pawnees had bartered away wagons, iron pots, and tinware. Burgess stamped what goods were left and gave all traders a written warning not to buy. The regular Quaker visitors from Baltimore noticed a new willingness among young Pawnee men to do agricultural and other work, so long as it paid. On their own part, the Pawnees recognized that money produced food by purchase when plowing and farming had produced few crops. Still, the summer hunt remained vital, and the Sioux remained a threat. Two hundred men, one hundred women, and fifty children left with John Williamson on July 3. This small number, compared to the more than fifteen hundred of the last winter hunt, was only a vanguard. The bulk of the four

bands delayed its departure to await news about peace overtures toward the Sioux.

In mid-July, a Pawnee delegation carrying letters from
Agent Burgess arrived at Fort McPherson, west of the reservation at the forks of the Platte. Baptiste Bayhylle explained in English that his fellow Pawnees wanted the
military to invite the Sioux chiefs to a meeting at the fort
in order to establish permanent peace between the two peoples. The Pawnees said that they were tired of fighting and
that the Sioux were too strong. Back at the reservation,
Agent Burgess waited to hear if the Sioux chiefs would respond. Then, on August 8, a runner arrived with the tragic
news that Sioux warriors had massacred many of the Pawnee
men, women, and children who had gone out on the summer
hunt.

A week after this disaster, John Williamson wrote a
straightforward report. On the morning of August 5, a party
of one hundred Sioux approached the Pawnee hunting camp
located on the north side of the Republican River near present-day Trenton, Nebraska. These Sioux earlier had surprised some Pawnee men as they butchered their morning
kill on the hunting grounds. Tirawahut-lasharo (Sky Chief),
the leader of the hunt, had died as he skinned a buffalo. The
Pawnees in camp removed their women and children to the
head of a ravine which ran for three miles to the Republican
River valley. Williamson and his white companion, L. B.
Platt, nephew of Elvira and Lester Platt, rode out toward
the Sioux party. They were fired upon and had to retreat.
The Pawnee men then came out to do battle. The contest had
lasted one hour with few killed when the main Sioux force
numbering seven hundred to a thousand appeared on three
sides. The Pawnees rushed back to the ravine, threw off the
robes and buffalo meat on their pack animals, and tried to
mount their women and children on these horses. As the
Pawnees fled south down the long ravine, the Sioux pressed
their pursuit and overtook many of the women and children.
Williamson and Platt successfully escaped down the ravine
and along the bank of the Republican River, where they met
a squad of forty-five soldiers from Fort McPherson. This

force, under the command of Capt. Charles Meinhold, returned with the two white men approximately ten miles to
the main scene of carnage. They found that the Sioux had
piled the Pawnee corpses and burned them. Williamson and
the soldiers gathered what wounded they could find along
the battle's path and took them to the Plum creek railroad
station for transport back to the reservation. Other groups
of Pawnees straggled back to their villages with news that
their running fight had lasted all day. They had escaped only
when night came.[3]

The Nebraska newspapers published sensational accounts
of the August 5 disaster, which they called "Massacre Canyon." Many settlers became excited by any Indians seen off
their reservations. When a company of Otos visited their
Pawnee friends to give condolences, Nebraska's governor
complained to the president as well as to Barclay White. The
governor claimed that Indians had no legal right to leave
their reservations. On September 23, the commissioner of
Indian Affairs met with the Quaker agents in Omaha and
announced that he wanted all buffalo hunts by Nebraska
Indians to cease. Commissioner Smith may have felt that
such decisions would keep the Indians on their reservations,
but he had in effect punished the Pawnees and other natives
for Sioux actions. Barclay White found himself in the strange
position of advocating one final winter hunt for the Otos and
Pawnees. White knew that these native people desperately
needed meat, and Congress, he felt, would be slow to appropriate funds for a beef ration.

Faced with possible starvation among the Pawnees,
Agent Burgess tried to add up the total losses at Massacre
Canyon. The Sioux — Spotted Tail's Brulés and Pawnee
Killer's band of Cut-Off Oglalas — had killed twenty men,
thirty-nine women, and ten children. Over one hundred of
the Pawnees' best horses had been lost, along with the dried
meat of about eight hundred buffaloes (approximately
twenty tons). Hides, tents, blankets, and saddles were also
gone. Burgess estimated that $9,000 would replace the prop-
erty and meat lost. When a grant for that sum arrived in
mid-November, the Pawnee chiefs asked that the full amount
be spent to feed their people.

Massacre Canyon produced more than just death and hunger among the Pawnees. In the aftermath of the slaughter, many Pawnees advocated leaving Nebraska and moving south to the Indian Territory. On September 25, two days after meeting with Commissioner Smith in Omaha, Barclay White arrived at the Pawnee agency to distribute treaty goods and funds. Just after the completion of his task, a Kitkehaxki man, Big Spotted Horse, approached the Quaker superintendent and asked that his name be stricken from the tribal roll. Big Spotted Horse wanted to move south to the Indian Territory and enroll with the Wichitas, a people considered close relatives by the South bands. White agreed to the request and then gave his permission on the same terms to two or three friends of Big Spotted Horse, most likely Lone Chief of the Kitkehaxkis and Frank White, a Chaui soldier. Other Pawnees, perhaps as many as forty, expressed a similar desire to move south, but Barclay White refused authorization. He insisted that only the men and their wives to whom he had given his approval could leave. At this point, White noted in his journal, "their chief Peta-la-sharo [Pitalesharo] appeared and made a speech stating that a large number of Pawnees were desirous of going to the Indian Territory and he wanted them to go." White rejected the Chaui leader's request. He claimed a large party would be intercepted by federal soldiers, arrested, and confined.[4]

Barclay White felt he had taken a firm stand against any large removal by the Pawnees. Yet Agent Burgess soon reported that Big Spotted Horse and his followers insisted on leaving "whether liberty is given or not." Perhaps sensing an internal threat to their political authority, some of the chiefs and the interpreter Baptiste Bayhylle requested permission to visit the Indian Territory in advance of Big Spotted Horse's party. Burgess refused such requests, but on October 16 he discovered that Big Spotted Horse had left, not with two or three friends and their wives, but with 285 Pawnees. Burgess immediately telegraphed Barclay White, who hurried by train to Columbus and arrived at the Pawnee agency that night. On October 18, White called for a council with the Pawnee chiefs, where he confronted Pitalesharo.[5]

White demanded to know why his positive instructions had been disobeyed. Why had Pitalesharo allowed the young men and their families to leave? Pitalesharo answered: "I will not hide anything from you. I did not do wrong. It is because two had passes to go south and the others followed them. I have felt bad since my people left but I will stay here as my Grandfather told me. . . . The Chowee band are going to the Wichataws." Ter-re-kaw-wah of the Pitahawiratas then explained that some of his band had followed Big Spotted Horse, but that he did not want to leave because "God gave us these lands." Lasharo-turi said that all the Kitkehaxkis "have made up their minds to go south & live," but had camped by the Platte River awaiting final permission to leave.

In a high anger, Barclay White replied to the chiefs' statements. He noted that in council the chiefs said they represented their bands, but White claimed the chiefs only wanted their special money payments and held "no control over their men and are nothing but women not chiefs." White concluded: "I want these chiefs to control their bands and if they cannot we will put men in who will control them." Pitalesharo seemed shaken by White's threat. He replied weakly: "I have been a chief a long time and this looks as if I was getting old. I wanted [the] Government to stop them. We done nothing wrong. I thought that you would take my part when the people left me so. I will send runners after them today." Pitalesharo attempted to keep up a brave front, and added that he could have stopped the Chauis but that he wanted "the white soldiers to stop them." He then indicated his own lack of authority over the removal issue when he concluded: "I am not afraid of the Chowees, if they want to kill me."

Emphasizing his position as the government's superintendent, White continued to express his displeasure. He wanted "every chief to know that when [the] Government speaks it will be obeyed. . . . I want you to know and remember that no large numbers can leave the Reservation without the consent of the Agent [Burgess]." White said that runners must be sent to bring back the 285 emigrants. His remarks seemed directed most especially at Pitalesharo, whom White still incorrectly considered the chief of all four bands.

Scar-rar-ra-re-sharo, Lone Chief of the Skidis, held no such illusions about Pitalesharo. The Skidis had always considered themselves separate from the South bands. Few had joined Big Spotted Horse, in part because the Skidis had shown the most interest in the assimilationist programs of the Quakers. Lone Chief expressed the Skidis' independent position by belittling Pitalesharo before Barclay White and the council: "If that man [Pitalesharo] could not manage his tribe he might have called on us and my soldiers would help him. I have made up my mind to stay here on my land. I am not going where I have nothing. This is my home. I want you to help me move up."

Not recognizing a possible schism among the Pawnees, Barclay White called Lone Chief's statement "wise words." Pitalesharo and the other chiefs did not respond, but they agreed to send out runners. Within days the 285 Pawnees returned, but by the end of October, Big Spotted Horse had left again. Agent Burgess reported that twenty-seven lodges (approximately 250 people) had gone quietly. No chiefs and only a few soldiers joined them. Burgess believed that the absent Pawnees were Chauis and Pitahawiratas. This time runners failed to overtake them. The actions of Big Spotted Horse showed that some of the chiefs could not maintain consensus and control their young men, but Barclay White did not carry out his threat to dismiss all the chiefs. He thus avoided the dilemma of a white official demanding political dominance over traditional Pawnee chieftainships.

In the fall of 1873, Pitalesharo, his Chaui band, and the other bands of Pawnees confronted problems only a few of which were influenced by Barclay White's threats. Food was scarce. Drought and grasshoppers reduced the harvests. Sioux raiders drove hunters off the buffalo range. White settlers stole timber. Three and a half years of Quaker administration had not brought peace with the Sioux or the end of white exploitation. The Quakers had effectively defended Pawnees accused of murder, but protection from Sioux raiders, white timber thieves, and avaricious traders did not follow. In addition, the Quakers wanted to break up the villages and put families on separate farms. Under these strains, the Pawnees survived. The earthlodges still stood. Then came Massacre Canyon. The consensus and status quo which the chiefs in each band had maintained in the face of so many pressures started to dissipate. Members of the South bands, which included some of Pitalesharo's fellow Chauis, left for the Indian Territory to live with their "cousins," the Wichitas. The Skidis had carried on trade with the Wichitas, but they did not have the same traditional relationship toward these people. So Pitalesharo may well have wondered whether the Skidis would join the South bands if they followed Big Spotted Horse and moved their villages.

Early in 1874, the Wichitas welcomed Big Spotted Horse and his fellow Pawnee exiles to the Indian Territory. At a council in February the Wichitas invited the South bands and the Skidis to settle on lands neighboring their reservation. The Orthodox Quakers who controlled the administration of the Wichita agency did not oppose this invitation. However, if all the Pawnees were to relocate in the Central Superintendency, the Orthodox Friends wanted certain social and financial stipulations. The Wichitas' agent, Jonathan Richards, insisted that the invitation for the Pawnees' removal indicated that the newcomers must cultivate the soil, raise stock, send their children to school, make advancement toward civilization, and, in general, live a quiet, peaceful existence. Both Richards and his superintendent, Enoch Hoag, wished to be certain that the Pawnees would continue to receive their treaty annuities if they moved south. Neither man wanted the Pawnees to rely solely on the hospitality of the Wichitas. Such concerns aside, Superintendent Hoag welcomed the idea of the Pawnees' relocation. He told the commissioner of Indian Affairs that he had long believed in the resettlement of all the native peoples of Kansas and Nebraska in the Indian Territory, and "the earlier accomplished — the better for the Indians and government."

Barclay White did not agree, for he viewed Big Spotted Horse as little more than a charlatan who had flimflammed an invitation from the Wichitas. White pointed out that in

Nebraska Big Spotted Horse was only a soldier, whereas in the Indian Territory he presented himself as a chief. In the summer of 1872, the Kitkehaxki brave had asked to permanently remove and join the Comanches. A year later, he had returned to the Pawnee reservation, collected his treaty annuities, and then asked if he could join the Wichitas. White expected Big Spotted Horse and his followers to return for their annuities in 1874. If they had been sincere about joining the Wichitas, the Quaker peevishly concluded, they would have awaited official permission from Washington instead of stealing off and eluding their pursuers by "forced marches."[6]

Barclay White's annoyance with Big Spotted Horse did not prevent the Hicksite superintendent from noting that the Wichitas' invitation, along with stories of the "fatness of land" in the Indian Territory, had made many Pawnees eager to remove. To prevent this exodus, Barclay White and William Burgess followed the familiar policies of attempting to negotiate peace with the Sioux, encouraging farming among the Pawnees, and discouraging depredations by neighboring whites.

On the night of January 16, 1874, a Sioux party led by Medicine Horse stole more than forty Pawnee horses from the Nebraska reservation. This raid caused Barclay White to renew his efforts toward a formal peace council. The Oglalas dismissed these overtures with derision, whereas the Brulés' agent said other internal problems prevented action on White's proposal. In late April, seven Sioux stole one hundred horses. The Pawnees gave chase, recaptured their horses, and killed six of the raiders. With horse raiding continuing and no hope for peace, Barclay White compromised his opposition to the Pawnee Scouts. He still would not allow General Ord to use Pawnee guides in campaigns against the Sioux for fear of retaliation. White said, however, that he did not object to the Pawnees helping troops seek out straggling bands of outlaw Indians who had left their reservations to engage in violence and theft. Such outlaws, of course, included the Oglala and Brulé raiders.

White raiders who stole timber instead of horses also victimized the Pawnees. In early January, William Burgess reported that white neighbors took wood daily, and so the Pawnees had started patrolling their forest. One white settler, delivered by the Pawnees to their agent, said his party had been chased, shot at, and a pair of oxen killed. The irate Nebraskan said whites would shoot back, but the Pawnees felt justified in their action because so little wood was left on the reservation. Agent Burgess nervously anticipated an escalation in violence.

Barclay White also feared the worst because Judge Elmer Dundy of the U.S. district court had recently ruled that federal courts had no jurisdiction over crimes committed on Indian reservations. In effect, state courts now held legal sway over the timber thieves. A great increase in thefts followed, and just as White feared, the county and state courts refused to act. White's efforts in the winter of 1872/73 had relied on the threat of dragging white offenders before a federal judge. Dundy's decision removed that threat, so White allowed the Pawnees to continue their patrols, but stressed that they should use no violence.

News of confrontations over timber resources led eastern Friends to fear a Pawnee-Nebraskan war. Benjamin Rush Roberts of the Hicksite Central Executive Committee suggested to the commissioner of Indian Affairs that the Pawnees cut and haul their wood across the frozen Loup River for sale to neighboring farmers. The Central Executive Committee claimed that enough timber existed to support this enterprise as well as to give each Indian farmer a portion of timbered land when the Pawnees finally settled on their individual farms.

Barclay White apparently recognized that the Pawnees could not afford to lose any more timber either by theft or by sale and requested instead that General Ord station a small company of mounted infantry on the southern boundary of the reservation. Commissioner Smith agreed, and by the end of January, General Sheridan directed General Ord to comply.[7] Thus the first request during the Quakers' administration for protection of the Pawnees by government troops came through the loss of timber to white neighbors, not through the loss of horses or lives to Sioux raiders.

White's action revealed that he could compromise his pacifism if white lives were threatened, yet he had made no such compromise when Pawnee or Sioux lives had been lost. Apparently, the concept of cultural inferiority preceded the concept of spiritual equality in this Quaker's mind, with the result that Indian lives, if not their spirits, would be seen as more expendable than the lives of whites. At least sixty-nine Pawnees had died at Massacre Canyon, but Barclay White had not requested military protection for the four bands. No one on either side had died in the confrontation over timber, yet White quickly appealed for military assistance. The possibility of Nebraskans slaughtering Pawnees, as Coloradans had Cheyennes less than a decade before at Sand Creek, may have provoked the Quaker superintendent's decision. Yet, the fact remained that Sioux raiders, not white neighbors, regularly killed Pawnees.

Two thousand members of the four bands remained in Nebraska after Massacre Canyon and the desertion of Big Spotted Horse and his followers. Barclay White and William Burgess still hoped to transform the majority of these Pawnees into farmers. The two Quaker officials recognized that more Pawnee men needed experience in farm labor before the reservation could be divided into family farmsteads. The Pawnee council realized that after the crop and hunting disasters of the past eighteen months any proposal to provide food needed immediate consideration, so the chiefs began to cooperate with the Quakers' plan. On March 18, the chiefs' council agreed to reserve $10,000 of treaty goods and funds for the payment of Pawnees who did farm labor. Delighted by this decision, Burgess wrote that "a harmonious feeling prevailed. They [the Pawnees] are now united, in good spirits."[8] Burgess's words revealed his hope that a successful commitment to farming would end all discord and talk of removal, but by May these sunny hopes had started to cloud over.

A work force of twenty men, predominantly Skidis, set about clearing the old Mormon fields and planting melons, corn, and beans. The agency farmer directed their efforts, for which each man was to receive between seventy-five cents and one dollar a day. By mid-May, no one had received his pay, and Burgess began to worry that he would be held personally accountable for funds committed to Indian labor. Indian Commissioner Edward Smith still maintained his ban on buffalo hunts, so agricultural production or government supplies would have to feed the Nebraska Pawnees during the next winter. Barclay White wrote Commissioner Smith pleading for official approval of the payment plan. By late June, the Pawnees had 1,300 acres of land under cultivation, and the agency farmer had planted an additional 330 acres. In early July, swarms of grasshoppers devoured nearly all the crops.

Twenty men plowing in the fields did not make a total conversion to "civilized" farming. In June, two Quaker visitors from the Baltimore Yearly Meeting arrived at the agency. They felt that the Skidis had made some progress toward "civilization," but the three South bands presented "a picture of degradation." The Baltimore Quakers made no note of the traditional division between the Skidis and the other Pawnee bands, nor did they explain why some Skidis seemed to accept white ways more readily. John B. Dunbar, an early ethnologist and son of the former Presbyterian missionary to the Pawnees, pointed out the role of Scar-rar-ra-re-sharo, Lone Chief of the Skidis. Dunbar claimed, in an article published in 1882, that Lone Chief had worked for the "advancement" of his people since the establishment of the Pawnee agency in 1858. The Skidi chief had set an example in his personal appearance, for he had adopted white dress and allowed his beard to grow. In addition, Lone Chief "was the first prominent man in the entire tribe who engaged personally in the labors of agriculture. He put his own hand to the plough."[9] The few Skidis who followed Lone Chief's example also opposed the intentions of other Pawnees, especially members of the South bands, to leave for the Indian Territory.

Dunbar in his article admitted that not all the Skidis, much less all the Pawnees, followed Lone Chief's example. Nonetheless, in the summer of 1874, Benjamin Rush Roberts and Chalkley Gillingham, the two Baltimore visitors, felt they should praise the Pawnees on the progress which some had made. The two Quakers presented their compliments to the assembled Pawnee chiefs at a meeting on June 26. They mentioned how much land had been broken for planting and how prosperous the Pawnees would be if they also raised chickens, hogs, and cattle. Roberts and Gillingham then asked the chiefs to respond. Their replies revealed not only the rejection of white ways, but also the desire of many to move south because of their poverty and hunger. As usual, Pitalesharo of the Chauis spoke first:

I stand before you poor and naked, — my feet are bare, and I have nothing to cover my legs, — I have but few Ponies and do not know how long I shall have them as the Sioux are making frequent raids on my people. When I lay down to rest I have to lay my head on my Revolver for the safety of my life and property — I want to go South where there will be no more war, and where my people can get something to eat. Not many snows ago we were rich, we had plenty of Ponies, heaps of Buffalo meat, and our children were fat, now they are crying for something to eat, we are poor, very poor.

The Quakers transcribed other speeches at the June 26 meeting. No Skidis appeared among the identified speakers, but a consensus among the South bands' spokesmen seemed evident. Ter-re-kaw-wah, the aged chief of the Pitahawiratas, referred to the rich life of the past and his warm friendship with Lester Platt, another former Presbyterian missionary. In those days, the Pitahawiratas "had Buffalo meat to feed our children and our dogs, now we have not any, and soon we will have to eat our dogs. — We are surrounded by pale faces, and cannot go out and kill game, and we want to go South and be free." Tie-ta-sha-cod-dic, a chief of the Kitkehaxkis, objected to white employees being paid when his children had no bread and the young men of his band would work for pay. Yet, he rejected the new agricultural effort: "You are plowing up our land we do not need it, there is more plowed now than we use, and is growing up wild again, and we need all the money to buy something to eat — we are compelled to go South where we can get game and shall not need the land."[10]

The implications of the three chiefs' words stretched beyond the issue of whether Chauis, Kitkehaxkis, and Pitahawiratas were willing to give up the hunt and rely totally on

agriculture. Less than two weeks before grasshoppers devastated all the crops, the chiefs expressed the consensus of
their bands. The South bands would not give up the yearly
cycle of hunt and harvest. They wished to maintain the traditions of Pawnee life which had produced the "rich" days
of the past. In order to keep their traditions, the South bands
were willing to give up their homeland and move south to
the Indian Territory. But these chiefs also recognized that
the Pawnees would need the aid and protection of the federal
government if they removed. This dependent relationship
had started as early as the treaty of 1833, and although the
Pawnees often had been disappointed by the extent of the
government's support, their dependence had grown over the
decades. The responsible leaders, true to their roles as chiefs,
would not act recklessly like Big Spotted Horse and leave
without permission. They awaited assurance of government
support from federal officials.

Benjamin Rush Roberts mentioned the meeting of June
26 in a letter to Barclay White at Omaha, but he ignored the
prospect of removal. The Pawnees, Roberts reported, insisted
on a summer buffalo hunt of at least three weeks' duration.
White later received transcripts of the meeting, but his own
letter to Commissioner Smith did not mention the South
bands' threat of an exodus. The Indian commissioner also
received copies of the chiefs' speeches, but he only granted
a pass for the summer hunt. All three men seemed willing
to treat the meeting of June 26 as a dispute over buffalo
hunting. Their inattention forced the Pawnee chiefs to seek
aid from others.

As early as May of 1874, some chiefs turned to Ter-re-
kaw-wah's old friend Lester Platt, whose trading post and
four-hundred-acre farm were located just to the east of the
reservation boundary near the Loup River. Platt and his wife,
Elvira, had worked off and on among the Pawnees since 1843,
at first as Presbyterian missionaries. Elvira Platt had started
teaching at the Pawnee Manual Labor School in 1867, soon
after the opening of the two-story brick building. Lester Platt
spoke Pawnee and had good cause to dislike the Quakers
because they had dismissed his wife from her teaching position two years before.

The white trader wrote down in English the statements of four chiefs and sent them to the commissioner of Indian Affairs. Pitalesharo said he wanted to come to Washington and arrange with the commissioner for the disposal of the Nebraska reservation "which is surrounded by the whites and get other land south." Tie-ta-sha-cod-dic and Lesharo-turaha of the Kitkehaxkis agreed with Pitalesharo. They emphasized that white settlers now surrounded the Pawnees. Ter-re-kaw-wah, chief of the Pitahawiratas for over thirty years, distrusted Agent Burgess. He claimed: "The Agent does not want us to go — he talks a plenty, but does nothing — we are poor and in a sad condition and the agent is afraid to have our wants made known, and forbids our going to Washington lest we tell of his misusing our money."[11]

Lester Platt would remain involved in the removal controversy. Eventually, potential profit as well as humanitarian service motivated his concerns. Three of the four chiefs who sought Platt out in May confronted the Quaker visitors from Baltimore on June 26. Eleven days later, soon after the grasshoppers had eaten all the Pawnees' crops, Platt wrote a wild, rambling letter to Commissioner Smith which blasted the Quaker management of Pawnee affairs. Without mentioning his own business, Platt bemoaned the Pawnees' poverty and the fact that they bought on credit from traders. He implied that the Quakers had embezzled $10,000 of the Pawnees' treaty annuity. Even after the grasshoppers' devastation, the agent had yet to allow a summer buffalo hunt. Platt felt that in his thirty-one years of association with the Pawnees, no management had been as "selfish and heartless and wasteful." Confusingly, Platt concluded: "All intelligent citizens feel that it would be a mercy to the Pawnees and a great benefit to the country for them to go from here." Whether Platt wanted the Quakers to leave, or the Pawnees, or both, remained hidden in his grammar.[12]

One way that Lester Platt could profit from the Pawnees' leaving did not remain obscure. In August a petition from a group of sixteen Pawnee "chiefs" arrived in Washington. The document claimed that Platt had not been compensated for the clothes and food he had given the Pawnee schoolchildren in the two years after he first arrived in 1843. He also had not been paid for 1,400 sacks of flour he had given the Pawnees during the winter of 1861. The petition concluded that in payment for these old debts, the government should grant Platt title to a full section of Pawnee land which adjoined his farm. The names of Ter-re-kaw-wah, Lesharo-turaha, and Tie-ta-sha-cod-dic appeared in support of the petition. Pitalesharo's name was not present and nearly half the names listed had not appeared on chiefs' council resolutions sent to Washington by Agent Burgess. Of course there were more chiefs among the Pawnees than merely the sixteen recognized as members of the agent's council, but no marks accompanied any of the names on Platt's petition. Perhaps Ter-re-kaw-wah and some of his fellow chiefs had agreed to help their "old friend." Two and a half years later, when Platt's widow claimed her husband had been promised a full section, the Pawnees remembered Platt as a good friend. But some of the chiefs listed on the petition, especially the Skidis, said they had not been at the council meeting in 1874.[13] Thus it appears that Lester Platt may have added names in order to have the complement of sixteen which normally appeared on council documents.

With the permission of Commissioner Smith, a few Pawnee men went out on a summer hunt in 1874 but found no buffalo. By mid-August, the Pawnees were pleading for government aid to purchase flour and meat. The chiefs' council asked for a $5,000 advance on their treaty annuity for the next year. They also asked that the salaries of some agency employees — the miller, the tinner, and all teachers — be applied to feed the four bands. Not wishing to lose these employees, Agent Burgess asked instead for permission to buy food on credit. He noted that the Pawnees would have no provisions until the crops of 1875 were harvested.

In the face of starvation, leaders of the South bands sought out another man, B. T. Spooner, a one-quarter Sac and Fox in his late twenties who had served as an interpreter for the Ojibwas in Michigan. He had lived with the Pawnees for two years, but had been ordered off the reservation by Agent Burgess in February of 1874. Spooner composed two appeals from the South bands. Both were dated August 21, 1874. One petition, attributed to seven chiefs, contained the familiar names of Pitalesharo of the Chauis and Ter-re-kaw-wah of the Pitahawiratas, plus Lesharo-turaha and Tie-ta-sha-cod-dic of the Kitkehaxkis. This letter mentioned the devastation of the crops and the lack of money to feed their people. The chiefs complained about the timber controversy with white settlers and said that the Sioux had stolen twenty-one horses the night before. If they moved south, the chiefs felt their bands could kill game, cultivate land, and have permanent homes. Their horses could graze at night and not be stolen by the Sioux. In the Indian territory, the South bands wanted "Wagons, and Plows and Schools as we had here when Mrs. Platt had charge of the School." In addition, they desired a new agent, Lester Platt, and a new interpreter, Jo Esau, because Baptiste Bayhylle "only works from his own band [i.e., the Skidis]." The petitioners asked that a reply be sent to Lester Platt and then concluded with the following plea: "We wish to go South before it is cold as we have no Blankets & nothing to buy with and wish to get buffalo robes for the winter, this is not an official letter but a friendly one that you may know our wants and advise us what to do."[14]

Spooner's second communication on August 21 included a request on the part of two Kitkehaxkis and a Pitahawirata soldier to visit the Indian Territory and select lands where they could settle. The white writer then explained to Commissioner Smith that "the large majority of the tribe have been asking for removal for a year at least, but the agent and superintendent are determined that they shall not be heard at Washington." Spooner felt "ecclesiastical interests" were preventing removal because the Hicksite Quakers did not want the Orthodox Quakers to have the administration of the Pawnees. In all probability the Presbyterian affiliation of Lester Platt was more germane to the Hicksites' opposition.

Whatever the reasons for delay, William Burgess and Barclay White soon found that among the South bands the issue was not if they would indeed remove, but whether they would leave immediately. On September 9, Burgess telegraphed startling news to Barclay White in Omaha. The Kit-kehaxkis had defied their agent's authority in a council meeting and announced that they were leaving to join the Wichitas. The Kitkehaxkis comprised one-quarter of the Nebraska Pawnees. Two other bands (presumably the Chauis and the Pitahawiratas) would leave if the Kitkehaxkis left. White telegraphed Commissioner Smith and asked for instructions. Both Quakers then wrote to the Indian committee of the Baltimore Yearly Meeting. Informed of the determination of so many Pawnees to leave Nebraska, the Baltimore Indian committee decided not to oppose removal if directed by the federal government. Now both the Quakers and the chiefs awaited the approval of the federal government in order to retain their own style of authority among the Pawnees.

Indian Commissioner Edward P. Smith drew up a plan of removal which constituted virtually a new treaty. He then delegated his authority to Benjamin Rush Roberts of the Board of Indian Commissioners. Roberts had visited the Pawnee agency in June as a member of the Baltimore Yearly Meeting's Indian committee. Now in early October he returned west to present the commissioner's plan to the assembled Pawnees. The choice of Roberts proved fortunate for the Quakers, because it undercut Lester Platt's efforts to gain recognition from Washington officials.

While in Columbus on business in mid-September, Agent Burgess had chanced upon Platt and a group of Pawnee chiefs who had an appointment with the mayor of Columbus. Burgess attended that meeting and heard the chiefs ask for local white support in their efforts to get federal approval of their emigration. Burgess said such requests should come from an open council for all the Pawnees. He told the chiefs that the superintendent and a member of the Board of Indian Commissioners would soon come to talk to them about these matters. Lester Platt then explained that he had visited Washington and talked to the commissioner of Indian Affairs, who had told him that if the Pawnees went south, they would be provided for.

Certainly the South bands were eager to leave. The Pitahawiratas and Chauis began tearing down their earthlodges in mid-September. They sold the lodge poles to Lester Platt and another trader, D. A. Willard. Neither man had a government license to trade legally with the Pawnees. By the time of Benjamin Rush Roberts's arrival on October 5, all three villages of the South bands had been dismantled. Only the Skidis had not destroyed their homes. The chiefs of the South bands said they had needed money for food and so had sold their poles and lumber to the two traders. Burgess said the Indians had been misled by their confidence in Platt and his assurance that they would be taken care of in the Indian Territory. Barclay White denounced Platt and Willard as "a greater curse to this tribe of Indians than even the Grasshoppers."[15]

As the feud between the Quakers and Lester Platt simmered, Benjamin Rush Roberts presented Commissioner Smith's proposals. Some Pawnees were not pleased. They took two full days to discuss the commissioner's plan among themselves. The question of whether the Skidis, especially the assimilationist group, would join the others may well have been part of these discussions. On October 8, sixteen "chiefs and head-men" gave their consent for all the Pawnees to remove. Two Skidi assimilationists, Eagle Chief and Lone Chief, who would stay behind in Nebraska, placed their marks on the document. They apparently did not want to block the will of the majority. Pitalesharo's name did not appear. His mark had been at the top of every official chiefs' list since the Quakers' arrival in 1869, but he had recently died of gangrene after receiving a mysterious gunshot wound. Still, the document claimed unanimous agreement among the Pawnees for removal, although the nature of the resolutions made such unanimity seem doubtful.[16]

The first article asked that the Nebraska reservation be sold at its full market value. Subsequent articles explained that this sale would pay for the purchase of a new reservation of "good agricultural soil," 300 square miles in size. On this new reservation, the Pawnees promised "to abandon the chase, and endeavor to get a living from the products of the soil and herding." To this end, each head of family would be "allotted in severalty" 160 acres of land. Each unmarried person over eighteen received 80 acres. Forty Pawnee men, ten from each band, were to leave for the Indian Territory with their families in order to select a suitable reservation. All expenses, including those for new agency buildings and schools, were to be repaid to the government after the sale of the Nebraska reservation.

Commissioner Smith had driven a hard bargain for removal, but acceptance by the council did not mean the ready transformation of the Pawnees into farmers. After the treaty of 1857, when they moved back to the Loup Fork, the South bands and many of the Skidis had maintained their cultural traditions. Now in 1874, through a series of supplemental resolutions, these traditionalists showed that they could use the trade-off system to support the retention of the Pawnee way of life. These additions to Smith's plan by the chiefs at the council were also "unanimously" approved but demonstrated clear benefits for certain groups at the meeting. The traditionalists would not give up the buffalo chase, so one resolution asked for a winter hunt with "our relatives, the Wichitas." The council requested that after this hunt the four bands then move onto their new reservation and "there engage in building houses and preparing ground for seeding and planting crops." Although all of these events were to be under white supervision, the sequence of winter hunt, seed-time, and planting followed the traditional Pawnee yearly cycle. Even the building of new homes on a new reservation could fit comfortably with the tradition of repairing the earthlodges' roofs after the winter hunt.

In return for the traditionalists going on their hunt, other supplemental resolutions supported Quaker and assimilationist desires. One request asked that a few chiefs and headmen stay on the Nebraska reservation with the old, the infirm, and the children of the manual labor school. By this trade-off, some of the assimilationist faction of the Skidis, including Lone Chief, could stay behind and their children could stay in school. Under government protection, supported by treaty funds, this remnant could move south at a vague future date, "when we [the Pawnees] are in a proper condition to receive them on our new reservation." As for the

Quakers, they wanted to keep troublesome traders such as Lester Platt and D. A. Willard away from the Pawnees. "Friendly" persuasion probably produced the supplemental resolution which denounced the purchase of material necessities, government goods, and "the poles of our winter lodges" by "outside traders." The statement bluntly concluded with a demand "that none of these parasites . . . be permitted to remove with us to our new home, or settle among us there. We have suffered from them in the past, we desire to be rid of them in the future."

The Quaker officials at the October 8 meeting had only reluctantly supported removal. They seemed to recognize the traditionalist sentiment which supported the exodus. They also recognized how grasshopper plagues, Sioux raids, timber thefts, and depletion of the buffalo had made removal imperative. As Benjamin Rush Roberts later explained to the Board of Indian Commissioners:

It is not in accordance with the view of the religious society, who have charge of these Indians, or of Superintendent B. White, that it is for their best interests, or for their more rapid advancement in civilization, that they are permitted to leave their reservation. . . . it is believed that though their progress may be retarded for several years by the move, their permanent rights, if they ever obtain such, may be better assured in the Indian Territory.[17]

Benjamin Rush Roberts's words held both prophecy and realism about the Pawnees. Barclay White retained a more sentimental view. At the October 8 council, Ter-re-kaw-wah of the Pitahawiratas had stepped forward, placed his hands on Barclay White's head, and delivered a short, earnest speech. White was moved by the aged chief's action after Baptiste Bayhylle explained that Ter-re-kaw-wah's words were a "blessing." White believed the chief had spoken "heart answering to heart" of the "satisfaction" the Pawnees felt about one Quaker's "administration of these children of the prairies."[18]

Bayhylle did not translate Ter-re-kaw-wah's words, which may have taken more the form of a farewell than a blessing. Ter-re-kaw-wah's name appeared on a letter and a petition shortly after the council of October 8. The letter said that "all chiefs" wanted Lester Platt to be their agent on the new reservation. The petition, signed by sixteen chiefs, made the same request. It also asked that the commissioner of Indian Affairs ignore the antitrader resolution of the recent council because Barclay White had "indulged his personal spite" against the chiefs' "old friend," Lester Platt, and the resolution had not been understandably interpreted. Both the letter and the petition requested that Elvira Platt teach the Pawnee children on the new reservation. The same sixteen names appeared on this petition in the same order as they had on the earlier August petition to grant Platt a full section of land. Once more Platt and Ter-re-kaw-wah may have cooperated for their anticipated mutual benefit. The prospect of the combined salaries of agent and school matron could have motivated Platt, whereas Ter-re-kaw-wah may well have desired removal from the Quakers as well as removal from Nebraska. Yet Platt's actions should not be seen as totally mercenary. An old friend and missionary to the Pawnees, he well knew the frustrations of working for the "advancement" of the four bands. Platt never gained his wish to become the Pawnees' agent because Commissioner Smith continued to support the Quaker administration. The Pawnee chiefs, well versed in the power structure of the government in such matters, stopped requesting Platt's appointment after they arrived in the Indian Territory. After all, some chiefs had requested Platt as their agent in order to win government approval of removal, but that victory had come without replacing their Quaker agent. As for Lester and Elvira Platt, they stayed behind in Nebraska. Their more than thirty years of close association with the four bands had ended.[19]

In October and November of 1874, the Pawnees began their southward journey. John Williamson had been chosen to travel with the Indians. He spoke Pawnee and was the same young man who had accompanied the hunters at Massacre Canyon. Williamson reported that Pawnee priests had consulted the Great Spirit (Tirawa), who they said did not want the Pawnees to live among the whites and had sent the grasshoppers and hot, dry winds of summer as a further sign that the people should leave. These religious interpretations underscored the traditionalist nature of the Pawnees' removal. As Williamson rode out to Grand Island to oversee the southern journey, he expected to find only the forty men responsible for choosing the new reservation. To his surprise, nearly fourteen hundred Pawnees had gathered along the Platte. Agent Burgess had hoped that most of the Pawnees would remain in Nebraska until a new reservation had been selected. He came to Grand Island to attempt to persuade a majority to stay behind. But he soon recognized the futility of his argument and gave his permission for all the Pawnees at Grand Island to leave.

Years later Williamson described the start of the Pawnees' exodus:

About the seventh of the month [November] we broke camp and started on our journey. None of us realized what hardships we were to suffer, as it proved to be a severe winter and game was very scarce, owing to the country becoming settled. We traveled in a southward direction, many of the squaws walking and carrying a pack upon their backs. This made it impossible for us to make over twelve or fourteen miles a day.[20]

Food shortages and hostile whites plagued the Pawnees on their journey. One group of white men stole a hundred ponies, but the Pawnees managed to steal them back again. At Great Bend, Kansas, Williamson received an emergency voucher from Barclay White for $1,800 in order to purchase food. Merchants in the Kansas town would not accept this document, but one individual agreed to sell a carload of substandard flour to Williamson. As had often been the case with their neighbors in Nebraska, whites along the route of the Pawnees' removal saw an economically exploitable situation.

Since the food supplies remained low, the Pawnee priests wondered if Tirawa had become angered by their exodus. One religious leader had a dream in which he saw that an ear of corn in one sacred bundle had been broken. The bundle was opened and a broken ear found. To repent for not having taken care of the bundle, the Pawnees tore up into strips many blankets and bolts of calico. They hung the strips from trees in order to pacify Tirawa. Shortly after these actions,

Williamson managed to purchase a hundred head of longhorn cattle on credit. This acquisition of meat on the hoof convinced the priests that Tirawa had forgiven them and sent food.

Remarkably, only one Pawnee died during the entire trip. In mid-February the great caravan arrived at the Wichitas' reservation, where it was reunited with the approximately 360 Pawnees who had already joined Big Spotted Horse in the Indian Territory. The Wichitas initiated a week of celebration at the arrival of their South band "cousins" and the Skidis. They all feasted, danced, raced, and exchanged gifts. Jonathan Richards, the Orthodox agent, issued cattle to the new arrivals. Such weekly beef rations were all the Pawnees had to eat until government funds arrived to support their immediate needs and to settle them on their new reservation. Whether the Skidi assimilationists, who were still in Nebraska, would rejoin the majority of the Pawnees remained an open question.

CHAPTER FOUR

Renting
Out Hell

The Indian Territory, the land in which most of the Pawnees wished to reestablish their villages, had not always seemed such an attractive haven for other native peoples. During the 1820s and 1830s, the federal government had pressured the so-called Five Civilized Tribes of the southeastern United States into the surrender of their homelands. Often under military guard, the Cherokees, Choctaws, Creeks, Seminoles, and Chickasaws had come to the new Indian Territory, west of the Mississippi River. These removals had been more by force than by choice. Yet, despite the massive loss of lives caused by their displacement, these southeastern Indians set up governments, laid out farms, raised livestock, and cooperated with Christian missionaries for the education of their children. After the Civil War, a new series of treaties established reservations in the western part of the Indian Territory for Plains tribes such as the Southern Cheyennes, the Comanches, the Kiowas, and the Wichitas. These native societies showed little interest in following the example of the Five Civilized Tribes, for they wished to maintain their Plains traditions. The Pawnees had similar feelings. They had removed to the Indian Territory in order to preserve their traditional way of life. But first, the question of exactly where they would settle had to be answered.

In order to find available land for the Pawnees, Agent William Burgess had come south in December of 1874 to consult with the Orthodox Quaker administrators of the Central Superintendency. These remarkable conversations between members of the two branches of the Society of Friends soon led to a conference on December 9 with a delegation from the Cherokee Nation. The Cherokees were willing to sell a tract of land to the Pawnees west of the ninety-sixth meridian on the forks of the Cimarron and Arkansas rivers. Superintendent Enoch Hoag and other Orthodox Friends told their Hicksite guest that this land would be appropriate for the Pawnees. Burgess rode out to examine the proposed reservation. In February, when the Pawnees arrived at the Wichita agency, Burgess took out to the site ten men from each band who had the power to select a new reservation. These forty Pawnees were not fully pleased with their agent's choice of location. They would settle too far from the Wichitas, and the Osages, old horse-stealing enemies of the Pawnees, had the reservation directly to the north. Only twelve names appeared on the document which approved the new reservation. Supposedly these twelve men now represented the authority of the original forty, but only one Chaui and two Pitahawiratas made their mark.[1]

Officials in Washington did not complain about the strange document, but swift settlement on the new land did not follow. The slow wheels of congressional legislation and the cautious actions of Washington officials, plus some resistance from the Indians themselves, prevented the final removal of the main body of Pawnees to their new reservation until late June of 1875. Although the Senate's Indian committee had ruled favorably on legislation to finance the Pawnees' removal and resettlement, Congress had adjourned its session without taking action. By early March, Indian Commissioner Edward P. Smith complained to the secretary of the interior: "As the result, the Department [of the Interior] finds itself with these 3,000 Pawnees, a large portion of them already in the Indian Territory . . . but without any means either to procure subsistence, or to commence preparing their homes, or to return to Nebraska, or to live in Nebraska, if they were returned." Smith believed an expenditure of no more than $150,000 would ease the emergency. He pointed out that the Pawnee lands in Nebraska were worth three to four times that amount, so the government could be confident of full repayment.[2]

The secretary of the interior allowed the "expenditure" of $150,000 but only as a form of nonbinding debt on the federal government. Agent Burgess would have to purchase food, buy construction materials for the new agency, hire labor and transportation — all on credit with no formal contracts. Parties willing to furnish such goods and services would have to await an act of Congress for their payment. Understandably, William Burgess worried that he might be held personally responsible for any purchases. He earlier had pleaded for a $10,000 emergency appropriation so he could buy beef, flour, and other supplies through open-market contracts. Now Burgess realized that if the Pawnees were to avoid starvation and finally settle in the Indian Territory, he would have to beg for the best terms available from white merchants.

In late April, two members of the Board of Indian Commissioners, F. H. Smith (the board's secretary) and Benjamin Rush Roberts, met William Burgess in St. Louis to assist him with his difficult purchases. A former board member in Chicago told the three men that only speculators would risk such sales and then for "a sufficient consideration." A similar authority in St. Louis called the effort "hopeless" unless they allowed "a liberal margin of profit" for speculation. Nonetheless, in Omaha wagons and agricultural implements and in St. Louis a second-hand sawmill and engine were received "upon reasonable terms." Proposals for flour, beef, and other supplies came at rates that the three men, "on our own responsibility, were unwilling to accept." A trip to Washington and a meeting with the commissioner of Indian Affairs produced no better solution, so William Burgess, with the authorization of the two members of the Board of Indian Commissioners, made his purchases on the "best terms" obtainable.[3]

With such financial vacillation, the main body of the Pawnees settled on their new reservation too late in the summer to plant crops. At first the Pawnees had refused to move at all because the Wichitas had invited them to stay. Two days of councils and parlays gained the consent of all the Pawnees except for some four hundred, many of whom had lived with the Wichitas for nearly a year and a half. This group wished to stay behind and harvest their crops. Their action did not create a schism. Instead, it produced additional food for all the Pawnees, and so gained the consent of Agent Burgess. Also, the fall harvest allowed continuation of the sacred celebrations associated with that event. After the harvest, these four hundred Pawnees moved to the new reservation.

Under the nominal leadership of Big Spotted Horse, this group of four hundred had served as the vanguard of removal when many of them came to the Indian Territory ahead of the majority of the Pawnees. Made up predominantly of members of the South bands, this vanguard, like the fourteen hundred who followed them a year later, had removed to preserve the Pawnees' traditional way of life. When the majority arrived in the Indian Territory and then moved to a new reservation, Big Spotted Horse again became merely a soldier of the Kitkehaxkis. He had not become the chief of a schismatic band of Pawnees, because even after removal the South bands emphasized unity and consensus. Big Spotted Horse returned to the traditional warrior's activity of horse stealing, which in a few years produced his violent end, shot either by a U.S. marshal or a group of Texas cowboys.[4]

Although the South bands had reunited on the new reservation, the Skidis remained divided, with an assimilationist faction still on the old reservation in Nebraska. After more than a year of Sioux raids and white depredations, this group of less than four hundred moved to the new reservation in the Indian Territory.

Eagle Chief, the primary leader of the Skidis, had stayed behind in Nebraska and had lost six of his best horses to the Sioux in late October of 1874. Lone Chief, the leading assimilationist, had found his farmer neighbors more rapacious than the Sioux raiders. Grasshoppers had destroyed white as well as Indian crops in the summer of 1874. Local relief associations told the destitute settlers to cut timber on the reservation. By late November, over a hundred loads a day were being stolen. Lone Chief caught some farmers cutting trees and beat them. The Skidi leader later explained that he could not remain idle while whites stole Pawnee timber. The secretary of the Platte County Relief Aid Association made unsubtle threats of armed retaliation, and claimed that 150 families needed fuel from the reservation. Barclay White resisted what he considered absurdly low offers of payment from the white relief groups. He felt the U.S. Congress should fully compensate the Pawnees for their losses. On the other hand, he warned the small Pawnee remnant that "the first bloodshed upon their part, would result in disaster to them." In mid-April, these Pawnees told two visitors from the Board of Indian Commissioners that they wanted to move south and join the main body of their people. The visitors, Benjamin Rush Roberts and F. H. Smith, replied that Washington officials would not allow this removal until the coming fall, after the crops had been harvested. A company of soldiers, at the request of Roberts and Smith, moved onto the reservation but provided inadequate protection from the Sioux, who killed Eagle Chief's wife and a Pawnee schoolboy in August.

Only the reunion of the Skidis in December of 1872 successfully removed all the Pawnees from the reach of plundering Nebraskans and Sioux raiders. Although Eagle Chief resumed his role as primary leader of the entire band, the fact remained that the assimilationists had given up their separate ways and rejoined the traditionalist band members. This event, however, did not produce the revitalization of Skidi, or more broadly Pawnee, society. Instead, the establishment of the Pawnees on a new reservation produced a rapid decline in population and an increase in destitution and disease. A census in 1872, before Massacre Canyon and Big Spotted Horse's emigration, revealed 2,447 Pawnees in Nebraska. The first full count in the Indian Territory, in the spring of 1876, numbered the Pawnees at 2,026. In July of 1877, there were 1,523. Murderous Sioux, the rigors of removal, and prolonged malnutrition contributed to this five-year decline in population, but the climate of the new reservation, combined with malaria, yellow fever, and typhoid, took the heaviest toll. In the fall of 1875 many died of what Agent Burgess called "fever and ague," and numerous horses died of a hoof disease. In the summer of 1876, the Pawnees suffered severely from what an inspector from Washington called "malarial and similar diseases." In August of 1878, nearly one hundred Pawnees died within two or three days. The agency doctor blamed yellow fever. Earlier that month, others had died of what the doctor called "typho-malaria."[5]

When Barclay White first saw the Pawnees' new reservation, he thought the land of "very fair quality," with some ripe hardwood timber, but located in "very miasmatic country." With one eye on his goal of assimilation and the other on the peoples' health, the Hicksite superintendent told Agent Burgess to locate the Pawnees on upland sections and to keep them out of village life. Contrary to White's wishes, "the Indians massed in the valley of the Black Bear [Creek] living in tents and tepees and drinking the Creek water, resulting in a great mortality among them."[6]

During the remainder of the Quakers' tenure among the Pawnees, no progress in breaking up the Pawnee bands or in ending village life would be made. Even in the face of demographic disaster, the Pawnees clung to their traditional ways. In Nebraska, because of the Sioux, the Pawnees had consolidated into two villages for the Skidis and the South bands. In the Indian Territory, the four bands established separate villages, each with its own cooperatively cultivated fields. The earthlodge also returned. By the summer of 1878, the traditional lodge predominated among the Pitahawiratas, and the other bands lived in lodges or in the canvas tents provided for them when they first arrived on Black Bear Creek. A few assimilationists, most notably the Skidi interpreter, Baptiste Bayhylle, built houses and started farms. Prairie land was broken for each band's use in the summer of 1877, but traditional bottomland agriculture remained preeminent, along with the familiar crops of corn, beans, and squash. Semiannual buffalo hunts occurred but with increasingly meager results. By the summer of 1878, these hunts had ended.

The Pawnees sought smaller game in the region of their new home, but the poor results left them dependent on government beef rations for their meat supply. In addition, spare harvests forced the Pawnees to get additional food through supplies from trade, begging, or more government largess. Merchants complained that the cheap trade in treaty goods created ruinously underpriced competition from the Indians. One clothing merchant in Arkansas City, Kansas, reported: "I have no doubt that 5/8's of all the clothing issued to the Pawnees is traded off before worn."[7]

Such desperate trading did not improve the Pawnees' food supply. Less than five months after the reunion of the four bands, in late March of 1876, William Burgess telegraphed the commissioner of Indian Affairs: "The Pawnees are out of subsistence. What is to be done?" Soon Burgess reported that hundreds had left the reservation seeking food. Those left behind dug for roots and gathered mushrooms. Mayors of towns along the Kansas border complained of Pawnees "prowling around." Aroused by the supposed threat to these towns, Congress rushed through an emergency appropriation of $10,000. Burgess then made the best bargains he could for flour, bacon, and beef. The cattle contractors knew his need was urgent and delivered animals grossly inferior to government specifications. The Quaker agent accepted these faulty beeves and allowed them to be overweighed. He would later have cause to regret his compliance. As for the wandering Pawnees, runners went out and brought them back to the reservation. By late June, the people again had nearly no subsistence, and Agent Burgess made another round of emergency purchases.

By August of 1876, Barclay White and William Burgess were so anxious to find some means of support for the Pawnees that they allowed Luther and Frank North to recruit one hundred men into the reestablished Pawnee Scouts. The North brothers came to the new agency in the Indian Territory and within an hour had signed up a hundred eager volunteers. The Norths found that the Pawnees could not furnish their own horses because so many had died. As for the Indians themselves, Luther North recalled that they were "in very bad shape. They were miserably poor, nearly all of them had ague, and many of them were dying. They were very much discouraged and many of them were longing to get back to Nebraska."[8]

In the summer of 1877, Barclay White openly reported to his fellow Quakers: "The movement of the Pawnees from Nebraska to the Indian Territory has been disastrous in its results." White estimated that at least nine hundred had died in the two years since the move. Among the dead, he numbered "some of the best and most progessive persons in the tribe." Although greatly distressed, the good Friend from New Jersey still hoped that separate farms, effective schools, and Christian values would improve the Pawnees' lives. In eight years in Nebraska and in the Indian Territory, the Quakers had proven powerless even to ameliorate the Pawnees' problems. Yet Barclay White still held his illusions about the future. With death and hunger in their villages, the Pawnees could not share his outlook.[9]

In the late 1870s and early 1880s several suicides occurred among the Pawnees. One man whose five wives died in succession shot himself in the forehead with a pistol. A younger man who had "consumption" took a butcher knife and stabbed himself in the heart. In one summer, 1881, nine young men between the ages of eighteen and twenty-five killed themselves. Pawnee elders believed that a suicide's spirit would wander over the earth and never be allowed to join his ancestors in the Spirit Land. Some Skidis claimed that suicide had been unknown among them. Despair had overcome tradition.[10]

In late May of 1878, a Skidi schoolboy mentioned another suicide in a letter he addressed to the commissioner of Indian Affairs as a classroom exercise. Only months before the Quakers would depart, this letter showed that the Pawnees retained their earthlodge villages, river-bottom corn plots, and buffalo hunts. Yet the flat tone and matter-of-fact style of the boy's English prose did not conceal the desperate conditions of Pawnee existence. The Indian commissioner may not have read this remarkable document, but the entire letter deserved his attention:

Pawnee Agency, I. T.
May 30th 1878.

Hon. Com. of Ind. Aff.

Dear Sir,
Today our teacher told us to write letters and I thought I would.... Last summer the Cheyenne came to visit the Pawnees[.] when they saw them they were very glad and they gave horses to them. There was one band near the Arkansas river[.] I was there we had houses all fixed up and all of the Pawnees got very sick and our chief died so we left the houses[.] all of the different bands were sick and great many of them died[.] I was sick too but I got well. The Pawnees were on hunt and they did not kill many buffalo[.] they were very hungry[.] ... Pete-how-e-rat are living in lodges and some of them are planting corn yet. I never heard about the Chowees they live far off from us And the Kit-ka-hock too and that is where the boys and girls come to school such a long way off. The Skeedes have planted their corn long time ago and it is about three feet high. Once three of us went to the river to plant corn[.] ... Last summer my brother had one spotted horse and two grays and one colt and that makes four[.] he got sick and he thought he would not get well so he got a pistol and killed himself[.] When we were up to Nebraska he went to visit the Cheyennes[.] he got two horses and he gave me one but when we came down here the Osages stole it And I can not find it any more[.] I have not time to write more[.]

Yours truly

Charlie Tatiah

Indian School boy[11]

Although the depressing realities of disease, malnutrition, and poverty caused some Pawnees to commit suicide, the collapse of the traditional village life did not follow. Few chose the Quaker model of assimilation. By the end of the 1870s, the Hicksite Friends had abandoned the Pawnees — more than a decade before the Pawnees would abandon their villages. This collapse of the Quaker effort occurred not because of the Friends' failure to "civilize" Nebraska's Indians, but because of developments in national politics. The end of the Grant administration in early 1877 brought on a new reform effort in Indian affairs. Quakers who had entered the Indian work as reformers now found themselves the target of reformers. The result in the administration of the Pawnee reservation proved to be chaotic.

When Rutherford B. Hayes succeeded U. S. Grant as president in 1877, he appointed Carl Schurz, a liberal Republican, as secretary of the interior. In a story of corruption too well known to be detailed here, the scandals of the Grant administration had soiled even the vaunted reforms of the Peace Policy. One spectacular revelation had brought about the resignation of the secretary of war, William W. Belknap, for accepting bribes from the government trader on the Kiowa-Comanche reservation. Despite the stated policy of church-approved agents, politicians in both the White House and Congress had interfered with the appointment process to serve locally partisan or personally pecuniary interests. To some eyes, the fraudulent operation of the Indian service before 1869 had merely continued for eight years as part of the general political corruption of "Grantism." Once in office, Secretary Schurz moved quickly to correct these abuses. In June of 1877, he appointed a special board of inquiry to investigate charges of wrong-doing.

The board of inquiry consisted of three members — Joseph K. McCammon of the attorney general's office, Maj. Thomas H. Bradley of the U.S. Army, and George M. Lockwood, chief clerk of the Interior Department. None of these men came from the ranks of the religious and humanitarian reformers who had supported the Peace Policy. Their conclusions reflected this fact, as they strongly criticized the appointment of agents out of "sentiment" rather than on a record of efficiency and business sense. Religious convictions and moral honesty, the board concluded, were not enough for an Indian agent, who must, in the course of his work, confront corruption, avarice, and "the sharp contests characteristic of western life." Not surprisingly, Schurz agreed with the findings of the handpicked board of inquiry. The new secretary of the interior wished to change the emphasis of Indian policy toward what he considered "practical" goals on the reservations, such as the establishment of farming, the private ownership of land, and the application of federal law over the Indian. These goals had been part of the Peace Policy, but Schurz viewed the religious overtones of Grant's program as a mistake, especially as religion influenced the selection of agents.[12]

The board of inquiry believed it had discovered some shady collaborations between the chief clerk of the Indian office, S. A. Galpin, and a few beef contractors who wanted to cover up an overpriced purchase of substandard beef at an Indian agency. Before the board published its report, Schurz dismissed Galpin for withholding information on the case. In his determination to reform the Indian service, Schurz insisted on choosing his own assistants, and Galpin, clouded by possible corruption, could not be one of them. Schurz also refused to retain John Q. Smith, who had followed Edward P. Smith as commissioner of Indian Affairs in December of 1875 and who was a good friend of President Hayes. To replace John Q. Smith, Schurz appointed Ezra A. Hayt, a recent member of the Board of Indian Commissioners who shared the new secretary's reformist zeal. Hayt set about removing a number of Indian agents because of improper practices or a lack of business efficiency. The new commissioner of Indian Affairs often ignored the denomination which oversaw an agency when he appointed a replacement. The church policy of the Grant years was in clear decline. Only those agents who were loyal to Schurz and Hayt, following instructions and acting in a practical, efficient, and businesslike manner, could prosper under these two reformers. The agents who remained from the previous administration almost automatically came under suspicion and investigation. For the Hicksite Friends in Nebraska, especially those at the Pawnee agency, the actions of Schurz and Hayt seemed to be a direct attack on Quaker integrity.

The substandard cattle which led to S. A. Galpin's dismissal had been delivered to the Pawnee agency in April of 1876. In his efforts to feed the starving Pawnees, Agent Burgess had purchased grossly inferior animals from the closely knit organization that nearly monopolized the supply of beef to the agencies of the Indian Territory. Thomas Lanigan, a cattleman from Fort Smith, Arkansas, dominated the beef contractors of the area. Using his partners as subcontractors, Lanigan and his pool could manipulate not only the price but also the weight of cattle. Galpin, an acquaintance of Lanigan and his associates, investigated Burgess's purchase but dismissed any allegations against the beef contractors. Schurz's investigation uncovered the chief clerk's report on the Pawnee agency and led to his dismissal for failure to vigorously prosecute dishonest practices.

When William Burgess arrived in Coffeyville, Kansas, in 1876 to make his emergency purchase of beef, most dealers would not sell at any price because the grass-fed cattle that had just come off the winter range were in poor condition and, with three additional months of good grazing, would take on considerable weight and value. R. C. Crowell and Company, who represented Lanigan, agreed to supply the Pawnee agency. Crowell purchased from two associates of Lanigan, T. F. Eldridge and Joseph Leach, a herd of eighty-two yearlings, two-year-old steers, and cows barely fit for food. Crowell's records showed that the cattle weighed 74,456 pounds gross at $3.10 per hundredweight, whereas Leach and Eldridge, who had purchased the eighty-two cattle earlier that month, listed a gross weight of 50,850 pounds at a price of $2.50 per hundredweight. These now supposedly well-fed cattle were delivered to the Pawnee agency. Immediately before the weighing, the animals were salted, watered, and fed fresh grass in open disregard of federal regulations. In the presence of William Burgess, as the cattle were weighed ten at a time, two cowboys stepped up on the scales to increase the amount. Burgess accepted a gross weight of 73,718 pounds and paid $3.50 per hundredweight. Crowell and Company received $2,580.13, which meant that the "Lanigan ring" had made $1,309.13 off an original purchase of $1,271 by Leach and Eldridge — a nice profit of 103 percent.

The cattle sale of April, 1876, underwent three separate investigations. In each inquiry more examples of Burgess's irregular administration of the Pawnee agency were uncovered. No evidence clearly pointed to personal profit on the agent's part. Indeed, Burgess was very candid in admitting his anomalous actions, but always in reference to the exigencies of his situation. Besides accepting underweight beef at inflated prices, Burgess regularly paid for labor by writing vouchers for purchases of nonexistent corn and potatoes. In the first case, he needed to feed starving Pawnees. In the second, he needed to hire men who would not work for the money budgeted, so he increased their salaries by commandeering funds appropriated to purchase corn and potatoes, two food items rarely available in the local area.[13] Yet, whatever his good intentions, Burgess had committed fraud.

The first two investigations of the Pawnee agency had not led to an indictment, but had produced strong criticisms of Burgess and his administration. Chief Clerk Galpin and Superintendent William Nicholson, an Orthodox Quaker, had visited the Pawnee agency in December of 1876. Galpin found many discrepancies in supply and pay records, which did not follow bookkeeping regulations. The agent, Galpin maintained, "appears to have complied with instructions when it suited his convenience so to do, but not otherwise." Nicholson agreed with the tone of Galpin's report, but took pains to point out that the Pawnee agency had not come under the Central Superintendency until May of 1876, a month after the notorious beef purchase from R. C. Crowell and Company. Still, the Orthodox superintendent found no criminal act on the part of his Hicksite agent. He later told a U.S. attorney: "I never had any reason to suspect a fraudulent collusion between the Agent and Messers Crowell & Co. who represented Mr. Lanigan. I attributed the circumstance to that general laxity and want of force so accurately depicted in Mr. Galpin's report and which was likely to prove quite unequal in dealing with positive men."[14]

A month after Galpin and Nicholson had visited the agency, William Leeds, representing the Board of Indian Commissioners, appeared at Burgess's agency for the second investigation of the notorious beef contracts. Like Galpin, Leeds strongly criticized Burgess's haphazard records. He believed that other beef purchases besides those of April had been of substandard quality. Burgess offered no formal defense of his actions. He simply asked to be relieved of his duties. The commissioner of Indian Affairs accepted his resignation, to become effective as soon as a successor was appointed.

William Burgess might have made good his awkward exit from the Pawnee agency if the new administration of Carl

Schurz had not launched its own examination of S. A. Galpin and the Indian service. This third investigation produced an indictment in October of 1877 against Burgess, William C. Masten, T. F. Eldridge, and Joseph Leach (the latter three members of the Lanigan ring). Criminal proceedings moved slowly, and a series of continuances prevented any formal trial. Meanwhile, witnesses scattered or disappeared. One cowboy, present at the fraudulent April weighing, died in a gunfight provoked while digging a grave. The Quaker clerk the Pawnee agency returned to his home in Mount Ephraim, New Jersey. Other important witnesses seemed hesitant to testify against the powerful cattle contractors. Finally, in April of 1881, the case was dismissed. William Burgess may never have conspired with the Lanigan ring to defraud the government for his personal gain, but his indictment along with the ring members proved the legal salvation of the former agent. The cattle interests would never let the case come to trial, so Burgess, who was certainly guilty of fraud, although perhaps without criminal intent, avoided the embarrassment of a court hearing or worse.[15]

The "irregularities" of the Burgess administration left such a strong suspicion of Quakerly corruption in the mind of Ezra Hayt, Schurz's new commissioner of Indian Affairs, that he insisted on installing his own clerk at the Pawnee agency. Hayt's spy, Joseph Hertford, reported zealously on every minute breach of regulations. These actions bedeviled and enraged the last two Hicksite agents to the Pawnees. They and their fellow Quakers took Hertford's presence as an insult to the Friends' reputation for honesty.

Charles H. Searing of New York had taken control of the Pawnee agency on May 16, 1877. The successor to Burgess had worked previously at the Santee Sioux agency. He was nominated by the Baltimore Yearly Meeting on the recommendation of its Standing Committee on the Indian Concern. President Hayes and the Senate had both approved. Searing's would be the last appointment to the Pawnee agency which followed the pattern of church-state cooperation established in the Grant administration. Jacob Troth had served as Pawnee agent for three years and eight months. William Burgess served for four years, four and a half months. Searing would be the Pawnee agent for only fifteen months. Samuel Ely, the last Quaker agent, stayed a mere three months.

The man most responsible for pushing the Quakers off the Pawnee reservation, Joseph Hertford, arrived at the agency on October 20, 1877. Hertford, a Catholic, had been born in Ireland but had lived in New Jersey prior to taking up his post in the Indian Territory. Married and fifty-three years of age, he brought a nearly fanatic energy to his work. In a three-month span from November, 1877, through early February, 1878, Hertford wrote at least fifteen letters directly to Ezra Hayt that focused on bookkeeping errors and personal misconduct. These accusations often implied criminal behavior but were based as much on hearsay and personal opinion as on direct observation. Hertford would report if signatures on annuity rolls seemed improperly witnessed. He complained when annuity funds went directly to the agency trader to pay Pawnee debts, instead of to the individual Pawnees and then to the trader. When Searing reported dwindling medical supplies, Hertford speculated that the agent either wished to fradulently obtain greater supplies or needed to cover up some shady dealings.[16]

Hertford's complaint about direct payments to the trader were justified, but in his speculation concerning the medical supplies, he ignored the recent epidemics among the Pawnees which might have prompted Agent Searing to keep extra medical provisions. Similarly, the commissioner's spy ignored the Pawnees' ongoing food crisis. Although game remained scarce, Pawnees still went out to hunt and allowed their relatives to claim their rations. Hertford believed such claims were merely a ruse to obtain double rations. Even if that were true in some cases, Hertford still seemed insensitive to the Pawnees' plight.

Hertford also claimed that Agent Searing acted like a feudal lord, that he kept the "Lion's share" of annuities, and that payoffs regularly flowed to the agent and his "ring." Such charges should have caused an investigation and trial, but Hertford had little evidence to support his accusations. Only one possible court case against Searing surfaced —

when he failed to record the sale of agency steer hides worth $200. Hertford eagerly charged the agent with embezzlement. After letters and visits from Hertford, U.S. attorneys in Arkansas and Kansas discussed the possibility of a legal case. Searing explained that he had neglected to record the sale of the hides to Artemus Patterson of Arkansas City, Kansas, and that the money had gone to buy medical and other supplies for the agency. No trial occurred.

Joseph Hertford disliked his servile position as clerk. He desired the status and authority at the Pawnee agency which he felt his special relationship with the commissioner of Indian Affairs implied. Soon after his arrival, Hertford claimed that Agent Searing "with an air of bombast . . . [demanded that I] . . . light the stove fire — bring in wood — sweep the office, etc., etc. If I had been a menial sycophant to succumb to such acts of tyranny he might next have required of me to black the stove or his boots, or clean his Fowling piece." Soon Hertford refused to appear at the office every day, and Searing cut his pay by a third. In effect, a government investigator sent to work at an agency where federal regulations about purchases and bookkeeping had been haphazardly obeyed was now contributing to the disorganization of the Pawnee agency. Gradually, he began to operate independently and refused to keep records or write correspondence unless he personally approved. Hertford functioned virtually as a second agent. If Baptiste Bayhylle, the official interpreter, said the stable boy abused the agency stock, Hertford wrote to Washington to have the boy removed. If Searing requested a new wagon, Hertford wrote to say the old wagon could be repaired.[17]

Part of Hertford's duties included the issuing of weekly supplies and rations to the Pawnees. Agent Searing discovered that clandestine gifts of government supplies were going to interpreter Bayhylle and some chiefs in order to build up support for Hertford's spy activities. Searing promptly removed Hertford as issue clerk. Hertford retaliated by refusing to sign three receipts issued under his authority. In addition, the Quakers believed that Hertford had influenced Bayhylle and others not to sign the annuity roll. By his actions, Hertford had left Searing with four imperfect documents totaling $18,000. If the annuity roll and receipts did not pass federal audit, Searing might have to pay the full sum out of his bond.

The agency interpreter had established a cozy alliance with Joseph Hertford. In March, Baptiste Bayhylle signed a letter to the commissioner of Indian Affairs which in all probability was written by Hertford. The letter denounced Searing for using "every means to keep us back in our wishes to become as good citizens as the Whites." Such statements could only impress an official unfamiliar with the Pawnees' tenacious traditionalism. Bayhylle claimed that if he came to Washington, he could reveal other problems which he could not put in writing because "Searing sees our letters." If true, Bayhylle ignored this danger at the end of this letter, where he claimed that Searing treated the Pawnees like "dogs" and had cheated them of their money and rations. Two weeks later Hertford wrote to Commissioner Hayt on Bayhylle's behalf. He requested a certificate, signed by Hayt and the secretary of the interior, which would certify Bayhylle as "Head Chief of the Pawnee Tribe of Indians." This certificate, he said, would be used primarily in dealings with whites. Hertford also forwarded Bayhylle's request for a $200 raise in his salary as interpreter, a 50 percent jump from the $400 he had received. Hertford said the Pawnee council would vote for the raise because the Skidi mixed-blood was their "head chief."[18] Conceivably, the "official" certificate and the $200 were to pay for Bayhylle's signature on the earlier letter.

Charles Searing had discovered that he could not fire Joseph Hertford because of the clerk's special relationship with the commissioner of Indian Affairs. So, by February of 1878, Searing asked to resign. Ezra Hayt did not consult the Central Executive Committee of the Hicksite Yearly Meetings for a replacement, but appointed a Hicksite Quaker, Samuel S. Ely of Pennsylvania, who had been the farmer at the Oto agency. Ely believed he was in line to become the Oto agent. He read of his appointment in the local newspapers and wrote to Washington to say that he and his wife, a former teacher at that agency, preferred to stay among the Otos.

Given no other choice, Ely reluctantly accepted the Pawnee position. Although February 18 was the official date on his new contract, by mid-March Ely had not left Nebraska. Hayt wrote: "You will go to Pawnee at once." Still slow to respond, Ely did not go to the agency for another month. Upon his arrival, a letter from Washington instructed him to reduce salaries and release certain Quaker employees "in order to free yourself entirely from the old regime." In his reply, Ely indicated that he wished to cooperate but that he wished to free himself of the petty surveillance of Joseph Hertford. As firmly as he could, Ely asked Hayt that his authority over Hertford be unobstructed because, although adequate as a clerk, Hertford was "not suited to the other requirements of the position [i.e., issuing weekly rations]." Ely knew that his situation at the agency was a delicate one. In a postscript, he told Hayt: "I wish this letter to be strictly confidential for as long as Mr. H. remains I want nothing to occur to prevent, our present, pleasant relation, so please let no one see, or know its contents but yourself."[19]

Ely wished to avoid the Searing-Hertford feud and for nearly two months he evaded a confrontation while awaiting word from Washington that his bond had been approved. Finally, on June 13, Ely officially replaced Searing as agent, but Searing did not leave. The matter of the $18,000 in improper receipts remained to be settled. Barclay White had arrived in early June, as a special agent of the Central Executive Committee, in order to straighten out Searing's records. White resolved as best he could the problem of Hertford's refusal to witness the supply receipts; a Pawnee who had seen the issues signed in place of Hertford. Government regulations required two "disinterested" witnesses, so the fact that the cooperative Pawnee had received his individual ration did not make the receipts "perfect." White still felt they would be accepted by a federal auditor. More than one signature, however, was needed on the incomplete annuity roll. In order to solve this problem, which involved $10,000, two councils were held with the Pawnees. In these councils, White, Searing, and Samuel Ely openly challenged Joseph Hertford and his ally Baptiste Bayhylle. The second meeting, according to Barclay White, "was the most exciting and disorderly Indian council I ever attended." It produced the needed signature marks but cost the Quakers control of the Pawnee agency after Hertford wrote to Washington about the incident.[20]

In the late fall of 1877, Charles Searing had decided to entrust Stacy Matlock, the agency trader, with delivery of the annuity payment from the National Depository Bank in Lawrence, Kansas. Searing had little knowledge of the region and feared he might be robbed on the trip. In return for Matlock's undertaking the journey to Lawrence, Searing agreed to pay directly to the trader all the debts owed Matlock by the Pawnees. In the past, as the time for the annual treaty payment approached, many Pawnees purchased trade goods on credit. After receiving their individual treaty funds, they repaid their debt. But in the late fall of 1877, the Pawnees who came to the agency office to get their individual payments found Matlock with his books before him seated next to the agent. As the Indians came forward, money was withheld from those who owed debts to the trader. Some Pawnees received nothing. In the final total, Matlock acquired $6,350, and the Pawnees received only $3,595. The remaining $55 was given Matlock to pay for his trip to and from Lawrence. Encouraged by Hertford and Bayhylle, a few disgruntled Pawnees did not place their mark on the annuity rolls. Others did not need this encouragement.[21]

Charles Searing had never overseen an annuity payment. Still, Barclay White knew that Searing had made a bad but honest mistake. So far as the Pawnees were concerned, his actions had "soured their minds" and made Searing "unpopular with the Indians." In addition, Searing had unwisely divided among the chiefs and soldiers $3,000 in salaries which they had voted for themselves in council ($80 to each chief, $60 to each soldier). Such "salaries" had been accepted in the past, but in this case the commissioner of Indian Affairs did not approve. Searing tried to hide these salaries by reporting that the Pawnees had received equal payments of $6.54, whereas he actually paid out only $5.00 per capita and used the remainder to pay the chiefs and soldiers. This action plunged the agency accounts into further disarray. Searing also had to inform the chiefs and soldiers that they could not get additional "salaries" in the future. All these financial problems, along with Searing's unpopularity, became the focus of the two dramatic council meetings in June of 1878.

Perhaps in anticipation of the possibility of future legal cases, Barclay White had notes taken at the two council meetings.[22] The first council, on June 19, began with a statement by the Pawnees' new agent, Samuel Ely. With no direct reference to Searing's financial problems, Ely requested that the Pawnees sign for all annuity payments and beef rations on the day of issue. When he finished his remarks an old, familiar figure rose to address the council.

Barclay White reminded the "chiefs and soldiers" that for several years he had been their superintendent in Nebraska, but on this visit he was in the service not of the federal government but of the Society of Friends. "That Society desires that all your business shall be, by your agent done in an honest manner." With the approval of the secretary of the interior, Carl Schurz, White had permission to look over the financial records in the agency office. He found that some certificates on former agent Searing's annuity payroll were unsigned. White explained the possible loss of Searing's bond and concluded firmly:

It is your solemn duty as honest men, to see that your receipts to him . . . are full and complete as the Government requires. I have paid your annuities to you during five years, you have dealt honestly with me, why are you not willing to be honest with Agent Searing[?] If you think your Agent has cheated you, you are mistaken, as I find by his papers that he has paid all that is coming to you.

Le-cuts-la-sharo, Eagle Chief of the Skidis, who, along with Lone Chief, had stayed behind in Nebraska with the assimilationist group, responded first to White's words:

We do not hate Mr. Searing. Our Great Father sent that money here for the agent to pay us. When you paid us, you gave us every cent, you know we always go in debt and always pay our debts. The trader never lost a cent. In this annuity payment by Agent Searing, all I did was to touch the Clerk's pen as my receipt and did not see any money for the receipt. When you paid us you paid us all the money, then we paid to the trader what we owed him and we always had some money left.

The reason we did not want to sign Agent Searing's payroll was because we did not want to be treated in his way.

La-ru-chuck-are-shar, "Sun Chief," a Chaui leader and the nephew of the deceased Pitalesharo, agreed with Eagle Chief. He said the Pawnees had to chop down trees to sell as rails so they could get something to eat. "It seems that our agent felt more interest for the trader than for us." Barclay White replied that he did not approve of Searing's paying debts before annuities but that Searing had not stolen any of the money. Good Chief of the Skidis pointed out that Searing had worked with the Santee Sioux and should know better. Using impressive logic, he told White: "You say these accounts are all right, that may be so, we do not know anything about it. We cannot read or write. We have had a good many agents and always got along right. This one commenced to do wrong at first."

Barclay White reminded the Pawnees of his personal honesty and of the money he got for them after the disaster at Massacre Canyon. "I have always worked for your interest," White pleaded, "and this day I am trying to keep up your reputation as honest men." The Pawnees seemed to recognize that the issue was not their or Barclay White's honesty, but the misjudgment of Charles Searing. Doctor Chief expressed this view and then Baptiste Bayhylle, who had interpreted all the Pawnees' speeches, addressed Barclay White: "Colonel Barclay! You have always been a good father, but I have reason for not signing that Pay-roll. I have been sworn as a Government Officer, and the agent . . . has cheated us."

Charles Searing now tried to defend his own actions. He said the Pawnees had received all their treaty annuities either in cash or as trade. The council seemed unimpressed. The next speaker referred to Searing's words: "It is not our fault . . . it is his own fault if he has done anything wrong." Ter-re-re-cox, "Warcry," seemed especially upset.[23] In reference to the treaty which created the annuity payment, he stated: "The Great Father at Washington owes us money. We are not dogs, we are men. . . . I have not refused to do anything for our Great Father. If our late agent loses money, it is his own fault and we are not to blame." Other speakers reemphasized the Pawnees' irritation with Searing. No one volunteered to sign the annuity roll, and on this obstinate note, the council closed.

White, Ely, and Searing had confronted Pawnee consensus, not the manipulations of Joseph Hertford. The Pawnees' anger with their former agent seemed very real. Hertford may have capitalized on this anger, but he did not create it. In order to offset the Pawnees' attitude, Barclay White turned to Tie-ta-sha-cod-dic, "Strikes Chief," who had not been present at the first council. The Kitkehaxki leader and the Quaker special agent were old acquaintances. Strikes Chief had testified at the murder trial of Yellow Sun, which Barclay White had attended. In addition, Tie-ta-sha-cod-dic had led the effort for removal along with his fellow chief Ter-re-kaw-wah of the Pitahawiratas. At a private meeting, Tie-ta-sha-cod-dic agreed to call a second council. Barclay White did not reveal in his journal whether any special arrangement induced Tie-ta-sha-cod-dic to cooperate. Later Pawnee statements at the second council showed that the usual trade-off was anticipated. In order to get the necessary marks on the annuity rolls, the chiefs and soldiers expected the reestablishment of their $3,000 in salaries.

The second council, on June 27, was held at the agency schoolhouse. Samuel Ely said that Tie-ta-sha-cod-dic had called for the meeting, but the Kitkehaxki chief took a more diplomatic tone, explaining that he had been away on a long hunt and wished merely to be informed about the first council. Barclay White gave the Quaker version of that meeting. Once more, he tried to intimidate the Pawnees. White claimed that anyone who "willfully" prevented the settlement of Searing's accounts "does wrong and commits a crime against the Agent and Government." Tie-ta-sha-cod-dic first spoke to the Pawnees without translation by Bayhylle. He then made a statement for the white officials. He said reassuringly that he did not think the trader, Stacy Matlock, took more money than the Pawnees owed him. He felt the Pawnees had received their full annuity, but he still did not like Searing's way of business. Ter-re-re-cox, who had spoken so angrily at the first council, addressed the Pawnees uninterpreted and then said through translation that the commissioner of Indian Affairs should decide. If the commissioner said to sign the annuity roll, the Pawnees would sign.

The suspension of translation had become a way for the Pawnees to argue among themselves with little white interference. Baptiste Bayhylle addressed the council and did not translate his own words. The next Pawnee speaker said that he agreed with Bayhylle's statement and would not sign unless the commissioner of Indian Affairs said he must. Samuel Ely replied sharply in an effort to prevent the decision from resting with Commissioner Hayt:

Chiefs and soldiers! One word more, this is a matter on which I have expressed no opinion. I have not been asked for it. I know something about honest business. You ought to stand up like men of honor, and if you have received your money, come forward and sign the receipt for what you have received. . . .
In a few days I will have to make a Payroll and I will have to pay the money into your hands. Now if some one comes in and says I have kept some, are you going to do as you have done this time and not sign a receipt for me?

The new Quaker agent, Samuel Ely, had recognized how unfriendly administrators in Washington and obstinate Pawnees at his agency could combine to sabotage his financial records. His words to the council contained the unsubtle threat of withholding future annuities. Baptiste Bayhylle hesitated in his translation. "I do not quite understand the last you said," he told Ely. The agent replied snappishly, "I have spoken in plain words and I expect to have it interpreted, that is your business." Ely repeated his last words, but Bayhylle remained silent. "Baptiste! Interpret to the Indians what I said," Ely then demanded. The Skidi employee turned to the agent. "I will interpret, and I will have a plain talk with you after Council." But Bayhylle did not address the council. Instead, he spoke directly to Tie-ta-sha-cod-dic, and then translated the Kitkehaxki chief's statement: "I received eighty dollars and paid Stacy Matlock, our trader, sixty dollars." Ely asked, "Will you sign the receipt for that money?" Tie-ta-sha-cod-dic replied, "I will."

These two words caused a near explosion in the council. Baptiste Bayhylle made another uninterpreted speech. Then much untranslated talk followed. Ter-re-re-cox seemed passionately opposed to the statements of another Pawnee. Excitement reigned. Tomahawk pipes were flourished. Bayhylle sent a messenger out to get him a weapon. He addressed the council once more without translation and then spoke in English: "Get your papers out and I will sign them."

Apparently, Baptiste Bayhylle had been the major obstruction to Pawnee consensus, in part owing to his alliance with Hertford and in part because of his desire to be recognized as the "head chief" by whites. As a Skidi chief, Bayhylle did participate in the councils of the chiefs and soldiers. Indeed, he was the only council member who spoke English. Bayhylle profited well from his role as both intermediary and interpreter between white officials and the Pawnee council. His bilingualism and mixed heritage made him a natural candidate for assimilation and for the positive attention of white officials. He had selected 160 acres of excellent land on the new reservation, built a house, and started a farm. He even employed some fellow Pawnees to work on his land. Yet Bayhylle remained an independent operator. Although he was the uncle of Lone Chief, he still did not become the leader of the assimilationist Pawnees, even among his fellow Skidis. As his alliance with Hertford showed, Bayhylle knew how to capitalize on factions among the whites, but his confrontation with Tie-ta-sha-cod-dic at the second council meeting also showed that traditionalist leaders, ruling by consensus, still limited factionalism among the Pawnees.[24]

Joseph Hertford openly tried to prevent Baptiste Bayhylle from signing Searing's incomplete annuity roll. He then told the council that their marks would be illegal, but Ely's threat of withholding future treaty payments had turned the tide. After they agreed to sign, Tie-ta-sha-cod-dic asked Ely to get more money for the Pawnees from Washington. Ter-re-re-cox told Barclay White to get eighty dollars for each of the chiefs and soldiers. Clearly, members of the Pawnee council hoped their cooperation had produced a trade-off and not a capitulation.

In late July, Samuel Ely paid the price of Pawnee cooperation. The new agent supported a resolution of the council to reestablish $3,000 in salaries among "Chiefs and the Headman of the Tribe, in payment for their services as business men and officers." As for Charles Searing, with his amended financial documents and the help of a U.S. senator, he managed to settle his accounts without personal loss.[25] Joseph Hertford, however, remained in his position as clerk and soon managed to remove the last Quaker agent among the Pawnees.

Hertford kept Commissioner Hayt well informed on the two council meetings. He denounced Barclay White for "sophistry" and called the newly signed roll "illegal." After the second council, Hertford said that Agent Ely intended to act toward him as Searing had done. Missing the humor of his own words, Hertford claimed that "the freezing out process has already begun" and pointed to his lack of a government stove to heat his cabin as an example of Ely's spite. In a personal confession to Hayt, Hertford revealed: "I feel bad occasionally to think, that I cannot live harmoniously. I have always led a cheerful happy life, and always loved, and do love peace, as I told Mr. Ely, but I further said I could not expect it as long as the ring existed here."[26]

With Hertford's reports and Hayt's cooperation, the exit of the Quakers from the Pawnee agency began. In July, two months before Samuel Ely's formal removal, an Indian Department clerk in Washington noted on the envelope of the Quaker agent's request to hire two employees: "As Mr. Ely is to go nothing need be done about this list." By early August, Ely had his first premonitions of doom. Commissioner Hayt revoked Stacy Matlock's license as agency trader. Hertford wrote, with some overdramatization, that at the news of Matlock's dismissal, "Mr. Ely then started like a man demented, and said in [the] presence of the Interpreter, and Chiefs, to me, 'that it was not in the interest of the Indians but it was striking at the Society of Friends.'"[27]

The Quakers soon launched a counteroffensive. In August, five different petitions from the Pawnee agency arrived in Washington. Four documents called for the retention of dismissed employees. Twenty-seven signatures and marks, including the name of Baptiste Bayhylle, supported Stacy

Matlock as trader. On the fifth petition, addressed to the president of the United States, ninety Pawnees asked that Joseph Hertford be discharged because "he is no friend of the Indians, he lies all the time . . . writes all kinds of lies to the Commissioner and begs us to go against our Agent." Baptiste Bayhylle remained somewhat loyal to Hertford and did not sign this petition. Other bilingual Pawnees, such as Joseph Esau and Nelson Rice, as well as many major chiefs, did sign or place their mark.[28]

Benjamin Rush Roberts, on behalf of the Baltimore Yearly Meeting's Indian committee, presented the petitions to Ezra Hayt in Washington. The commissioner of Indian Affairs told the Hicksite representative that "it was insubordination on the part of Agent S. S. Ely to be forwarding petitions of the Indians, for the removal of Clerk Hertford." Other arguments could not sway the commissioner. After an examination of the voluminous correspondence from Hertford to Hayt, Roberts called the charges against Agent Ely "trifling." However, in order to secure the "unmolested" operation of the Pawnee agency, the Baltimore Friends committee recommended that both Hertford and Ely be withdrawn. Commissioner Hayt ignored this suggestion. He could not be influenced even by a final petition in support of Ely signed by the major chiefs (with only Baptiste Bayhylle absent).[29]

On September 16, 1878, acting on instructions from Ezra Hayt, Inspector John McNeil suspended Samuel Ely from his office as agent. Although Hayt and McNeil vaguely talked of Ely's "countenancing frauds in the construction of an apothecary shop," the major reason for Ely's dismissal, as explained to the secretary of the interior, rested on "an utter disregard of orders." In short, Ely, like Charles Searing, had proved himself more loyal to the Quakers than to the new regime in Washington. His replacement, Andrew C. Williams of Kansas, was not a member of the Society of Friends.[30]

As for Joseph Hertford, he stayed on, but his independent ways soon created a feud with the new agent. Charges of fraud and theft passed between the two men. Hertford became clerk of the Sac and Fox agency in April of 1879. Once there, he continued to write special letters to the commissioner of Indian Affairs. Williams only stayed until the end of May, 1879, at which time the Pawnees welcomed their fourth agent in a little more than two years.

The dismissal of Samuel Ely left the Hicksite Friends in great confusion as to their responsibilities toward the Pawnee agency. Benjamin Rush Roberts and two other members of the Central Executive Committee met twice with President Hayes in late September of 1878. Much to the Quaker delegation's surprise, both President Hayes and Secretary of the Interior Schurz expressed a strong desire for the Friends to continue their management of the Pawnee agency. They asked for a new Quaker agent promising that he could nominate his own employees.

Filled with renewed determination, Benjamin Rush Roberts returned to Baltimore, where the Standing Committee on the Indian Concern began its search for a new agent. Out of approximately ten applications, a suitable candidate was selected and his name sent to the office of Indian Affairs. After an interview in Washington at the Interior Department, the Quaker nominee returned home to await word of his appointment. No letter arrived, so Benjamin Rush Roberts called on Commissioner Hayt in Washington. Hayt informed Roberts "that the department considered the applicant entirely unfitted for the position." Roberts and the Baltimore Friends could not ignore this final affront from the commissioner of Indian Affairs. Three days later, on March 21, 1879, at the instruction of the standing committee, Roberts wrote to Secretary Carl Schurz that the Baltimore Friends relinquished "all charge, or responsibility" for the Pawnee agency and declined to make "any further nominations for Agents." Appropriately, Commissioner Hayt, not Secretary Schurz, acknowledged Roberts's letter and released the Baltimore Friends from their duties.[31]

Ezra Hayt had been the key figure in driving the Quakers from the Pawnee agency. His determination to expunge what he perceived as Friendly corruption had overridden the weak promises of President Hayes and Secretary Schurz. Hayt's actions revealed the uncompromising zeal of the reformer —

a zeal similar to that which the Friends had demonstrated when they took up their duties under the Grant administration. Indeed, their insistence on controlling all agency appointments rested on the ideal of moral Quakers improving the "corrupt" Indian service. The traumas of the antislavery crusade and the Civil War had shifted the Quakers' attentions from internal denominational discipline to a renewed effort in race relations. This shift had allowed the Friends, as a body, to become more active in social reform efforts such as the Freedmen's Bureau and later the Peace Policy. Ironically, Ezra Hayt's administration of Indian affairs reemphasized the concept of discipline through strict adherence to regulations. He would have fitted in well with the conservative Hicksites of the antebellum period who tried to maintain unity in their branch of the Society of Friends despite the challenges of radical abolitionism.[32]

For a postbellum, altruistic Quaker like William Burgess, the starving Pawnees' need for food superseded the government's strict requirements for beef contracts. The substandard, fraudulently weighed cattle which Burgess purchased in 1876 allowed the Pawnees to survive one episode in their continuing food crisis. If Burgess had followed government regulations, Ezra Hayt would have had no significant grounds for purging all the Quakers at the Pawnee agency, but then more Pawnees would have starved. Burgess had brought himself and his fellow Quakers under a cloud of corruption, but his motivations were humanitarian. Ezra Hayt's motivations were bureaucratic.

Whether Quaker or bureaucrat, each side believed that an effective Indian service on the local level rested with the character of the Indian agent and his employees. Whether honest, altruistic Quakers or well-disciplined Washington appointees, the quality of the people working at the agency was supposedly the key. Yet the tragic, complex history of the Pawnees during the administration of four Quaker agents demonstrated the fallacy of such thoughts. In nine years, the Quakers made little progress toward their goal of transforming the Pawnees into educated, Christianized farmers. They simply did not have the power to force such a transformation. At his most powerful, the agent merely controlled the agency. Assuming approval and funding from Washington, he could hire teachers, doctors, and farmers; construct dams, houses, and schools; clear, plow, and plant fields. The employment of some Indians, the example of white employees, and the education of children supposedly aided assimilation.

Control of schoolrooms, hired labor, and work projects did not mean, however, that the agent controlled the reservation lands or the Indians who lived on them. In Nebraska, Quaker agents could not stop Sioux raiders or white timber thieves. They could not even prevent the Pawnees from abandoning their reservation. Yet what the agent did control brought its own controversies. In Nebraska, white neighbors complained of Quaker "exclusiveness" in jobs and tried to have the agents removed. In the Indian territory, such exclusiveness prompted fears of conspiracy and corruption, and finally led to the Quakers' removal.

As for the Pawnees, they confronted the extermination of the buffalo, the depredations of the Sioux, and the devastations of drought, grasshoppers, and disease. In the face of such disasters, the four bands did not allow their traditional social organization and way of life to collapse. Factions developed but did not permanently rupture Pawnee consensus. The followers of Big Spotted Horse and the Skidi assimilationists eventually settled with the rest of the four bands in the Indian Territory. In addition, the chiefs continued in their primary role of defenders of consensus. Their authority still rested with the extended family structure of the village. This structure could not be maintained if the Pawnees moved onto farmsteads, so the chiefs, except for Baptiste Bayhylle, usually ignored the allotment plans of their agents. Some chiefs, especially among the Skidis, did not ignore the possible benefits of white agricultural techniques. Plowed fields could mean more crops for their hungry people.

Indeed, the chiefs realized that federal funds, government supplies, and meat rations, along with plowed fields, had replaced the buffalo as the four bands' major food supply. Consequently, the chiefs continued to refine their negotiation skills in council and experimented with letters and petitions to Washington. The next fifteen years would demand more adaptations for the Pawnees on their reservation until its dissolution in 1893. But the future would not produce new Quaker "fathers." Of the seven Nebraska tribes under the care of the Hicksite Friends, the Pawnees saw the earliest termination of the "Quaker Policy." Still, the Pawnees' traditional village life would slowly collapse by the mid-1890s. Under the pressures of government programs and through profound changes in their own economy, the Pawnees became a loose aggregate of people living, not in villages, but on farm tracts.[33] This transformation could be attributed only in part to an earlier "Friendly" persuasion.

CHAPTER FIVE

The Otos and Factionalism

Unlike the Pawnees, another Nebraska tribe, the Otos, and their affiliates, the Missourias, could not avoid a lasting schism in the 1870s.[1] The Pawnees weathered the crisis of removal and the factions it produced. After the Otos considered moving south, however, the people remained split into two divisions. The disruption of traditional social structures, especially in the leadership role of certain families, contributed greatly to the Otos' factionalization. The Quaker agents helped create this division, but the Oto case does not fit easily into the models of American Indian schisms presented in other historical studies. For example, religious differences did not explain the divisions which arose among the Otos. Under two Hicksite agents, no religious conversions to Friends' Christianity occurred. Yet, confusingly, the two Oto factions called themselves the "Coyotes" and the "Quakers." This latter name indicated the willingness of one faction to cooperate, at least for a time, with its Quaker administrators. On the other hand, the Coyotes, or Mine-cot-tees in the Oto language, did not reject the political importance of white officials. They recognized the power of officials in Washington and tried to have these officials overrule the decisions of Quaker administrators in Nebraska. Each of the two Oto factions, therefore, demonstrated a mixture of independent action and reliance on government authority.[2]

Eventually both factions agreed that the entire society should move south and asked for approval from Washington in order to override the opposition of their Hicksite agent. Though by 1878 each faction wished to leave Nebraska, neither group could agree on whether the Coyotes or the Quakers should lead the people once they settled in the Indian Territory. As a result of this conflict, the Otos did not reunite after their removal.

Among the Otos, the idea of removal had occurred well before the arrival of their first Hicksite agent. In 1847, in a pattern familiar to the Pawnees and other Plains groups, the Teton Sioux had driven the Otos off the buffalo ranges north of the Platte. Although the Pawnees and the Otos had fought each other in the earlier years of the nineteenth century, by the 1830s the two tribes had established friendly relations based, in part, on a shared defense against Sioux raiders. Perhaps because the Otos were so small in number — between five and six hundred in the 1850s — the Sioux did not carry out against them the same extensive war of attrition that they waged against the Pawnees. Still, Cheyennes and Osages continued to trouble the Otos, as well as occasional Sioux parties. In addition, white emigration and settlement threatened to overrun the Otos' villages on the Platte. In 1851, the government agent reported that the Otos were exceedingly anxious to sell their lands and leave.

Instead of removal to the Indian Territory, the federal government responded with the treaty of 1854. In an arrangement similar to the Pawnees' agreement of three years later, the Otos in 1854 relinquished their claims to all lands except for a tract twenty-five miles long and ten miles wide, south of present-day Beatrice, Nebraska. The Otos' reservation extended some two miles into Kansas. When they moved south to their new home, the Otos objected to the Big Blue River serving as the eastern boundary of their reservation. They pointed out that the river formed a natural barrier against raiders out of the west and that the other side of the river also contained better timberlands. Accordingly, the federal government agreed in 1855 to move the whole reservation five miles east, with the Big Blue now flowing through the Otos' land. Other aspects of the 1854 treaty remained in effect, especially the payment of $12,000 a year for thirty years and the articles which talked of the promotion of agricultural pursuits. This section even provided for the issuing of patents of ownership to individual Otos after the allotment of farms.

The first Hicksite agent to the Otos, Albert Green, arrived at his post in southeastern Nebraska in late May of 1869. At age twenty-four, he had left his home near Philadelphia to take up his new position. The previous Oto agent, John L. Smith, welcomed Green and handed over his office to the young Quaker. Six days after his arrival, Green wrote to his fellow Hicksite and new superintendent, Samuel Janney: "Although my predecessor has, as I believe endeavoured faithfully to execute the duties of his office, I am sorry to report that the condition of affairs here is far from satisfactory." Smith had neglected both farming and education. Green complained that no schoolhouse had been established and little land had been cultivated. Soon Janney and Green understood the reason for Smith's neglect. Along with Janney's predecessor, Hampton B. Denman, Agent Smith had managed to produce a treaty for the removal of the Otos and Missourias to the Indian Territory.[3]

Superintendent Denman had also tried to remove the Pawnees before the Quakers' arrival, but his efforts with that tribe had not progressed as far as the negotiations with the Otos and Missourias. On February 13, 1869, in Washington, D.C., five Oto leaders, including Medicine Horse, Buffalo Chief, and Little Pipe, had signed an agreement to sell their entire reservation and purchase a new home in the Indian Territory. Medicine Horse and Buffalo Chief had been two of the seven leaders who came to Washington in 1854 to accept the treaty which established their people's original Nebraska reservation. Both men soon became opponents of the 1869 treaty.

In 1854, Medicine Horse (or Shun-gech-hoy), the son of a Missouria mother and an Oto father, had just become primary chief of the Otos' Bear clan. The most powerful of the Oto gentes, the Bear clan by tradition produced the hereditary chief of the entire society. A heavyset, muscular figure, five feet, nine inches, in stature, Medicine Horse possessed a keen political intellect and a fierce determination to preserve the traditions of his people. In time, he would become a stern foe of the Quakers and their plans for assimilation. But in 1869, both Medicine Horse and the new Quaker administrators found they agreed in their opposition to the new removal treaty.[4]

The Quakers objected to the treaty because it absurdly undervalued the Otos' reservation lands. Two railroad companies had the privilege of purchasing nearly 92,000 acres, over half of the reservation's approximately 162,000 acres, at $1.25 per acre. Samuel Janney conservatively estimated the land's value at double the treaty price. Albert Green ignored the offer of a bribe of 640 acres from representatives of the railroads and instead produced a petition against the treaty that 125 Oto men had signed. Marks on the January, 1870, petition included those of Medicine Horse and the other leaders who had gone to Washington. The document denounced "corrupt and designing men" who had misled the chiefs into an agreement which stood "at variance with the wishes of the tribe." After this petition arrived in Washington, President Grant asked the Senate to return the treaty to him. The Senate complied, and the treaty never took effect. The president's decision for rescission had been guided by the advice of his good friend and commissioner of Indian Affairs, Ely Parker, who had been informed about the Otos' opposition to the treaty through letters from Green and Janney and through visitations from eastern Friends.[5] In this way, the Quakers had blocked the ratification of an unfair treaty, but they had not ended the idea of removal among the Otos.

When Albert Green arrived in 1869, the Otos had not left for the Indian Territory, but they had not, in white terms, settled down and become farmers. Oto families relied on garden agriculture along the river bottoms, small game hunting in nearby areas, and biannual buffalo hunts on the western prairies. Fewer than 450 Otos lived primarily in one twenty-five-acre village consisting of as many as thirty earthlodges, each forty feet in diameter, as well as a few bark lodges. As with the Pawnees, the lodges were not occupied in the winter. Skin tipis located among the trees or along creek bottoms had proved easier to keep warm in the coldest months. In social organization, the Otos seemed more formal than the Pawnees but not as complex as the Omahas (to be discussed in chapter 6). As opposed to the four bands and two divisions of the Pawnees, the Otos had nine gentes, all named for animals. These nine exogamous, patrilineal clans had their own origin myths, hierarchies, and privileges. For example, Medicine Horse's Bear gens always supplied the leader of the fall buffalo hunt. The Buffalo gens, on the other hand, claimed that they brought corn to the Otos and supplied the leader of the summer hunt.

The gentes did not dictate a formal arrangement of lodges in the village or produce a full moiety division of Earth and Sky in the society, as they did among the Omahas. Yet the separation and individuality of the nine clans made the Otos more a confederation of gentes than a unified community. The basis of lodge residence and gens affiliation was the blood tie of family. The key element of Oto social organization, therefore, was the family. The Oto clans, in general, recognized three classes of people: the chiefs, the people who held secular and supernatural power, and the common people. An Oto could not move easily between classes because rank was determined by heredity, which was jealously maintained. Sons of chiefs became chiefs or, failing that, brothers' sons became chiefs and so forth. The emphasis on class rank may be seen among the Missourias, who were absorbed into the Otos' gentes by the 1830s but retained their own distinct chiefs rather than lose this status to the Oto families.[6]

Factions may have already existed among the Otos because of the distinctions between clans, classes, and families. For this reason, it is unclear whether the Quaker agents created, increased, or merely rearranged divisions among the Otos. It is clear that the agents played havoc with the chiefs' class, so that a prime reason for Oto factionalism in the 1870s may be traced to the disruption by the Quaker agents of traditional class structure and family privilege.

Like the other Quaker agents in Nebraska, Albert Green hoped to establish individual farms among the Otos. He had little success. Article six of the 1854 treaty provided for the allotment of the reservation into farmsteads. In late August of 1869, three months after his arrival, Agent Green reported to the Board of Indian Commissioners: "I despair of inducing these Indians to accede to an allotment in severalty of a portion of their lands." In eleven years, although many Oto men expressed interest in learning white agricultural techniques, neither Green nor his successor, Jesse Griest, would be able to move the Otos out of their villages onto individual farms. Within a month of his arrival, Green recognized the source of his opposition. He told Samuel Janney that the old chiefs opposed breaking up the village system because they feared the loss of their authority.

Green told the Otos that no man would be recognized as chief who did not himself show a willingness to farm and who did not encourage the young men to farm. Some chiefs responded positively. They chose their land and started to make improvements. The Otos' primary chief, Arkeketah (or Stand-By) refused to cooperate, so Green removed him from the chiefs' council in the summer of 1871. The signature mark of Medicine Horse now appeared at the top of the list of names on council resolutions, a sign of his elevation to primary chief. Medicine Horse had gained his new status partly through traditions of family and gens, and partly through Quaker action. Arkeketah could still exercise his influence among the Otos through his family's status, but the Quaker agents controlled the makeup of the official chiefs' council. Only that council could officially petition the federal government, and the Quakers could ignore tradition in changing its membership. By early 1875, all the traditional chiefs, including Medicine Horse, had been replaced.

Despite Arkeketah's refusal to farm, many Oto men demonstrated a willingness to do farm labor, but only if they were paid. To the Otos, agricultural work could produce two benefits: more food and additional income to purchase trade goods. Yet the Otos would not make the logical move, in white terms, from working in the fields to living in them. Jesse

Griest, who replaced Albert Green in 1873, operated a system of what he called "tribal farming" that employed Otos as laborers with their pay coming out of their annuity funds. Pay was the same as under Agent Green, a dollar a day. The crops did not go directly to the men who cultivated them but were distributed to all the Otos by Agent Griest. Through the employment of Oto men, the distribution of crops, and the dismissal of chiefs, the eleven-year reign of the Quaker agents undercut the role of the traditional chiefs. Wealth and power rested more with the agent than with the leading families of the gentes. Agent Griest employed 130 Otos in one year, which was easily a majority of the adult males. Indeed, Griest claimed that more men sought jobs than he could employ.[7] With such eagerness for work and income, an agent could "appoint" a new chief and have many Otos recognize his decision. Not surprisingly, the traditional chiefs dismissed by the agent led a faction which did not recognize the agent's "power" to select chiefs. This group would, for several years, refuse to accept any annuity payments, which was a clear effort to negate by boycott the agent's economic power.

Over eleven years, other confrontations occurred between the proagent faction, eventually called Quakers, and the traditional chiefs' faction, known as Coyotes. Although disagreements over money and power helped produce these confrontations, the key issue became the sale of the entire Nebraska reservation and the removal of all the Otos to the Indian territory. The Coyotes seemed to believe that a move south would leave the Quaker agent behind and allow them to regain their position of authority. The Quakers, on the other hand, did not wish to give up their new status and income, which was tied to retaining their agent. Entwined with Oto factions and the issue of removal was the question of selling all or part of the reservation. Unwisely, Superintendent Janney and Agent Green had not let this question rest. In a meeting at Omaha in August of 1870, Samuel Janney suggested that in order to build better schools and establish operating farms, each tribe under the Quakers' administration should sell a portion of its reservation. Although he had just helped Janney defeat a treaty to sell the entire Oto reservation, Agent Green agreed with Janney's plan. In 1870 and 1871, Green suggested a sale of 80,000 acres on the west side of the Blue River for market value or for the highest bid.

As the two Oto factions evolved and formalized during the first half-decade of the 1870s, the dispute over how much land to sell and where the people should live became an indication not only of growing factionalization, but also of the instability of the Otos' existence. Variations in food supply and community health affected many Otos' willingness to leave or stay. Pressures from whites also had a varying influence both on the local level from squatters and timber thieves and on the national level from congressional legislation and bureaucratic policies. Recalling their visits of 1854 and 1869, and hopeful that consultations with the "Great Father" might resolve many problems, the traditional chiefs began to demand a trip to Washington. This trip, when it occurred, revealed much but accomplished little.

Albert Green pointed out that ever since their visit to Washington in 1869, the Oto chiefs had advocated moving to the Indian Territory. As agent, Green had opposed such plans. He had attempted to direct the Otos toward a more "civilized" existence, but in fact, the Otos' situation had hardly become stabilized, much less "civilized." Before Green arrived in 1868, Agent Smith reported that grasshoppers and drought had destroyed the Otos' crops and that the people could not hunt buffalo because of Sioux raiders. In the summer of 1869, Green called the Otos "destitute" and reported that forty-eight children had died since winter because of damp lodgings and squalid conditions. In 1870, drought severely damaged all crops, but the Otos did have a successful buffalo hunt. The next summer, insects destroyed the wheat crop and many children died from illness.

Relations with the Otos' white neighbors created another set of problems. Landmarks defining the boundaries of the reservation disappeared, and the Otos complained that white squatters had settled on their land, and were also stealing their horses and timber. Yet, when desperate for food, the

Otos cut their own timber and sold it to white farmers and railroad contractors.

These timber sales showed that many Otos preferred to use their own money and resources in their own way. The chiefs argued tenaciously over any adjustment in annuity payments. They rejected Green's suggestion that the government supply more goods instead of cash. They kept reducing an initial commitment of $3,000 for farming tools until it reached $1,000. Green complained that the council would only support the salary of one blacksmith and one teacher. Despite their reluctance to financially support their agent's plans, however, the Otos willingly spent the cash they received. By early 1872, the Otos owed $3,000 in debts to white merchants.

Other developments also demonstrated the Oto chiefs' attempts at independent action. For example, in an effort to establish peace between the Osages and the Otos, Green had managed to set up a meeting between the two tribes with the cooperation of the Osages' Orthodox agent. The Osage delegation received forty horses from their Oto hosts, smoked the red-stone peace pipe, and departed as friends. But these new friends created a new avenue for removal. The Oto chiefs demanded that they be permitted to visit the Indian Territory to see if they could settle on lands next to their Osage "brothers." In late April of 1872, the seven members of the chiefs' council, led by Medicine Horse, requested an appropriation of $200 for a trip south. Agent Green allowed some twenty Otos to go. He hoped that they would weigh both the advantages and disadvantages of removing their entire tribe. After a month among the Osages, Medicine Horse and the other chiefs returned with a favorable report, only to learn that Congress on June 10, 1872, had approved the Quaker plan of selling 80,000 acres to keep the Otos in Nebraska.

The chiefs responded with a request that they be allowed to visit the commissioner of Indian Affairs in Washington. Barclay White refused to grant his permission. In a letter dated July 5, 1872, and addressed to "Medicine Horse and other Chiefs of the Oto and Missouria tribe of Indians," the Quaker superintendent explained why he believed that the congressional bill for the sale of half the Otos' reservation would benefit their people:

This law . . . was intended with the money received from this sale, to build you better houses than you now have, buy you more horses, oxen, wagons, plows and mowing machines; . . . educate your children; help you to help yourselves, or in other words, teach you how you may, when you are hungry, always find flour in your bag, and a Buffalo near your lodge.[8]

Although White may have considered his final statement a metaphor, the Oto chiefs — with their cultural traditions and after crop failures and poor hunts — may not have seen it that way. In any event, the Quaker superintendent had made a strange, impossible promise which did not lessen the chiefs' desire to go to Washington.

White concluded his letter with the instructions that an open council must produce a written document which said whether all or half of the reservation should be sold. The Otos had reached no agreement on this issue, but neighboring whites eagerly claimed that they had. Sen. Phineas W. Hitchcock received two petitions with seventy-two signatures from residents of Washington County, Kansas, and Gage County, Nebraska. The petitions claimed that Agent Green did not fairly represent the Otos' desire to sell all of their reservation. Whether they knew the Otos' true wishes or not, these white neighbors did covet the Indians' land. Senator Hitchcock went on to produce a bill for the sale of the entire reservation. Meanwhile, the Oto chiefs' council came to a partial resolution of the issue. In early September, they refused the sale of 80,000 acres but said nothing official about selling all of their land. Albert Green told Barclay White that the Otos wished to sell all of their reservation or none of it. White believed that some chiefs still wanted to go to Washington so they could negotiate a treaty of removal. He told the commissioner of Indian Affairs that at recent councils "the Chiefs have avoided the topic, and shown by their manner that there is a division of sentiment among them upon the subject."[9]

Senator Hitchcock proposed to purchase the Oto reservation at no more than $1.25 per acre, despite the fact that railroad companies had recently offered $12.00 an acre for rights of way over the reservation. Spurred by Hitchcock's low purchase price, the Department of the Interior submitted an act to Congress for the fair appraisal and disposition of the entire Oto reservation. Barclay White praised the "just and honorable" nature of this action. Meanwhile, the Nebraska state legislature passed a joint resolution imploring the U.S. Congress to purchase all the Otos' lands because they "are in a wild and uncultivated state, presenting a barrier to the settlement of that portion of our State."[10] Under all these combined pressures, the Otos made no clear statement on the matter through their chiefs' council.

In April of 1873, Jesse Griest from Gettysburg, Pennsylvania, became the Otos' new agent. Griest would prove more rigid in his opposition to removal than had Albert Green. Still, the Coyotes, or "wild faction" as Griest called them, managed initially to work out a compromise with their new agent. At a large council on May 26, nineteen chiefs and headmen of the Otos and Missourias agreed to the sale of 80,000 acres of their reservation. In addition, the council selected Jesse Griest as its choice for one of the three government appraisers. Yet the council also said: "We are fully united in requesting that a delegation of our Chiefs be permitted to visit Washington as soon as practicable, to consult with the Hon. Commissioner of Indian Affairs." Medicine Horse, Little Pipe, and even the formerly dismissed Arkeketah placed their marks on the council's resolutions.[11] As their interview in Washington would demonstrate, the traditional chiefs hoped to go above their Quaker "fathers" in order to sell the entire reservation and move to the Indian Territory.

Barclay White wrote to Edward P. Smith, the new commissioner of Indian Affairs, trying to explain the Oto chiefs' anticipated visit: "I cannot account for the ardent desire of all Indians with whom I have had business relations, to visit the City of Washington. It appears to be the Mecca of their hopes. The Otoes have been particularly anxious to go there, and I do not think any arrangement of their affairs at another place, would be satisfactory to them." White's words proved prophetic. Edward Smith passed through Omaha late in the summer, but the Oto chiefs refused to meet with him. Only Washington would do, so in October, Jesse Griest with five chiefs made the long trip to the federal capital.[12]

The Oto delegation consisted of Medicine Horse, Big Bear (also called Joe John or Joseph Powell), Little Pipe, Missouri Chief, and Arkeketah (or Stand-By). Battist Deron, the massively proportioned son of a French father and Oto mother, served as interpreter. Francis M. Barnes, the agency trader and white husband of an Oto woman, also joined the party. Griest and his seven companions arrived in Baltimore in late October. Some Quakers from Philadelphia joined the delegation and traveled down to Washington, where on October 31 the Otos met for the first time with Commissioner Smith. Two other meetings occurred on November 1 and November 4. Transcripts of the three meetings have been preserved and present a fascinating study of one confrontation between the commissioner of Indian Affairs and a group of Native American leaders.[13]

The first meeting opened with a flourish of rhetoric. Commissioner Smith welcomed his visitors and observed: "You are elderly men, and probably have children, and what you say today, will not only be for today, but will live after you." Medicine Horse, who would be the primary spokesman for the Otos, responded to the commissioner's greeting: "Grandfather. I have wanted to see you. Our father has brought us down here and it is a very nice day. We came here on business. We did not come for nothing, but we are tired." Medicine Horse's form of address was significant. As noted earlier, the Oto family was the primary unit of social organization. Within the family, the Otos cherished the relationship between grandfather and grandson. Traditionally, it was an affectionate, close relationship with little tension and conflict. The father-son relationship, on the other hand, involved more teaching and discipline, although children were never whipped and rarely scolded.[14] Medicine Horse could clearly distinguish between Edward Smith or Jesse Griest and his Oto grandfather or father, but his words should not be viewed as merely figurative. His frame of reference, after all, was Oto. In addition, Medicine Horse and his fellow chiefs had already shown that they hoped their "grandfather" in Washington would support their wishes better than their Quaker "fathers" in Nebraska.

Medicine Horse asked if Smith had granted permission for a fall buffalo hunt. Smith said he had, although he preferred to "make you like white men; and nothing keeps up this wild living, and habits like hunting." Smith explained that the Pawnees had asked to go on a hunt, "but we are going to do better for them. We are going to take some provisions from the Sioux to give them." With no attempt at a full explanation, Smith glossed over the Pawnee disaster at Massacre Canyon only three months before which had created the justification for taking treaty goods from the Sioux. But the Otos did not ask why the Sioux would give up their provisions to the Pawnees. Instead, the chiefs said they were tired and wished to rest before discussing their business at length.

After a night's sleep, Medicine Horse presented the main topic for discussion: "Father, I have only one thing to talk about and that is what I came for. We are all made up on one plan, white men and Indians, and we can talk together. My tribe has sent me down here to do the talking for them." Despite his eloquent idea of brotherhood ("all made up on one plan"), Medicine Horse had demoted Edward Smith from grandfather to father overnight. The Oto chief continued: "We would sell our land. . . . White men near our reservation have all good homes and farms. We would like to have the same. . . . Some of the chiefs went with me to see another country. I like it and want to go there." Rather cleverly, Medicine Horse seemed to have anticipated the government argument that the Otos should stay in Nebraska and start farms. He claimed that the Indian Territory offered better farm land.

Commissioner Smith asked where the Otos wished to settle. Medicine Horse said they wanted land near Beaver Creek. Smith claimed that the Kaws owned the land and that, besides, "one acre of your land in Nebraska is worth one hundred acres of that kind." (In a little more than a year, Edward Smith would help resettle the Pawnees in the same area that he now disparaged.) The commissioner pressed on, asking how the Otos would live if they moved. Medicine Horse replied: "If I move there I will live as well as the other Indians

there. I can work[;] I can hang on the plow as others do."
Smith thought the Otos might just "go wild again," but Medicine Horse explained that the Otos did not want to live near
white men who "steal everything they can from us and kill
our boys every once in a while."

Smith seemed to ignore Medicine Horse's complaint about
wild white neighbors. Incredibly, he suggested: "What you
ought to do is get ready as fast as you can to be like white
people." If the Otos were going to "live wild," Smith said he
would not let them move. A sharp exchange then followed:

Medicine Horse: I have always worked for my living. I have never lived
wild. I am like other people. Always was. I have always raised corn.

Comm. [of Indian Affairs]: There is no better place to raise corn than
where you are.

Medicine Horse: Where we live now the white people take our timber.

Comm.: The Indians cut it and sold it to them.

Medicine Horse: We sold some. We had to do it to get food for our
children.

Comm.: You have been a long time in that country and have nothing to
show for it. No farms opened, . . . no houses or anything like white people.

Medicine Horse: For several years we have wanted to move and that is
why we have done nothing there. White men when they want to move do so,
and I think we have the same rights. We are not satisfied and we want to
sell. We can sell our own land.

Comm.: That is your mistake. The Government has to take care of you
and see that everything is done for your benefit. When you get so you can
read and write and are able to take care of yourself then you can have your
land to take care of or sell if you wish. You call the President your Great
Father. He is going to take care of his children.

The views presented by Edward Smith and Medicine
Horse in this rapid exchange had implications beyond the
Otos' case. Indeed, their argument neatly encapsulated some
basic issues of Indian-government relations which still have
impact on contemporary affairs. Medicine Horse argued for
the legitimacy of the native way of life, freedom of action
based on native values, and the right to be left alone without
oppression. Edward Smith talked of the government's responsibility to care for the Indians until they proved their
competency in a white world. He made the case for government paternalism. Arkeketah now entered the argument. He
tried to show that government promises in the form of treaties were not reliable.

Arkeketah had come to Washington to sign the 1854 agreement that established the Nebraska reservation. He claimed that "in the treaty it is all different from what was said." He especially disliked the policy of paying some of the annuity in goods instead of money. The lands in Nebraska had not been sold "for paper money but for hard money." Smith said the treaty annuities went to "advance civilization," to buy wagons, houses, and cattle. "You certainly need other things much more than you need money," the commissioner concluded. Arkeketah was not convinced. He had been told in 1854 that if he were "dissatisfied to come here and visit the Great Father again and he would make it alright." Arkeketah now heard that his people were to fence their fields and farm the land like whites. They must not be "wild," the commissioner demanded, and they should get their living "from the ground." Arkeketah replied snappishly: "I was never wild, and I don't want to be. . . . We always raised something from the ground to support our families, before we ever saw the white man."

Still upset that they could not get more of their treaty payments in money, Arkeketah asked: "How would these white men feel to have their property used in this way?" Once more, Smith turned to paternalism for his answer: "If the white men are children and you are their guardian, you can do what you please . . . provided you do what is good for them." Medicine Horse could take little more of this argument. "We are not children. We are men," he insisted. Recalling important developments in the previous decade in race relations, Medicine Horse observed: "Those black curly haired people I have always heard were made free. I thought I was always a free man. I am free yet."

Unwittingly, Medicine Horse had expressed an equation between money and freedom which tenant farmers, millworkers, and coal miners could have understood. In the late decades of the nineteenth century, the use of scrip, or even simple credit in advance, allowed country merchants and company stores to force farmers and workers to purchase goods at a premium. Especially in the South, poor blacks and whites received their income, in effect, as goods instead of money. They had little or no choice of where to shop, and they had to accept the price and quality of goods offered at the local store. The Otos and other treaty Indians shared a similar problem, because they had to accept the annuity goods sent to them by the government. These goods could be traded with white merchants at a loss; but if the Indians had received from the government the same amount in money, they would have had more income and more freedom to purchase what they wished. A major American historian has called the system of scrip and credit in the South "mill-village" and "crop-lien paternalism."[15] In 1873, the shrewd and independent-minded Medicine Horse had already noted the paternalism of the federal government in its policy of supplying goods instead of money.

The argument over government paternalism and Oto freedom continued in the third meeting, on November 4. Yet the chiefs also demonstrated the Otos' dependence on the federal government for annuity funds. Little Pipe showed how the chief's role had changed as benefits of the buffalo hunt gave way to benefits supplied by the government: "I came here to do business for our tribe. All our tribe has gone on a hunt. They don't expect to make a good hunt and we came for our Annuity. We came on a hunt." As Missouri Chief explained, the Otos would expect their treaty money at its regular time when they returned from the buffalo range. In effect, the decline of the buffalo herds had been mitigated by the regular payment of annuities after the fall hunt. Commissioner Smith, however, planned to commit more of the Otos' funds to the development of farming and the purchase of livestock. Big Bear expressed the chiefs' disappointment:

Our tribe is very poor for the last few years and we thought we could come and make a plan so not to be so poor. . . . Our women do not wear good clothes, we have so little and we thought we could come and see if you would not do something for us. But you have a plan very different, for two nights we could not sleep. We came to fix everything. We thought that our Great Father would do everything for his children as they wished but you do not do so for us.

Big Bear's words demonstrated that the Otos viewed the government's paternalism in terms of Oto child raising. Otos not only indulged their children and applied little formal discipline; they also respected and honored them. The latter behavior would be especially true for the children and chiefs and headmen. An Oto child of the upper classes was honored publicly from birth to maturity, which impressed on the child the importance of his family and its place in society. In addition, a well-behaved child whom the community respected supported the status of his mother and father and thus helped maintain the status of his family.[16] Given the primacy of responsible social behavior in their culture, it is little wonder that the Oto chiefs were offended when Commissioner Smith called them "wild." Indeed, children were so obviously a part of the family-centered structure of their society that the Otos could not easily conceive of a parent mistreating a child or denying a responsible request.

The Oto view of parenting and child raising may explain in part the chiefs' great faith in the benefits of a visit with their "father" in Washington. Commissioner Smith challenged their faith in such government "parents." The commissioner emphasized discipline and "adult" domination of his Oto "children." At the third meeting, he told Medicine Horse: "You are my children. . . . It takes you a long time to find out that I am going to do what I think best for you." Medicine Horse replied: "There is such a thing as children being whipped to death." For an Oto, whose people never whipped their children, such words were damning.

The five Oto chiefs found their meetings with Edward Smith an exercise in frustration. They received no clear decision about their right to sell all the reservation. Medicine Horse said that if they could not sell all, then they would no longer agree to sell 80,000 acres. Smith claimed that the decision to sell the western half of the Otos' reserve could not be changed. Medicine Horse had asked that the commissioner not let the Oto be "scattered" and that he let them "all live in one place." But the commissioner's intransigence would increase factionalism among the Otos and help produce the opposite of what Medicine Horse desired. The traditionalist Coyotes would become a separate division of the Otos. Four of the five chiefs who had come to Washington in 1873 became part of this faction. Big Bear, the one chief who did not join the Coyotes, warned the commissioner that even cooperative Otos had their limits. Speaking with some sympathy for his more traditional fellow chiefs, Big Bear told Commissioner Smith: "You can not make white men of us. That is one thing you can't do."

A survey of the Otos' entire reservation was completed in 1874, with the 80,000 acres in the western half subdivided into 40-acre tracts. No sales of this western land followed, although the congressional act of June 10, 1872, had provided for its disposal. The presence of a surveying team mapping, not half, but all of the reservation may well have confused and angered many Otos. Yet other events in 1874 proved more troublesome. White neighbors continued to cut timber on the reservation despite threats of prosecution by Agent Griest. The plague of grasshoppers which devastated the Pawnees' crops and helped drive them to the Indian Territory also struck the Otos' fields that summer. In early October, Medicine Horse led fifty hungry families south to visit the Kaws and join in a buffalo hunt. Half the families soon returned to Nebraska, but the rest, approximately 150 people, pressed on. Agent Griest telegraphed Gen. John Pope with instructions to turn back the remaining families. He also directed Pope to arrest Medicine Horse and two other leaders in order to "promote peace and benefit the tribe." Pope more than followed his instructions. He arrested eight Oto men, including Medicine Horse and Little Pipe, and kept his prisoners for more than a month at Fort Hays, Kansas. When the men returned to the reservation, Griest dismissed all the chiefs from the agency council. He appointed "younger," "progressive" men in their place.[17]

Griest had mixed feelings about the return of Medicine Horse and his faction. During their October sojourn, Griest had wondered in a letter to Barclay White whether the "stable portion" of the Otos would benefit if the "wild ones" stayed away. The agent explained how the disaffected faction had refused the goods which had replaced cash in the last annuity. Because they would not take the provisions offered, their hunger increased and they had to go south for food.

Griest said that a division had existed for years, with the "wild faction" holding back the "progressive" group. They "stigmatize the others as wanting to have houses and become white men, which they regard as a great disgrace." Still, Griest seemed most upset that Medicine Horse and his cohorts had left without permission. A little more than two weeks after that unapproved departure, Agent Griest granted a request from progressive leaders for a buffalo hunt along branches of the Solomon River.[18]

The danger of Sioux raiders brought a quick end to this approved fall hunt, and approximately two-thirds of the Otos had to rely on government rations until spring. The most uncompromising of Medicine Horse's group did not accept this subsistence and survived by selling timber to neighboring whites. In addition, this recalcitrant faction refused to send their children to the Quakers' new industrial school. Barclay White explained to the commissioner of Indian Affairs that these "old chiefs" ignored the government's policies in order "to keep power." In turn, White and Agent Griest said that they ignored the old chiefs and only recognized progressive "headmen" in order to reduce the influence of these "refractory ones."[19]

Estimates of the number of Otos in either faction varied greatly, but Quaker observers always put the Coyotes in the minority, with an estimated membership of one-third of the people. By 1876, the Coyotes had a separate village only a few miles south of the main settlement. Not all of the Coyotes may have lived there, because individual Otos shifted back and forth between the factions. Nonetheless, the most adamant Coyotes continued to refuse their annuities. In 1876, 157 Otos boycotted not only payments in goods, but also the payments in cash. In 1878, this boycott of all payments continued when 175 refused their annuities; 292 accepted them.

Over the years, up through the Otos' removal to the Indian Territory in 1881, the leadership of the two factions remained stable. Medicine Horse was regularly recognized as the primary chief of the Coyotes. Many other prominent chiefs, including Little Pipe and Arkeketah, also affiliated with this faction. The new chiefs and headmen who sat on the agent's council were a mixture of mostly unfamiliar names. They supplied the leadership for the Quaker, or "progressive," faction. The sixteen names that appeared on the last major council petition of May 26, 1873, changed dramatically after Griest's purge in late 1874. At the top of the list of chiefs, where Medicine Horse had once made his mark, the name of Harre-gar-row (or Big Elk) appeared. Only two chiefs from the old council remained, Big Bear and Whan-a-ga-he. Two former "braves" or headmen, White Horse and Jim Arkeketah, had been elevated to chiefs by Agent Griest. Two other "braves" retained their former status. None of the other ten, including the primary chief, Big Elk, had been recognized as part of the council two years before.[20]

In December of 1875, Sen. Phineas Hitchcock began to reapply legislative pressures for the removal of the Otos. He introduced a bill to spend treaty funds for the relocation of the Otos on a new reservation in the Indian Territory. This bill also instructed the secretary of the interior to sell land on the old reservation only to actual settlers. These homesteaders could make claims for $2.50 per acre under the law of preemption. Such generous terms for settlement and purchase must have pleased Hitchcock's constituents in Nebraska.

Jesse Griest reacted swiftly. He called an open council at the Oto agency which met on New Year's Day in 1876. The resolutions of that council called Hitchcock's bill "unjust" because the Otos' consent had not been given to the sale and because the bill grossly undervalued the Otos' land. The council members denied that their people wished to settle in the Indian Territory. Instead, they said, "we want to hold on to the eastern half of our reservation; . . . we want to open farms, and improve them." Eighty-six Oto men placed their signature marks on the petition. In a long letter which accompanied this document to Washington, Agent Griest blamed both the faction of "the old hereditary chiefs" and the "political element of the state" for trying to sell off all the Otos' land. He said that for future "personal profit," whites had conspired with these "discharged chiefs" in "secret councils" held off the reservation.

Some Otos reported to Griest that the white men had made extravagant promises, such as annuity payments in gold and silver, a sale price double that of the Hitchcock bill, and freedom for the Otos to travel as they liked. The provocation of the opposition chiefs made the administration of the agency, in Griest's account, "very unpleasant and in a measure, ineffective." If the government sanctioned the sale, the recalcitrant faction would triumph and the progressive Otos would be so discouraged that their "improvement" would end "for an indefinite period." Griest urged the commissioner of Indian Affairs to support the "young chiefs" and to punish the leaders of the Oto opposition through "arrest and detention."[21] He made no suggestions about mendacious whites.

The new Indian commissioner, John Q. Smith, who had replaced Edward P. Smith in late 1875, did not follow Jesse Griest's recommendations, but the Quaker agent's accusations were not unfounded. On January 17, 1876, a group of local white citizens met with members of the "wild" faction on a remote part of the reservation. William Anyan, who was a member of the Nebraska legislature, attended this meeting, as did a local minister, a notary public, and at least five other whites. With the aid of two interpreters, these white neighbors helped the Coyotes write a petition to the U.S. Congress. On such occasions, distortions and misrepresentations were always possible, just as they were at any agent's council meeting, if the literate people who participated were unscrupulous. However, the document produced at this gathering contained many of the sentiments already expressed by Medicine Horse and his cohorts:

Some of our Nation have visited the Indian territory, and brought back very favorable reports of the country. There is more game there. The winters are milder, and we shall not be obliged to put up hay for our ponies. There is more rain there, and not so much danger from grasshoppers. There is more timber there than here, and the land is good. We shall be away from the whites. The Pawnees, who are our friends, have gone there, and we would like to live near them.

The petition went on to say that Agent Griest, "for his convenience or interest, or both, . . . keeps us here permanently against our often expressed desire to remove . . . he misrepresents us to our great Father." It also claimed that of the 460 Otos on the annuity payroll, 330 supported the sale of the entire reservation. For this reason, the petition urged the passage of Senator Hitchcock's proposed legislation. It indicated that $2.25 per acre, plus compensation for any improvements, would be acceptable to the Otos. Although this last claim seemed out of character for the financially astute Medicine Horse, his name appeared on the petition along with those of Buffalo Chief, Arkeketah, Big Soldier, Little Pipe, Missouri Chief, and 88 other Otos.[22]

Two petitions from the white citizens of Gage County soon followed this document. In response, Agent Griest launched a countercampaign directed at the commissioner of Indian Affairs. Griest emphasized the role of "outside parties" in league with the "refractory" Indians. "The whites had pecuniary and political purposes," Griest insisted. The Otos, on the other hand, did not desire and had not agreed to the sale of their entire reservation. Other letters supported Griest. Mary Barnes, the educated Oto wife of the agency's white trader, told the commissioner that the "politicians and citizens of Nebraska" wanted the Otos moved, but that she and her husband had put their "life time earnings" into their farm and did not want to give it up and be forced to take their five children to the Indian Territory. Mary Barnes might have been an exceptional case of assimilation to white values, but her handwritten words could still sway a Washington official. Similarly, F. O. Wallis of Beatrice, Nebraska, tried to influence the secretary of the interior. Wallis said that land speculators wanted to rob the Otos. After talks with Agent Griest, he agreed that "outside forces" and one faction "not amiably reunited" with the majority of the tribe had produced this plot. The Otos wanted to be "let alone," Wallis concluded.[23]

In their fight to keep the Otos in Nebraska, Griest and his fellow Quakers acquired an unexpected ally. Sen. Algernon Sidney Paddock, a resident of Beatrice, became a major force in amending his fellow senator Phineas Hitchcock's bill. The House of Representatives, unlike the Senate, had refused to accept Hitchcock's proposal to remove the Otos and sell all their Nebraska land. Following the advice of eastern Friends, the House agreed to reserve 40,000 acres for the Otos and open 120,000 for white settlers. The Otos would lose the western three-quarters of their reservation, but they would not have to move. Paddock agreed with the House amendments, which he helped steer through the Senate. He believed, as did members of the House, that removal could be unjust and disastrous. Minor opposition from the commissioner of Indian Affairs, based on questions of relief for the Otos and effective sales to the settlers, at first convinced President Grant to veto the bill. Then the president reconsidered his action and tried to recall his veto. The Senate and House avoided any legal entanglements when on August 15, 1876, they simply overrode the president's veto.

In June of 1872, the Congress had approved a Quaker plan to sell 80,000 acres. Four years later, in order to keep the Otos in Nebraska, the Quakers had agreed to increase that figure by 50 percent. This four-year inflation may have indicated the high price of congressional support — especially from someone like Senator Paddock. As in 1872, an open council of the Otos and Missourias had to approve before the land could be surveyed, appraised, and settled. Nebraska citizens and other prospective homesteaders from Kansas and Iowa ignored this legal requirement. The congressional act of August had authorized the sale of 120,000 acres to actual settlers only, in tracts not to exceed 160 acres. In order to gain rights of preemption, by late September white families had marked off all the quarter sections of the most desirable land. Not surprisingly, these white squatters had chosen the fertile creek bottoms where the Otos carried on their traditional agriculture. They ignored most of the higher and drier prairie lands.[24]

By the late summer of 1876, factional squabbles, white squatters, and talk of land sales had shaken the determination of the progressive chiefs to stay in Nebraska. In early August, Agent Griest's handpicked chiefs had asked to visit the Indian Territory to see if they could find a better home there. If no good lands were available, the council resolved to live on the eastern quarter of the Nebraska reservation. Earlier that summer, some of the same chiefs had asked to send a delegation to Washington to talk to the commissioner of Indian Affairs. These two requests produced no results, but indicated that the supposedly cooperative faction of the Otos had begun to share some of the views of the "wild" faction. Still, the "new" chiefs of the agent's council did not reunite with the traditional chiefs. Big Elk and the other council leaders understandably chose to retain their recently acquired rank and power. They even told Agent Griest to declare forfeit and to distribute to the rest of the Otos the annuity goods and monies which the wild faction had refused. As with the two earlier requests, authorities in Washington ignored this resolution of the agent's council.

The inaction of the Office of Indian Affairs on earlier proposals may explain, in part, the council's reluctance to approve the sale of 120,000 acres. The "progressive" chiefs wanted some sign of reassuring support from the powers in Washington if they were to reduce their reservation by 75 percent. Medicine Horse and the traditional chiefs had insisted on a visit to Washington when they agreed to sell 80,000 acres in 1873. Big Elk and six progressive chiefs now made the same request when they and sixty-nine Otos finally approved the sale of 120,000 acres on December 23, 1876. Whereas Medicine Horse in 1873 had come to Washington to sell the entire reservation, the progressive chiefs wanted their delegation to visit Washington "in order to have a free talk with our Great Father, and those who have charge of the Indian business; that we may learn for ourselves our true position, and the wishes of the Government towards us."

The progressive chiefs knew they could only plead for fair treatment from the federal government. The agreement of December twenty-third reflected their desperate anxiety about this dependent relationship. The council mentioned how the Otos could no longer hunt "wild animals which the Great Spirit placed here with us for our food." Instead, they had to "believe the intentions of our Great Father" and "look for protection" to Washington. They therefore asked that *"good honest men"* be appointed to oversee the appraisal and sale of the 120,000 acres. After their disposal, the progressive Otos recognized, "we will have no more land to sell." Still, they understood why they had lost so much:

We have given one piece of land after another to our Great Father on which white men have made good homes. Now they seem to be angry with us because we still have a small piece of good land to stand on, and want to get it from us. We will have to let them have part of it, because we have grown so poor that we have very little to live on, but we do not want to sell it as was done in former times when our old Chiefs sold large tracts of land for very little & eat [*sic*] up and wasted what little they got.[25]

Although the appraisal of the Otos' reservation soon began, the commissioner of Indian Affairs rejected the council's request that a delegation come to Washington. In early February, the progressive chiefs again petitioned for a Washington visit, but were ignored. Such disregard could only increase the progressives' feelings of powerlessness, and the presence of white squatters on their land could only amplify these same feelings.

By February of 1877, whites had marked off claims, cut timber, put up houses, and formed vigilance committees. The latter threatened to shoot anyone who tried to occupy lands already claimed. All this activity occurred on Oto land that had not been fully appraised and opened for settlement and sale. Agent Griest discovered that most of the squatters planned not to pay for the land or make any proper legal claim. He then requested the un-Quakerly use of military force to remove the illegal settlers. President Grant and the secretary of war cooperated. In March and early April, one officer and ten enlisted men assisted Griest with his evictions. Despite Griest's pleas, the troops did not stay on to prevent the squatters from returning. Over the next two years, they became well established on what had been the Otos' land. In February of 1879, George Fink of Blue Springs complained to Griest: "The cream of the reserve is held by a set of squatters and desperadoes who are daily stealing timber off the lands, and are a burden to every tax payer; and if there is not a change made so as to give a man a chance to buy land in a peaceable way that land will never be sold."[26]

Eventually, the 119,846.17 acres on the western portion of the Otos' reservation would all be sold, at an average price of $3.85 per acre. The three government appraisers — including an appointee of the chiefs' council, Francis M. Barnes — had valued the land at an average of $3.56 per acre, nineteen cents less than the price received. Yet the money gained from the sale of the western tract would create a great controversy between the Otos and the federal government, a controversy which was not settled until the early 1950s, when the Indian Claims Commission decided that the Otos and Missourias had received a fair price. The United States Court of Claims upheld this decision.[27]

As for the issue of removal to the Indian Territory, it remained unsettled until 1881. The progressive, or Quaker, faction of the Otos supported the idea by the end of the 1870s, but not as a way to reunite with the Coyotes. Instead, continued pressure from neighboring whites and a profound disillusionment with Agent Jesse Griest led to the progressives' change of mind. As for Griest, he opposed removal up until his own exit from the Oto agency in June of 1880.

At times, Griest seemed unwilling to continue the fight. In the fall of 1877, he submitted his resignation, which, at first, both the secretary of the interior and the Hicksite Central Executive Committee accepted. The eastern Quakers nominated Samuel S. Ely, who had served as a teacher and farmer at the agency six years before, for the position. Ely closed his business in Philadelphia and arrived at the Oto agency in early December. Yet no official letter of appointment from Washington followed Ely west. He stayed two months before reading in the local newspapers that he had been appointed agent to the Pawnees, not the Otos. Ely reluctantly accepted this post, although he preferred to stay in Nebraska. In a surprisingly candid letter, Ely criticized the administration of his fellow Quaker, Jesse Griest. This letter may have been calculated to please the new commissioner of Indian Affairs, Ezra Hayt. Still, it revealed Ely's assessment of Griest's negative influence with the Otos. Ely recommended that the commissioner relieve Agt. Griest and make it more satisfactory to the Indians, for they feel that they are through with him, and very much desire, an agent who will look more to their interest and less to his own. Agent Griest is a very fair talker, but his work has amounted to but little. The Indians are no better off than when we left six years ago, and I know they have been obedient, and are anxious to become farmers . . . a great many [are] half-fed, some starving and all poorly clothed. . . . The wild part of the tribe came to me a few days ago, and said they wished to be one tribe, again, and settle down to civilized life, but that they would never have anything to do with the present Agent, for he had wronged them, and misrepresented things to them, until they had no faith in him.[28]

Samuel Ely's letter did not turn Commissioner Hayt against Jesse Griest. Indeed, it may have done the reverse. News that the "wild" faction resented Griest may only have convinced Hayt that this Quaker agent could take a strong stand against recalcitrant Indians. Hayt offered Griest a reappointment as the Otos' agent, and in May of 1878, Griest accepted.

Yet even before Griest received this continuance, his influence over the progressive chiefs seemed to be slipping. A rambling petition from a council meeting on March 13, 1878, demonstrated the frustrations felt by the eight progressive chiefs and thirty-five other Otos who signed the document: "We have been very much unsettled for several years, & while this is the case, we cannot do much. Our money is wasting away; our timber is being cut down; we look every way to find the right path for our tribe, but we do not get along well. We do not know which way to look, or who to believe."

Apparently, one individual the progressives had started to doubt was Jesse Griest. On the other hand, local whites near the reservation willingly gave the Otos any aid that supported removal, regardless of faction. In late April, W. V. Lagourgne, who had served as one of the three government land appraisers in 1877, witnessed another petition along with three white citizens. In this document the same eight chiefs who had signed the March petition, Big Elk, Big Bear, James Arkeketah, and five others, made their intentions clearer. In March, these Otos had asked to visit Washington to seek good advice. Griest had approved this request. He would not have approved the April petition. The chiefs wished to "place before the [Interior] department and the *Great Father proposals* for the sale of the remaining part of our reservation." They further explained that, "as we do not have confidence in our present agent, we do most earnestly desire . . . to personally make our wants known."[29]

The April petition indicated that the progressives were willing to leave Nebraska, but that they wished to control any such removal. These chiefs had lost confidence in the authority of their agent, but an invitation from the "greater" father in Washington could continue to certify their political leadership and establish their control over removal. As they explained in the April document: "We regret to state a division exists in our tribe, but [we] are sure a visit to Washington would restore peace." If the progressives were to be peacemakers, it meant their hegemony over the Coyote faction.

However, the reverse seemed the case among the Otos, because by the summer of 1878, the Coyotes had renewed their efforts to move the Otos out of Nebraska. In late May, Little Pipe and nine Oto men left for the Indian Territory. This group planned to visit the Kaws, the Osages, the Pawnees, and the Poncas, as well as other tribes. Agent Griest complained that he had no means to compel the ten men to return. He blamed white neighbors, who wanted all the Otos to leave, for encouraging Little Pipe and his cohorts. In late June, this group visited the Pawnee reservation and according to their old acquaintance, Samuel Ely, were not impressed with the Pawnees' new home. Ely claimed that the Otos "could see for themselves, that the Pawnees have not been benefitted by the change [in reservations]. I think they left here feeling that they had better land, a better climate, at their present home."[30]

Samuel Ely's wishful impressions would not prove true. On July 11, Medicine Horse held a well-attended medicine lodge dance at his own lodge in the Coyotes' village. The colorful crowd, which visitor Barclay White observed, demonstrated that the Otos could still participate as one people in a religious ceremony. The crowd also showed that Medicine Horse, despite what Quaker observers considered a quarrelsome personality, had not lost his standing as a traditional leader. Indeed, by late fall Medicine Horse and the traditional chiefs showed that they had in fact expanded their leadership.

William Leeds, the acting commissioner of Indian Affairs, had become convinced that the Otos would have to yield to the pressures of white settlement, and so he sent Inspector John McNeil to the reservation. At a large council on November 15, McNeil oversaw a vote on the question of removal. The Coyotes won on a vote of 229 to 213, with 17 people recorded as absent. This vote gave the traditional leaders a narrow victory, but the progressives responded swiftly. Eight days after the council, Big Elk and twenty-four other "chiefs and leading men" signed a long letter to the commissioner of Indian Affairs written on Agent Griest's official stationery. The letter focused on the disruptive influence of the Coyotes, who "threw away their chiefships" and had "caused all the trouble in our tribe." These men would not follow the commissioner's "plans." Yet, the progressives continued,

> in a council that one of your officers had with us lately, about half of the tribe decided to go with them [the Coyotes]; it looked as if you were going to help them carry out their plans. This we think is very bad; it looks as if you were not going to help the Indians that have taken your plans, and are trying to make homes for themselves, but instead you help them that have always worked against improvement, and it is not worth while for us to try to do anything.

The progressives, who would leave only if they controlled the removal, said they did not want to leave Nebraska "until we know all about what kind of a place we would have to live." They asked the commissioner to keep all the Otos together, "but if some of them get away we do not want them to have any of the tribe's money; that is too small to divide and will all be needed here."[31]

The progressive chiefs seemed to recognize the connection between federal monies and power in their society. Jesse Griest bluntly told commissioner Hayt that the "old chiefs" wished to regain their former power through removal and that they should not be recognized. Inspector McNeil, however, had talked to Little Pipe, who said his group had selected land near the Sac and Fox reservation during their summer trip. McNeil told the council on November 15 that the commissioner of Indian Affairs wanted the Otos to settle on the west side of the Kaw reservation. Jesse Griest did not want the Otos to move at all. The progressive chiefs now supported Griest's position, but would continue to do so only until they felt confident that Washington upheld their leadership.

A stalemate continued on the Oto reservation for eighteen more months. Petitions and letters from all factions, white and red, flooded into Washington. Both groups of chiefs asked for permission to visit the commissioner of Indian Affairs. Both were ignored. The Coyotes continued their boycott of annuities. The progressives fulfilled their threat not "to try to do anything." In September of 1879, Agent Griest returned from a trip east, where he had met with the commissioner of Indian Affairs. He discovered that all farm work had stopped. The progressives had refused to plant their fall wheat. Griest also became upset by the small number of children at the agency school; an average of only ten students attended. The chiefs' council informed Griest that they must visit Washington before they could do anything about education.[32]

On April 9, 1880, James Arkeketah tried to bypass Agent Griest because of the progressive chiefs' impatience to hear from Washington. Arkeketah telegraphed the following message to the commissioner of Indian Affairs: "Major Griest refuses telegraph you for us[.] this message is sent to you by Chiefs and policemen & men of the tribe [who] wish to move to Territory soon as you give us permission[.] Otoes very dissatisfied. Have written you often, no answer. Please answer at Earlier [sic] date."[33]

The commissioner of Indian Affairs had also received charges of corruption against Agent Griest in a letter signed by the fictitious name F. M. Munroe. This letter made broad, outrageous accusations. For example, it said that the Coyotes had lived in houses and cultivated the land but that Griest had driven them "from the house to the wigwam." The letter also claimed that the agent "laughs at religion" and would not open a Sunday school even though the Indians had requested one. Other charges included neglect of the agency cattle and refusal to provide comfortable beds for white employees. Griest believed that Dr. William C. Boteler, the new agency physician, had written this strange document. To Griest and his fellow Quakers, Boteler was yet another spy sent to disrupt the Friends' work among the Indians.[34] These Quaker fears seemed well founded when Inspector William J. Pollock arrived at the Oto agency in early May, in part to investigate the charges against Griest and in part to calm the fervor over removal.

Inspector Pollock held a council with the Oto chiefs on May 3. Representatives of both factions appeared, and the troublesome Dr. Boteler made notes of the speeches at this meeting. The chiefs insisted on discussing the possibility of removal. Most said that all the Otos wished to leave. James Arkeketah insisted:

We have but one plan. We want to move to Indian Territory. . . . We have sold the west part of our reservation and if our Great Father desired us to remain, he ought not advised us to sell. We are now surrounded by white men and have a railroad which brings men who steal my ponies, and the settlers plow over our line. Our reservation will soon be too small, our Agent don't pay any attention to this; . . . It is hard to live here; whites are stealing our wood, you cannot find a good tree here; we want to go to Indian Territory to farm; we will live there together forever.[35]

White Horse agreed with James Arkeketah's statement. Then, as though some form of unity and commitment to farming had appeared, Little Pipe and Pipe Stem of the Coyotes talked about what they considered to be the good quality of the farm land in the Indian Territory. Medicine Horse then spoke up: "I agree with the rest. . . . [Because in the Indian Territory] . . . all there have a red skin . . . we all have our hearts turned that way."

Inspector Pollock questioned Medicine Horse directly: "Do you think young men will farm better in Indian Territory than here[?]" Always the shrewd debater and negotiator, Medicine Horse replied: "Father we have the same hands that the white-men have. God made the Indians to support themselves[.] You can't expect men to lie down and have plenty to eat — we know it. Come and see us after one year and we will have farms, pigs and cattle — that is a fine country for cattle."

Inspector Pollock did not give the government's approval of these removal plans, because he had other matters to investigate. At a second council, on May 5, Pollock asked the chiefs to comment on the "honesty" of their agent and his employees. Jim Arkeketah and White Horse said they preferred to discuss removal. Big Bear bluntly stated that the chiefs had "plenty" to say about Agent Griest but only after the removal issue had been settled. Pollock refused to cooperate, so the chiefs began to talk about their Quaker agent. White Horse complained that "he has been here seven years and we are still getting poorer." Medicine Horse then demonstrated his bitter sense of humor: "The reason this fellow (agent) stays here so long a time is he wants to *make money*, maybe he belongs to the tribe! . . . I think their [his] belly ought to be pretty full by this time." Little Pipe agreed. He bluntly concluded: "We don't want this agent retained."

Seven years may well have been too long for Jesse Griest to stay on as agent. Clearly, both factions wanted him to leave, but their demand centered more on their people's poor condition than on any dishonesty by Griest. For seven years, Griest had retained the modest salary and comfortable living conditions of a government employee while the Otos sank into greater poverty. His economic condition caused great resentment, as did his opposition to removal and his imposition of "civilized" white ways. After seven years, Griest had lost any chance to be a positive influence. Inspector Pollock rightly concluded in his report to the commissioner of Indian Affairs that Griest should be replaced, but he wrongly attempted to base this conclusion on "dishonest" actions. For these charges, Pollock had only vague examples and no clear evidence. Griest furnished all the accounts and receipts that Pollock demanded. No record of personal gain by the agent appeared, although Pollock attempted to make the most of the technically improper care and sale of fewer than a dozen cattle and hogs.[36]

As for the Otos, Pollock's visit did not reunite the tribe, but it did convince each faction that the federal government might soon approve removal. The progressives had made strong statements about leaving, but the Coyotes left first. As early as February, four families of this faction had settled among the Sacs and Foxes in the Indian Territory. Then, on May 18, Jesse Griest reported that the "wild faction of Otos, believed to number about one hundred, left for Territory last night." By early July, 181 Otos and Missourias had arrived at the Sac and Fox agency. Their leaders included Medicine Horse and Little Pipe. The agent in charge of the Sacs and Foxes reported that these Otos had talked to Inspector Pollock and were fully aware that they had left without permission and at their own risk. They said they had moved because "their stock is being constantly stolen, their timber cut, and other depredations committed by the whites."[37]

The Coyotes appear to have taken a calculated risk. White pressures would soon end the Otos' days in Nebraska, so the Coyotes left early. They may have hoped to claim Coyote dominance by arriving first in the Indian Territory and establishing themselves on the land. If so, they miscalculated. The progressives waited behind in Nebraska for a clear sign from the federal government. In March of 1881, Congress passed an act for the sale of the last portion of the Nebraska reservation. In May, a delegation of five progressive chiefs visited the Indian Territory and selected lands on Red Rock Creek, south of the Ponca reservation. They rejected a location west of the Sac and Fox reservation where some 238 Coyotes were already living. In October, the 234 Otos and Missourias who had stayed in Nebraska moved to the new reservation.[38]

The selection of an official reservation different from the Coyotes' location effectively split the Otos in two. The Coyotes persistently refused to move to the new reservation, but the progressives held the upper hand. They had removed with an Indian agent and thus retained the vital legal and financial link with the federal government. Their agent, however, was not a Quaker.

Jesse Griest had submitted his resignation even before Inspector William Pollock had arrived at the Otos' Nebraska agency in May of 1880. Pollock's report on the charges of corruption against Griest produced a careful, detailed rebuttal from members of the Philadelphia Yearly Meeting. No legal proceedings followed, and the secretary of the interior, Carl Schurz, invited the Philadelphia Friends to nominate a new agent for the Otos. The Philadelphia Indian committee refused to nominate a replacement because of its continued protest against government "spies." This "irresponsible surveillance" had already ended the Quaker oversight of the Pawnee agency and was now blamed for the unfounded charges against Agent Griest. All the other Hicksite Yearly Meetings supported Philadelphia's position. On June 16, 1880, Jesse Griest, the second and last Quaker agent to the Otos, was officially relieved of his duties.[39]

Until mid-May of 1880, the Otos had remained in Nebraska as one tribe with two sets of chiefs. The authority of one set, the traditional chiefs, rested with the central organizing factor of Oto society, the family. Chiefs inherited their power through their families' status. Medicine Horse and his fellow chiefs did not move to the Indian Territory between 1874 and 1880, because in order to maintain their status, they needed a large number of Oto families to move with them. Most of the "progressive" chiefs did not owe their status to an inheritance from their Oto families, because in 1874, Jesse Griest had demonstrated how a white "father" could create a new set of Oto chiefs. Indeed, the fact that Griest and other government officials were called "father" by the Otos signified more than just a gesture of respect. A new, powerful family, which could be called the "Washington family," had become a highly influential force among the Otos. This family had numerous members on the reservation: clerks, teachers, and farmers, as well as an agent-"father." The Washington family helped supply food, employment, and cash gifts. The traditionalists tried to attack this economic connection. They boycotted annuities and sold reservation timber to get money. In addition, both the traditionalists and the progressives recognized that powerful members of the Washington family — in effect, "greater" fathers — resided off the reservation. For this reason, both sets of chiefs regularly demanded to visit the "Great Father" (the commissioner of Indian Affairs or the president). Both factions were aware that control of the Washington family did not rest exclusively with their agent.

Significantly, the progressive chiefs did not become members of the Washington family. They did not become white men. In fact, the term "progressive" overstated these chiefs' commitment to assimilation. Barclay White called the Otos "among the slowest of our tribes to advance in civilized pursuits." Observers often blamed this "backward" condition on the disruptive influence of the traditional chiefs, but the so-called progressives also lacked commitment to "civilized" ways. These chiefs did not fence off individual farms or build separate houses. Like the traditionalists, they stayed in their villages and lived in earthlodges. Many resisted sending their children to school.[40] Like the traditionalists, the progressives seemed to recognize that effective leadership still required recognition by a large number of Oto families. A strong commitment to assimilation could destroy such recognition. In addition, the progressives managed to maintain recognition of their leadership by the Washington family. This recognition involved limited — often lip service — cooperation with the government's goal of assimilation. After all, the government agent, Jesse Griest, had chosen the progressive chiefs to counter the traditionalists and not vice versa. In 1874, Jesse Griest had hoped that by creating a faction of new, forward-looking chiefs he could accelerate the Otos' progress toward "civilization." Over the next six years, no such acceleration occurred, but the formal factionalization of the Otos increased greatly.

Even after both factions had settled in the Indian Territory, their division did not heal quickly. At the official reservation on Red Rock Creek, the federal government continued its financial support of the Otos. Such subsistence attracted many disaffected Coyotes, but they came to Red Rock reluctantly. Medicine Horse did not come to the reservation and accept his annuities until 1892. His granddaughter had married an Iowa man, and for at least five years, from 1887 to 1892, Medicine Horse lived in the Indian Territory as an adopted member of a traditionalist group of Iowas who, like the Coyotes, had split from their larger native society. As for the rest of the Coyotes, in 1889, seventy-five still lived near the Sacs and Foxes, although they occasionally visited Red Rock. As late as 1921, government officials continued to make note of dissident individuals who stayed away from the Oto agency.[41]

Such prolonged antagonism was familiar to the Society of Friends, which had undergone its own schism in the 1820s. At that time each side had been convinced that it held the best traditions and brightest future for the Quaker religion. Half a century later, an heir of the Hicksite schism helped split a small Indian tribe in two. Yet each faction of the Otos also believed that it held the best traditions and brightest hope for its people's survival. Just as the Hicksite and Orthodox Friends would eventually settle their differences in the twentieth century, the two factions of the Otos and Missourias would drift back together. Nonetheless, by the early decades of this century, both the Society of Friends and the confederated tribe of the Otos and Missourias had learned how slowly schisms heal.

CHAPTER SIX

The Omahas and Accommodation

During the 1870s the Otos and the Pawnees resisted most of the assimilationist plans of their Quaker administrators. The Omahas, on the other hand, responded in a distinctly different manner. The idea of accommodation to white, Euro-American culture had taken hold among this group of Native Americans before the first Quaker agent arrived. Many Omahas already had shown great interest in setting out individual farms and in sending their children to school. They appeared to be an ideal society for Quaker administration. However, this willing accommodation to white ideas of "progress" did not mean that all Omahas wished to surrender their native identity and totally assimilate. The Quaker agents also learned that some Omahas preferred other religious denominations and other missionaries.

In addition, the Omahas were not immune to the trials which plagued many Indian tribes. Eradication of the buffalo, failure of crops, factionalization of leaders, decimation by white diseases, and depredations by red neighbors — all these problems afflicted the Omahas. But unlike the Otos and Pawnees, they did not leave Nebraska and instead managed to retain a viable existence. Soon after the Quakers left, Congress passed the Omaha Allotment Act of 1882, which divided much of the reservation among the individual native residents. This law served as a model for the infamous Dawes Severalty Act of 1887. By the early decades of the twentieth century, the Dawes Act and other statutes of its kind had drastically reduced Indian landholdings and thus helped impede the farming efforts of many Native Americans. The Omahas did not escape these frustrating developments. Unfortunately, during their few years together neither the Omahas nor their Quaker agents had foreseen such results from allotment.

The Omahas were already a society in cultural transition at the time the Quakers arrived in the late spring of 1869. Their fertile reservation lay along the Missouri River approximately eighty miles north of the city of Omaha, Nebraska. In 1854, the Omahas had ceded all their hunting grounds to the federal government in return for a 300,000-acre tract and forty years of treaty payments at $20,000 a year. Another treaty, in March of 1865, sold 95,000 acres along the northern part of the original tract to the United States. On this northern section, the federal government established a reservation for the Winnebagos, who had been removed from their homelands in Wisconsin and Minnesota. The treaties of 1854 and 1865 contained provisions for the expansion of agriculture and the allotment of landholdings to individual Omahas.

When the Omahas settled on their reservation in the mid-1850s, they divided into three villages. The largest, called Middle Village, was located near the agency and consisted primarily of earthlodges. A smaller village to the north also contained these traditional lodges, which, as with the Pawnees, were large enough to shelter two families. The third village lay south of the Middle Village, near where the Presbyterians planned to build a new mission. Residents of the other two villages called this settlement "the village of the 'make-believe' white men." Under the leadership of Joseph La Flesche, the Omahas in this southern village built homes, started farms, and sent their children to school. The example of this assimilationist group would influence the entire society. By 1868, most of the Omahas wanted to acquire their individual allotments, build houses, and start farming.[1]

Joseph La Flesche (Inshtamaza or "Iron Eye") was the son of a French fur trader and an Omaha woman. Raised among his mother's people, La Flesche spent three years of his youth among the Sioux and also accompanied his father on trading expeditions. On one such trip he visited St. Louis. Eventually, he hunted and traded on his own. All these travels made him aware of the onrush of white settlement west of the Mississippi. As a young man, La Flesche had become a favorite of the old Omaha chiefs, especially Big Elk. Unlike the Otos', the Omahas' traditional chieftainships were not strictly hereditary. An individual could advance in rank by "count," in effect giving away gifts such as horses or holding many feasts. Actions which brought honor but no material return, such as saving a comrade's life, also advanced an individual's standing. Under Big Elk's guidance, Joseph La Flesche began his rise toward chieftainship. When his own son died, Big Elk recognized La Flesche as his new son and brought him into the Elk gens, although La Flesche should have been in his mother's gens. Big Elk shared his adopted son's awareness of the expansion of white settlement. After a visit to Washington, D.C., the elderly chief gave a foresighted address which the Omahas would retain in their oral traditions:

My chiefs, braves and young men, I have just returned from a visit to a far-off country toward the rising sun, and have seen many strange things. I bring to you news which it saddens my heart to think of. There is a coming flood which will soon reach us, and I advise you to prepare for it. Soon the animals which Wakon' da has given us for sustenance will disappear beneath this flood to return no more, and it will be very hard for you. Look at me; you see I am advanced in age; I am near the grave. I can no longer think for you and lead you as in my younger days. You must think for yourselves what will be best for your welfare. I tell you this that you may be prepared for the coming change. You may not know my meaning. Many of you are old, as I am, and by the time the change comes we may be lying peacefully in our graves; but these young men will remain to suffer. Speak kindly to one another; do what you can to help each other, even in the troubles with the coming tide.[2]

On the death of Big Elk in 1853, Joseph La Flesche, at age thirty-five, took the old leader's place as one of the two principal chiefs on the Council of Seven Chiefs. This elevation made La Flesche a major figure at the treaty negotiations of 1854. In Washington, La Flesche argued successfully for annuity payments in cash instead of goods. This clause of the treaty allowed the Omahas to buy tools, food, and clothing as they saw fit. Having demonstrated his independence of mind to Washington officials, La Flesche returned to Nebraska, where he helped organize what later became known as the "young men's party." Once the Omahas moved onto their new reservation, this group, seemingly in response to Big Elk's farewell address, helped establish the "village of the 'make-believe' white men."

The residents of this southern village showed great enterprise. They cut logs and hauled them to a sawmill which produced boards for their frame houses. La Flesche hired white carpenters to construct his own two-story home with a trading store on the first floor. These carpenters then directed other men in the village as they constructed small frame houses with shingled roofs. A team of oxen broke, by plow, a hundred acres of bottom land which was fenced and divided into separate fields for each man of the village. On this land, the villagers raised the first wheat grown on the reservation. Other small fields were cleared, and large crops of corn and some sorghum were grown. In winter, these Omahas hauled their produce across the frozen Missouri River to Sioux City for sale to the new settlers on the Iowa side. The "'make-believe' white men" also laid out a system of roads leading from their village to the agency, to a steamboat landing on the Missouri, and to the new boarding school established by the Presbyterians. All the children of the village attended this missionary school.[3]

Despite their derogatory name for the southern village, the Omahas in the two northern villages shared one major goal with the "'make-believe' white men." The residents of all three villages had no desire to move from their traditional homeland in Nebraska. The Omahas in their own Siouan language considered themselves the "uki'te," or "tribe." This word had double importance, because as a verb, "uki'te" meant "to fight" as one body against external foes. The noun "uki'te" therefore carried the idea of community, but also the idea of common defense. Thus preservation of the community and protection of it were merged in the Omahas' self-concept.[4]

Other concepts enhanced this Omaha self-image. Separate parties hunted the buffalo in the late fall and winter, but in the summer one large common hunt was undertaken. At this time, the Omahas symbolically demonstrated the overall unity of their society in the highly structured pattern of their camp, which was a great circle called the "hu'thuga." In addition, the Sacred Legend of the Omahas' creation revealed how the people themselves improved their own condition and, in effect, produced their own society. As a preamble to major events such as the acquisition of fire or the use of bark to cover their dwellings, the Sacred Legend regularly employed the phrase "and the people thought," followed by questions such as "What shall we do?" or "How shall we better ourselves?" The answers to these questions emphasized a practical, self-reliant process of thought rather than the actions of mythical, spiritual intermediaries.[5]

During the late 1870s the buffalo hunt, and with it the "hu'thuga," would disappear. Nonetheless, the Omahas' community based on the ideals of common defense, social unity, and practical thought remained. These ideals help explain why the Omahas, unlike the Otos and the Pawnees, did not leave Nebraska in the 1870s and 1880s.

In many other respects, however, the Omahas resembled the Otos and the Pawnees. All three native societies had biannual buffalo hunts, lived in earthlodge villages, and cultivated garden patches along streams. The Omahas also had traditional social structures as complex as those of the other two. For example, they had more elaborate gentes than the Otos and, in addition, recognized formal moieties of Earth and Sky. As with the Pawnees, the Omahas had a traditional chiefs' council (the Council of Seven) which emphasized peace and order within their society and did not, as with the Otos, insist on hereditary status for membership. Despite such similarities, the Otos and the Pawnees removed from Nebraska in a desperate attempt to maintain their traditional way of life, while the Omahas adjusted their habits and patterns and appeared to acquiesce to assimilation. But they still maintained a form of cultural independence and successfully retained their reservation in an area they considered their homeland.

Joseph La Flesche and the "'make-believe' white men" had begun this process of partial acculturation soon after the Omahas moved to their reservation in the mid-1850s. The new southern village, however, did not transform the whole society. On the buffalo hunts, all the Omahas still camped in a single circle strictly organized according to moieties and gentes. Most Omaha men retained the blanket or "robe" as their form of dress. Pipe dances and exchanges of gifts with other tribes continued. Even striking changes of behavior could be explained by some traditional influences. For example, once they had moved to their new reservation, the incidence of drunkenness among the Omahas was drastically reduced. Joseph La Flesche had sworn to end drinking among his people when, as a young man of seventeen, he had witnessed a horrifying murder by a drunken Omaha. Yet La Flesche had to wait until he obtained the traditional powers of a principal chief before he could forbid the consumption of alcohol. To enforce his ban, he even applied a traditional punishment, flogging.[6]

La Flesche and his followers did not wish to abandon all Omaha traditions, but they did wish to adopt some white ways to better their people's condition. For example, La Flesche himself followed Omaha custom and married several wives, yet he insisted that most of his children receive a "white" education at missionary schools. Such selective adaptation of white ways helps to explain why the "'make-believe' white men" did not create severe factionalization among the Omahas. In addition, the Omahas recalled Big Elk's plea to "speak kindly to one another; do what you can to help each other." They also retained a strong sense of "uki'te." This Omaha unity, plus the traditional appreciation of practical ideas for the common good, allowed the influence of the "'make-believe' white men" to increase throughout the 1860s.

During this period, the influence of the government agent also grew. After the establishment of the reservation, the Omahas set up a council of chiefs distinct from the traditional Council of Seven. Up to nine "chiefs" were appointed to this new council. With continued cooperative behavior, these chiefs could hold office for life, but they also could be removed by the agent at any time. The Omahas called such leaders "paper chiefs," because they relied on government recognition for their status. Still, the expediencies of the Omahas' relationship to the federal government gave these "paper chiefs" considerable influence.

Finally, in 1868, the "paper chiefs" were ready to see the allotment provisions of the 1854 treaty carried out. In a series of petitions, these chiefs requested government funds to plow fields, build houses, and set up individual farms. Surprisingly, Joseph La Flesche, the leader of the "'make-believe' white men," was not a member of the council which made these requests.[7]

In 1866, for reasons which remain obscure, La Flesche had moved his family off the reservation because of a dispute with the Omahas' government agent. That agent, Robert W. Furnas, told the director of the Presbyterian Board of Foreign Missions that he had not ordered La Flesche to leave the reservation as some claimed. Yet Agent Furnas also stated that in order for La Flesche to return, "he *must . . .* conduct himself properly, and *be subordinate to the agent.*" Furnas called La Flesche "a shrewd, cunning, ambitious and aspiring Indian *politician,* who has never been willing to be subordinate to an agent, or even [to] the Hon Comr of Indian Affairs." Evidently Furnas and La Flesche had clashed over the issue of political authority, and the agent had won. When La Flesche returned to the reservation, he did not serve as a "paper chief" and his influence as a traditional chief may have been limited to some loyal followers among the "'make-believe' white men," or the "young men's party," as they came to be called. Whatever the case, La Flesche's leadership among the Omahas had waned. The political role of the traditional chiefs disappeared, and the agent's council of "paper chiefs" replaced the Council of Seven as the governing body of the society.[8]

By the time the Quakers arrived, the domination of the government agent over "his" chiefs had been established. The trade-offs and disputes which marked the interactions of Quaker agents with the Pawnee and Oto chiefs did not become a part of the Quakers' relationships with the Omaha chiefs until the final years of the Friends' administration. Although he lived until 1888, none of the Omahas' Quaker administrators appointed Joseph La Flesche to the agent's council. La Flesche did not possess the pliant, cooperative attitude preferred for "paper chiefs." So as the Quakers carried out allotment and helped the Omahas establish a farm economy, they continued to ignore the role played earlier by Joseph La Flesche, a traditional chief. Nonetheless, during the 1870s the Omahas retained La Flesche's balance between accommodation and tradition, and resisted the Quakers' goal of full assimilation.

The first Friends agent to the Omahas, Edward Painter, was an elderly medical doctor from Fallston, Maryland. On his arrival in June of 1869, Painter found nearly one thousand Omahas living "in miserable mud huts and tepees, where light and air are almost wholly excluded." Painter also noted that "disease mostly of a scrofulous character is prevailing amongst them to an alarming extent." General Augur's ban on summer buffalo hunts for all the Nebraska Indians left the Omahas "entirely cut off" from their "customary" meat supply. Incongruously, Painter also claimed that the Omahas wished to give up the chase. "The men are ready and anxious to go to work, and support themselves," the new agent reported. A short buffalo hunt that summer helped the Omahas avoid a food crisis. They would continue these hunts until 1877. Even while they maintained this "customary" activity, however, the Omahas also allotted their lands and established individual farmsteads. Edward Painter had been partially correct in his first reports — the Omahas did wish to "go to work" farming, but they did not want to give up the "chase."[9]

During his first year as agent, Edward Painter carried out the allotment in severalty which the Omahas had requested before his arrival. Although the chiefs of the agent's council had preferred the plan set up in the 1854 treaty, they accepted the less generous provisions of the 1865 agreement. Under this later treaty, each head of a family received 160 acres, with each unmarried adult over age eighteen entitled to 40 acres. The treaty of 1854 would have simply granted 80 acres to each Omaha.

A previous agent in 1868 had estimated that among the 1,002 Omahas, families ranged from 6 to 10 members. Edward Painter, however, reported that 248 "families" could receive 160 acres each. The complete allotment roll showed 254 grants of 160 acres or more with another 39 grants ranging from 70 to 159 acres. Thirty-seven individuals received allotments of approximately 40 acres. If the 76 individuals with grants of less than 160 acres were considered separate from families, then the 254 "families" given at least 160 acres averaged only 3.65 members per family. Of course, this figure does not take into account Omaha polygamy. Fifty-one women received tracts of 160 acres or more. Some of these individuals may have been plural wives, as indeed may have been the case for the eight women who were assigned more than 70 acres each.[10]

The striking statistical fact remains that the Omaha "family" which acquired a full quarter section (160 acres), whether headed by husband, plural wife, widow, or widower, averaged fewer than four members. This remarkably small "family" size probably reflected a high mortality rate among the Omahas. Statistics of Omaha fertility for this period are not known, but it may be safely estimated that Omaha women typically would have given birth to more than two or three children in their lifetime. Indeed, a reasonable estimate could reach as high as twelve. Although they may not have been typical, two of Joseph La Flesche's wives each bore and raised five children. With high mortality, particularly among infants, and with the resulting small families, many farms on individual allotments would operate with a distinct labor shortage. Thus, if the Omahas followed the "civilized ideal" of separate "families" on separate farms, they could expect hard work and meager results.

The Omahas did not immediately transform their social economy after they gained their allotments. Cooperation among themselves and the maintenance of such traditional activities as hunting eased their transition from village agriculturalists to independent farmers. As the Omahas cleared and plowed fields, constructed houses, planted and harvested crops, the cooperative efforts of the men and women of the society, rather than the solitary work of the individual family, provided the labor force. Occasionally the men received pay from treaty funds for their efforts, but these payments stopped after 1873. Although assigned to separate farms, the Omahas did not work in isolation; yet they did not see their farms as communal property. The Omahas had never held food as common property — instead they believed in hospitality and the sharing of food as long as it lasted. A similar cooperative attitude seemed to support the Omahas' establishment of a farm economy.[11] White farmers on the frontier also emphasized hospitality and "neighborliness." They too believed in cooperative labor, especially at house raisings, plantings, and harvests. Among white farmers, such cooperation came out of economic necessity and family kinship. The Omahas, as they established their farms, also were responding to social and economic factors, but their cooperation had the added dimension of cultural tradition and "uki'te."

After the allotment of 1869, in the eyes of their white agent, the Omahas commitment to farming grew steadily. In 1870, Edward Painter proudly reported that a large portion of such outdoor labor as cultivating crops and gathering wood, previously reserved for women, was now done by men. Even the chiefs had taken up the axe and plow and helped bind up the grain. The agent's council approved treaty funds to pay Omaha men to clear and plow lands. Five to ten Omahas also were employed as carpenters to build frame houses. Samuel Janney marveled that the Omahas "do an astonishing amount of work." At Painter's insistence, the council agreed in 1871 to the sale of 50,000 acres from the western part of the reservation. Congress approved this sale the next year, and the profits helped to fence fields, build houses, and purchase implements, livestock, and machinery as well as to establish and maintain new schools. These 50,000 acres included the better unallotted farm land, but at $2.50 per acre, sales went slowly.[12]

As the Omahas continued their efforts at farming, their white neighbors did not pilfer timber in the outrageous manner which so disturbed the Otos and Pawnees on their own reservations. Indeed, during the 1870s — except for two murders, the loss of several horses, and the theft of some wheat — the Omahas had remarkably few complaints about the whites who lived near them.[13]

By the 1870s, the Omahas, unlike the Otos and the Pawnees, no longer lived on the edge of the expanding farmers' frontier. This fact alone may explain the relatively peaceful relationship between the Omahas and their white neighbors. Once white farmers had survived the desperate early years and established their homesteads, the need to exploit all possible resources, including their red neighbors' timber, may have subsided. In short, the first rush to build homes and fence fields had passed. The farmers were well settled and a demand remained only for firewood and some occasional lumber for the repair of buildings and fences. With their farms located near the fertile course of the Missouri River, these established white settlers had enough timber on their own land to meet their own needs. Thus, the Omahas were spared excessive raids on their timber lands by white neighbors and had enough wood available to undertake some house building of their own.

In 1871, Edward Painter asked for $49,650 to build 331 houses for the Omahas. Painter's plans were never carried through on such a grand scale, but when the last Quaker agent left in 1880, 111 houses were occupied by the Omahas. Painter had great enthusiasm for these "frame cottages." He believed a five-room house measuring twenty by twenty-four feet could be erected in three to five days with "almost exclusively" Indian labor. Painter thought each home should contain a sitting room, a kitchen, and three private bedrooms. The foundation walls and chimney would be made of brick and each room would contain a fireplace.

The modest homes which were constructed fell short of Painter's dreams and eastern Friends who visited the Omaha reservation were not impressed. In 1870 two visitors from the Ohio and Genesee Yearly Meetings said that two or three houses had been abandoned for the summer because they were infested with vermin. In June of 1875, four delegates from the Indiana Yearly Meeting found the present frame housing untenable. Vermin permitting, the Omahas had taken to inhabiting their new houses only in warmer months. They preferred their tipis in colder weather. The four Quakers from Indiana approved the logic of the Omahas' choice. As they explained in their report:

> The policy heretofore pursued of building houses for the Indians is, in our judgment, a grave mistake, because they *do not* know how to use them, and *do know* how to live in tents or tepees. They require a large amount of wood to warm them in winter, and the owners do not enjoy cutting and hauling it several miles. The teepee requires but little fire to make them comfortably warm. The Indian can live in the teepee on his farm as well as he can in the village of tents. His forefathers lived in them in all the long ages past, and he knows, nor thinks of, nor is comfortable, nor at home in any other kind of a house.[14]

Such heretical appreciation of native housing did not end the building program on the Omaha reservation. More frame houses would be built until, for many Omahas, the frame house on the farm allotment replaced the earthlodge in the village. The Indiana Quakers noted in 1875 that more than half the residents of the northern village had moved to their farms, and that only three lodges and a few tents remained in the Middle Village. They did not mention Joseph La Flesche's southern village, which may already have dispersed. Still, many Omahas did not emulate their white neighbors and live exclusively in their houses. Some moved into their warmer tipis in cold weather or others moved out completely for the biannual buffalo hunts. Six hundred Omahas had gone on the winter hunt of 1874/75. The Indiana delegation reported that they went "out of necessity" and without their agent's permission.

Theodore T. Gillingham of New Holland, Indiana, was the agent who opposed the buffalo hunt. He had replaced Edward Painter in the fall of 1873. Gillingham and his wife, Elizabeth, who had taught freedmen in the South after the Civil War, had first come to the Omaha agency as teachers. After his appointment, Gillingham remained among the Omahas for less than three years. He regularly tried to end the biannual hunts, but with no success. In 1876 Gillingham issued thirty beeves so the Omahas could hold a feast in place of their winter hunt, but as they had done the year before, the Omahas went out anyway. Anticipating a more profitable use of his time, Gillingham resigned his post in 1875 in order to join a mercantile firm in Chicago. The slow operations of the Washington bureaucracy delayed for nearly a year the arrival of his replacement. Jacob Vore, himself a former mercantile businessman from Dublin, Indiana, took control of the Omaha agency on September 20, 1876. For his fellow Quaker and successor, Theodore Gillingham had one final word of advice: "The Omahas are becoming much excited over the hunt, and I recommend that effective means be taken to prevent it this fall, as it each year puts them back."[15]

Jacob Vore found the Indians eager to leave for their winter hunt. They had little food. In the summer of 1876, grasshoppers had decimated their crops. Disease, aided by malnutrition, had taken its toll. The Omahas explained to their new agent that they needed their buffalo hunts to secure their meat supply, to provide robes for trade, and to produce new hides to repair their tipis. The year before, Agent Gillingham had announced proudly that the Omahas had received no rations or regular subsistence from the federal government. Except for a small cash annuity, Gillingham claimed that the Omahas were self-supporting, with treaty funds helping to increase farming and all "able" men working on the land.[16]

Actually, the Omahas' self-sufficiency relied on a dichotomy between their approaches to hunting and agriculture. The people continued to hunt in the "old" way, following the rituals and social organizations of their own traditions. They farmed in a "new" way, but the accommodations which characterized the Omahas "allotted" agriculture had not carried onto the buffalo range. A balance between tradition and accommodation had helped produce the Omahas' food supply until the summer of 1876, when the grasshoppers struck.

From 1873 to 1877, the farm lands of Nebraska were devastated by the summer swarms of grasshoppers. These devouring insects proved far more destructive than storms, drought, or fires, but they also seemed fickle in the areas they ravaged. Fields in one location would be stripped bare, whereas lands planted in the same crops only a few miles away would be untouched. The Pawnees and the Otos had lost their crops in the summer of 1874, but the Omahas' fields had not been affected, although crops in neighboring Dixon county to the north-northwest were devoured. In 1876 the swarms came to the Omahas' lands. The year before, fifteen hundred acres had been planted, with corn as the predominant crop. Five hundred more acres were planted by 1876, but corn production, because of the grasshoppers, dropped from 25,000 bushels to only 3,500. A modest wheat crop of 5,500 bushels was not destroyed. Such devastation two years before had speeded the Pawnees' removal from Nebraska and sent the Otos on a desperate, but unapproved, buffalo hunt. In the late fall of 1876, the Omahas responded in a manner similar to the Otos. Approximately six hundred left on a winter hunt, although their new agent, Jacob Vore, thought such hunts should be "positively disallowed."[17]

The Omahas stayed out on the buffalo range for five months, but with such limited success that by late February of 1877 they were starving. They begged for food at Fort Hays, Kansas, and Gen. John Pope gave them $340 worth of rations. The Omahas' last formal buffalo hunt had failed. On their return to the reservation in late March, the destitute hunters informed Jacob Vore that they now wished to put in a full spring crop. Vore warned Washington that he needed more seed and relief rations if the Indians were to survive until the fall harvest.[18]

Government aid and the absence of grasshoppers allowed the Omahas to produce 27,000 bushels of corn and 9,000 bushels of wheat. After 1877 the grasshopper plagues ended, and the Omahas continued to expand their agricultural lands and livestock holdings. These advances would be modest. By the time the Quakers left in 1880, only five hundred new acres had been added to the two thousand cultivated in 1876. Yet by 1880, the Omahas owned 166 cattle and had owned as many as 291 pigs (in 1879). Still, horses, a traditional source of status and wealth, outnumbered cattle by an approximate ratio of three to one, and less than a quarter of the Omahas wore what their agent called "citizen's dress."[19] The buffalo hunts may have ended in 1877, but not all signs of tradition disappeared with the bison.

Cultural traditions may only in part explain the Omahas' cautious acceptance of white agriculture. During the 1870s, white farmers on the Central Plains provided no real model of successful husbandry for Native Americans. The white man's fields had no immunity to drought and grasshoppers. Indeed, local businessmen and state and local politicians feared the depopulation of frontier farm lands in areas such as Nebraska. For this reason, massive amounts of private, state, and federal aid flowed out to the farmers during the hard times of the 1870s. Ironically, the U.S. Army became a major supplier of food and clothing. In the fall of 1874, more than two years before the starving Omahas came to his post, Gen. John Pope issued rations to destitute farmers in Kansas. Gen. E. O. C. Ord dispensed similar charity in Nebraska. Other support came from private groups and special legislation. One private relief society in Nebraska, in a little more than seven months, raised over $74,000 in cash and thousands of dollars more in commodities. State and federal legislation provided funds for food as well as financial support to continue farm operations. Nebraska, for example, appropriated $50,000 for new seed.[20]

The Omahas, in the winter of 1876/77, had looked to the buffalo hunt for relief from the grasshoppers. White farmers had looked to private and political charity. The Omahas failed on their hunt and returned to their Nebraska reservation. On the other hand, white farmers received much charitable support, but many abandoned their homesteads on the Central Plains and moved back to the more fertile Midwest and East. In the mid-1870s, the impact of drought and the onslaught of the grasshoppers proved that the white model of diversified subsistence farming could fail on the Central Plains. Yet for most well-meaning social reformers this farming model remained the "ideal" solution for Indian assimilation throughout the rest of the nineteenth century. Larger-scale single-crop or pastoral enterprises, plus the techniques of dry farming, eventually produced agricultural prosperity on the Central Plains. But before these developments, the Indians who stayed in the region suffered under the wrong "ideal."

The experience of Quaker farmers in Kansas and Nebraska should have tempered the Friends' enthusiasm for this farming "ideal." Eastern Orthodox Friends contributed generously to fellow Quakers in Kansas who had suffered the devastations of drought and grasshoppers. Among the Hicksite group, former Pawnee agent Jacob Troth complained that "our highly favored friends of the East" had not sent enough aid to his Quaker neighbors around Genoa, Nebraska. Troth's letter appeared in the April 10, 1872, issue of the *Friends' Intelligencer* of Philadelphia. He reported that all other Protestant denominations, including the Orthodox Quakers, had made large donations. The eastern Hicksites needed to send aid, because some Nebraska Hicksites had been forced to seek work away from their farms in an effort to support their families. Concluding dramatically, Troth reported: "I lived in Virginia during the war, from the beginning to the close, and in that part of it occupied by the contending armies, and I think I know something of its ravages, but [I] saw nothing equal to the ravages of grasshoppers in this State the last year, so far as crops were concerned."

Troth's letter generated a charitable response from some eastern Hicksites, and he organized a Friends' Relief Committee in Genoa which distributed funds to twenty-six needy Quakers. No funds were needed for Troth's Indian neighbors because the Pawnees had left the state. In his correspondence Troth did not compare the plight of Quakers driven from their farms to seek work with the recent exit of the Pawnees to the Indian Territory. The Pawnees, however, may have made such a comparison.

With their exodus in 1874, the Pawnees demonstrated that they did not accept the farming "ideal" as a solution to their problems; clearly they would rather move than farm. The Otos and Missourias showed a similar determination when they removed in 1881. External pressures plus indigenous cultural and political factors had justified removal within each tribe. Such indigenous factors also explained the rejection of the farm model by both groups, but this rejection had an added dimension of simple observation. In the mid-1870s the Pawnees and the Otos could easily see that farming was not working for whites, so why should it work for Indians?

The Omahas, because they would not consider leaving Nebraska, reached a different conclusion. Beginning in the mid-1850s, a spirit of accommodation, especially toward white agriculture, spread across the society. But such accommodation never produced a capitulation to white ways. Like the Pawnees and the Otos, the Omahas could observe the hardships of white farmers in the 1870s. These observations, combined with cultural traditions, slowed the Omahas' acceptance of the white farm model. With the end of the buffalo hunts, however, agriculture became the dominant source of the Omahas' food supply.

Beyond the increased commitment to agriculture, another factor which explained the Omahas' continuing accommodation to white ways was the acceptance of schooling. As had been the case with farming, the Quakers were also not the original source of the Omahas' interest in education. In 1846 the Board of Foreign Missions of the Presbyterian church established a mission among the Omahas at Bellevue, Nebraska. Two years later, the Presbyterians opened a boarding school at Bellevue which welcomed Omaha, Oto and a few Pawnee children. In 1857, after the relocation of the Omahas on their new reservation, the Board of Foreign Missions constructed a new school overlooking the Missouri River near the headquarters of the new agency. This school building, constructed of native stone, had three stories and seventeen rooms. It was designed to house the Presbyterian missionaries, their families, and some fifty boarding students. Indian boarders shared meals and worshiped with the missionary staff. Church meetings were held in the school assembly room, and several Omahas became active Presbyterians. The school's curriculum included farm work for boys and domestic training for girls. Classroom instruction stressed reading, geography, writing, and arithmetic.[21]

By 1868, two teachers instructed a total of sixty students. Yet Superintendent H. B. Denman of the Northern Superintendency complained that William Hamilton, the director of the mission school, had meddled in Omaha affairs and created "domestic dissensions." Because the Presbyterians received $3,750 out of the Omahas' annuity to operate the school, Denman felt he had the right to call for Hamilton's dismissal. The actions of this Presbyterian missionary had already caused some Omahas to stop sending their children to the school, Denman claimed.[22]

In all likelihood, William Hamilton had been caught up in the reaction to Joseph La Flesche and his "young men's party." Those Omahas who saw La Flesche and his cohorts as "'make-believe' white men" may have resented Hamilton and the mission school because many children of the "'make-believe' white men" had attended the school. At least two of La Flesche's children had studied with the Presbyterians. In addition, the agent's council of chiefs was dominated by critics of the "young men's party." When a new agent, Edward Painter, arrived in 1869, these "paper chiefs" asked that the $3,750 given to the mission school be used instead to establish day schools.

Both their new Quaker agent and the superintendent, along with the commissioner of Indian Affairs, approved the request of the chiefs' council. Samuel M. Janney informed the Board of Foreign Missions that he wanted the boarding school to stay open, but as a majority of the Omahas' children had not attended that school, he felt day schools would succeed better. John C. Lowrie, secretary of the Presbyterian Board of Foreign Missions, already had complained to the new commissioner of Indian Affairs, Ely S. Parker. Lowrie wrote: "Day schools cannot succeed among those who do not value education, and unhappily it is true that it is the nonprogressive part of the Omahas who have applied for the termination of the contract. The more enlightened, better civilized though smaller part of the tribe, do not wish the existing arrangements to be materially disturbed."[23]

Despite Lowrie's protest, the Presbyterian boarding school would remain closed for a decade while the Quaker experiment with day schools ran its course. The Board of Foreign Missions still retained a missionary among the Omahas during this period, and his presence created some tensions with the Quaker administration of the agency. Yet enrollment figures vindicated the Quaker decision to establish day schools. With their children taken away for class instruction only during the day, more Omaha families sent their children to school. In 1871, with three teachers at three schools, the Quakers gave instruction to 144 children. Two of the Quaker teachers reported that they had made a great effort to get Omaha parents involved in sending their children to school. They described the children as thoughtful but shy students: "The greatest obstacle in the way of educating these people is their great reluctance to practice speaking our language even after they understand it. They are timid and sensitive, afraid of using it incorrectly. One thing particularly noted by us is their uniform kindness to each other; we never taught among any class of people where unpleasant differences so seldom occurred."[24]

In 1873, Agent Painter reported that only a few Omaha families were still indifferent to the educational opportunities on the reservation. Of the approximately 160 children of school age, 110 had enrolled in the three day schools. An average of 70 students a day had attended during the ten months of classes. Painter claimed that more children would attend if there were more room in the schools. The agent's report showed that the classroom curriculum paralleled the former offerings of the Presbyterian boarding school. Reading, writing, arithmetic, and geography were still the major subjects, with the addition of a practical course in bookkeeping. The Quakers operated the three day schools at a total cost to the federal government of $2,663.65 per year. With grants from the Board of Foreign Missions, plus $3,750 in treaty funds, the single Presbyterian school had cost twice as much. The Quakers, however, did not give specific instruction in farm labor and domestic work to the children. Such instruction was given to all the Omahas, adult and child, by the agency farmer and by the Quaker women on the reservation. This form of general education also supported the

Friends' efforts to "instill precepts of Christian religion" among all the Omahas. In a letter to the Board of Indian Commissioners, Edward Painter defended the Quakers' "sedate" efforts to produce moral and religious awareness:

> It may not be out of place for me briefly to refer to the work now being done here [at the Omaha agency] to "Christianize the Indians." It is well known to those familiar with the principles and practices of the Society of Friends that they do not send out their members to preach at stated times, believing that a divine and renewed qualification is necessary to fit them to do this effectually; yet it is not to be inferred, on this account, that those sent among the Indians are indifferent to their spiritual welfare.[25]

Painter had stated sound Hicksite theology, but other Protestant denominations did not appreciate the Friends' generalized approach to Christianity. In June of 1873, John M. Peebles, who for six years had preached in neighboring Decatur, Nebraska, complained to the commissioner of Indian Affairs. Peebles claimed that the only hope for the Indians was to make them Christians. He leveled the difficult-to-believe charges that Agent Painter opposed Bible reading in the schools and "pays no regard to the Sabbath." Peebles did not identify his own denomination, but he bitterly denounced the closing of the Presbyterian boarding school and Painter's antagonism toward the continued missionary work of William Hamilton, the school's former director.

Peebles's letter documented the interdenominational tensions which swirled around the Quakers' administration of the Omaha agency. These tensions produced a recommendation from Superintendent Barclay White that Edward Painter resign his position. With the usual Quakerly obliqueness, White explained to the commissioner of Indian Affairs that Agent Painter had raised great hopes among the Omahas for their general improvement, which, when not fully realized, became the opportunity for "outside parties . . . to make him unpopular with the tribe."[26]

Painter acquiesced to White's suggestion, but he also identified "the missionary stationed here" as one of the "designing persons" who manipulated the Indians. The "young men's party," which included Joseph La Flesche, would have been the group most open to William Hamilton's advice, because it contained many Presbyterian converts. The closing of the boarding school in 1869, along with a lack, in Presbyterian terms, of Christian zeal, had brought on Edward Painter's downfall. The opposition to Painter spread among all the Omahas, finally reaching the chiefs' council, which began to refuse approval of any suggestions for the allocations of treaty funds. Without the council's approval, Painter could not spend these funds to plow fields, harvest and thresh wheat, or purchase supplies.[27] Rather than replace the entire council, as Jesse Griest would do with the Otos, Painter resigned.

All nine of the chiefs who created this deadlock and resignation in 1873 had sat on the agent's council in June of 1869, when the council ended the funding of the mission school.[28] In both cases, four years apart, the chiefs demonstrated that although they were nominally the agent's appointees, they could act independently and express the preponderant views of their society. In 1869, the chiefs opposed the "young men's party" and closed the mission school. In 1873, they agreed with this group and helped oust the agent. Their actions in 1873 showed that their earlier rejection of the "young men's party" had not hardened into consistent opposition. Indeed, the influence of the "young men's party" had spread by 1873, so the chiefs could continue to act out of "uki'te," rather than out of factionalism. Four years later, the "young men's party" would not be so generous. It would join with a new Quaker agent in an effort to abolish chieftainships entirely.

The appointment of a new agent, Theodore T. Gillingham, seemed to calm the troubled waters at the Omaha agency. Gillingham, a former teacher at one of the day schools, continued the educational program on the reservation. Overall enrollments increased to 160 students in 1874 and 156 students in 1875. These figures marked the highest enrollments during the Quakers' administration of the agency. Gillingham left his post in the early fall of 1876 because he felt that agents received too little pay for the responsibilities they bore. His replacement, Jacob Vore, arrived after the grasshoppers had decimated the Omahas' corn crop. Vore had to adjust to severe cuts in the Omahas' educational budget because of government budget restrictions on hiring employees such as teachers and because of the Omahas' desperate economic situation. During his three years as agent no more than two schools were in operation at any time.[29]

Jacob Vore's administration produced more controversy than that of any previous Quaker agent among the Omahas. His first dispute came in the fall of 1876, with his choice of teachers. Because of limited funds, Vore felt he should change teachers and hire only females, whom he could pay less. One excellent candidate for a teaching position, the twenty-two-year-old daughter of Joseph La Flesche, was ignored by Vore. Susette La Flesche (also called Inshtatheumba, or Bright Eyes) had attended the Presbyterian mission school for two years, and then had gone on to the Elizabeth (New Jersey) Institute for Young Ladies. The principal of the institute said that La Flesche had "outstripped" the white children in her studies and had stood "at the head of her classes." In her last year in New Jersey, La Flesche had taught classes at the institute. On her return to the Omaha reservation, Susette La Flesche worked as an assistant teacher under Agent Gillingham. When Jacob Vore initiated his austerity program, La Flesche lost her position, and Vore refused to appoint her as a full-time teacher. La Flesche then rose to her own defense and wrote to the commissioner of Indian Affairs. As an educated Omaha, she pointed out to the commissioner that "it all seems like a farce, when the Whites, who came here with the avowed object of civilizing and teaching us to do for ourselves, what they are doing for us, should, after we are prepared to occupy positions, appropriate those positions to themselves."[30]

Jacob Vore lamely explained to the commissioner that he had relied on La Flesche's fellow Presbyterians for an evaluation of her teaching abilities. They considered her an excellent assistant teacher with fine educational training, but lacking in the "energy and self-control" to carry on full teaching duties. Commissioner John Q. Smith rejected Vore's explanation and directed the Quaker agent to give preference to the employment of qualified Indians, who were to be paid at reasonable rates. Vore complied, and La Flesche took charge of an agency school. She received only half the pay of previous white teachers, but this low income may have been due as much to a limited budget as to any spite on Vore's part.[31]

In 1879 and 1880, to eastern audiences concerned with the plight of the "red man," the name of "Bright Eyes" (Susette La Flesche) became well known as a result of her participation in a lecture tour undertaken to inform concerned American citizens about the mistreatment of Standing Bear and his fellow Poncas. Although Standing Bear's story outraged many white reformers, the plight of the Poncas had a more profound impact on their old friends, the Omahas. The Omahas and the Poncas belonged to the same Southern Siouan language group, along with the Osages, Kansas, and Quapaws. Common traditions and similarities of social organization indicate that all five peoples were once united. In 1865, the Poncas, who numbered around seven hundred, moved onto a reservation along the Missouri River, north of their Omaha friends. Three years later, at the treaty of Fort Laramie, the United States ceded the entire Ponca reservation to the Teton Sioux. The Poncas had not been consulted. The Sioux, who had waged the same war of attrition against the Poncas that they had carried on against the Pawnees, now had the small Southern Siouan tribe in an impossible situation. During these desperate times, to avoid Sioux raids and find food, the Poncas often visited the Omahas. Like the Omahas, many of the Poncas had taken allotments and started farming. They now considered leaving their reservation and settling with the friendly Omahas. A joint council in 1873 agreed to this resettlement, but the federal government, which admitted it had created most of the problem, decided to resettle the Poncas in the Indian Territory.

The removal of the Poncas in 1877 produced a tragic story that became a *cause célèbre* for Christian reformers. As with the Pawnees, who had removed on their own, relocation to the Indian Territory brought greater poverty and many deaths to the Poncas. One of their chiefs, Standing Bear, after his son died of malaria, led a small number of Poncas back to the north. In the spring of 1879, Standing Bear and his followers had reached the Omaha reservation. Their plight became known to a group of concerned citizens in the city of Omaha. When federal troops arrived to arrest Standing Bear, these citizens produced a writ of habeas corpus to prevent the return of the Poncas to the Indian Territory.

The trial that followed produced a landmark decision. Federal District Judge Elmer S. Dundy, who had ruled so skillfully in the murder trial of the Pawnees, *Yellow Sun et al.*, ruled that "an Indian is a 'person' within the meaning of the laws of the United States, and has, therefore the right to sue out a writ of habeas corpus in a federal court." Such a legal right for Indians had never been recognized before, because Indians did not hold citizenship in the United States. Dundy also found no authority for returning the Poncas to the Indian Territory, so he ordered their release.

Thomas Henry Tibbles, an assistant editor of the *Omaha Herald*, had been, by his own accounts, the most active supporter of Standing Bear's case. Tibbles launched a campaign for the return of the Poncas' old reservation on the Missouri. He organized the lecture tour which brought popular renown to both Standing Bear and Susette La Flesche, who served as the Ponca chief's interpreter. La Flesche soon noted that eastern audiences preferred her more romantic Omaha name of "Bright Eyes." She shrewdly accepted the preference and added her own dramatic touch by appearing on stage in traditional native dress.

The tour's greatest success occurred in Boston, where civic leaders organized an Indian Citizenship Committee and Helen Hunt Jackson resolved to include the Ponca case in her book *A Century of Dishonor*. This volume became a popular, sentimental exposé of Indian-white relations. In response to Jackson's book and to the speeches of Standing Bear, some heated arguments about abuses of the Indian service arose in the U.S. Congress. These debates produced legislation in 1881 to repay the Poncas for their losses and to allow individuals to choose allotments on either the old or the new reservation. As for Susette La Flesche, she married Thomas H. Tibbles that same year.[32]

Leaders among the Omahas, such as Joseph La Flesche, had dictated letters of support in their native language for Tibbles's campaign. J. Owen Dorsey, an Episcopal minister, wrote down these letters and then translated them. Dorsey, who would spend two years among the Omahas, had become engaged in a philological study of the Omaha language. The letters that he translated revealed the anxieties which the Omahas felt over the possible loss of their lands. The Omahas asked Tibbles to represent their cause in the East and to secure clear title for the Omahas' allotments. One Omaha, Two Crows, complained: "Though we employ the agents to write (to the President about these things), behold, they do not write for us! Notwithstanding they say that they have written for us, the agents do not speak the truth."[33]

Quaker administrators had ignored consistently the trauma which the removal of the Poncas created among the Omahas. In the spring of 1877, when news of this event reached the Omahas, they had already experienced the devastation of the grasshoppers and the failure of their final buffalo hunt. Agent Jacob Vore noted at the time a renewed commitment to farming; yet, even as the Omahas were coming to recognize farm agriculture as their primary food source, they saw their friends the Poncas, who also had taken up farming on allotments, forcibly evicted by the federal government. Agent Vore observed great agitation among the Omahas, but he blamed factional politics between the "young men's party" and the chiefs' council. In 1877 Vore reported: "With the Omahas the chiefship is a source of more strife and disaffection than any other source of difference. There is a large party opposed to their present hereditary chiefs, and desirous of either electing the chiefs or of having none."[34]

A long letter of January 12, 1878, to the president of the United States expressed the views of the young men's party. The names of fifty-one Omahas, including Joseph La Flesche and his educated son Francis (Frank), appeared at the end of this letter. The writers confessed that they wanted the old chiefs "put away like an old wagon . . . that is worn out, or an old mud house that is going to fall on us and hurt us." The letter made clear, however, that the reason for this suggested dismissal lay in the fear that the chiefs' council would agree to the sale of the Nebraska reservation. The seductive promise of "plenty of money" could easily persuade the chiefs, because "they are too much like children and bad men can easily impose upon them." The young men's party knew how government agents had created the paper chiefs who made up the council. If the government wished to impose removal on the Omahas, as it had with the Poncas, the chiefs' council would comply. To avoid this possibility, the letter asked for protection under the law: "We want to be like good white people and be under good laws, and we are willing to pay taxes to be protected as white people are protected. We are not living in a village now as we used to do but have selected farms, and are living on them. but [sic] we have no title to our farms and our homes, and if our Great Father buys our chiefs and our lands, we will lose all."[35]

The young men's party was also aware of how the federal government manipulated native political organization for its own policy goals. By asking for individual legal titles, the party sought to ensure that, though common ownership of the land would no longer exist, the native community could remain in Nebraska on adjoining farms. The young men's party had revised the concept of protective unity, or "uki'-te," to end the threat of removal. As the letter showed in an early passage, the young men's party remembered that "we and our Fathers for many years past have lived together as one people . . . for the sake of protecting ourselves." The letter went on to explain that the people had chosen where they wished to remain "as long as we live and our children after us."

Although the writers claimed that they wanted "to be citizens like white people," they also had heard "that if we become citizens, we must forsake our tribe and give up our annuities." They explained that the threat of losing annuities helped the "wild Indians" and the old chiefs, who argued that, through removal and the sale of the reservation, annuities would be maintained and new monies acquired. The writers found these recalcitrant Omahas to be "just like white people . . . they love to go where the money is. But if our Great Father will give us our lands [by title], and give each one his share of our annuities, we think almost all our young men will become farmers and support themselves."

This letter of January 12, 1878, revealed how well the young men's party, with its educated, Presbyterian members, understood the use of the law to block threats of removal. Jacob Vore, however, would not be the individual to help the Omahas gain legal land titles and U.S. citizenship. In 1871 Edward Painter had distributed certificates of ownership to the individual allottees. From 1878 until he was replaced in the spring of 1879, Vore ignored requests for a new set of more legally valid titles. He continued to see this issue as a mere byproduct of the dispute over the abolition of chieftainships and the termination of "old customs" such as feasting, dancing, and visiting other Indians. The young men's party, in its letter to the president, had expressed discouragement with the agent, yet Vore saw the young men's party as his ally in the confrontation with the chiefs. Vore gained permission from Washington to end the chiefs' salaries, which had been paid out of treaty annuities. When he announced this new policy at an open council in December of 1878, Vore was amazed to notice how the "chief and anti-chief parties" began to "fraternize more than at any time since I have been on the reservation."[36]

Apparently, the members of the young men's party believed that Vore's termination of the chiefs' salaries had created another economic pressure which might encourage the chiefs to sell all the reservation. Vore's action gave the young men's party a new reason to distrust their agent, but his decision also gave this party a topic of agreement with the chiefs. Both groups disliked Jacob Vore. Letters and petitions from the Omaha chiefs denouncing the Quaker agent quickly began to arrive in Washington. The longest and most reliable letter, dated January 16, 1879, came from Henry Fontenelle, a schooled Omaha who, like Joseph La Flesche, counted a French fur trader among his ancestors. Fontenelle said that all the chiefs had come to him and requested that he write to the commissioner of Indian Affairs. The chiefs had a long list of complaints against their agent, many of which centered on the employment of his family at the agency. Vore's son was the agency farmer; his son-in-law, the agency physician; his daughter-in-law, the salaried matron. The chiefs said that Vore himself was too old and infirm to fulfill his duties, and claimed that he ignored the chiefs, who were "the lawful representatives" of the people. Fontenelle's letter included a strong slap at all Quakers, as represented by Jacob Vore:

> Our Agent is a member of the society of Friends or quakers. We hailed with much gladness and joy the just policy of Gen'l Grant in appointing christian denominations as our Agents, we dreamed of a brighter future in our welfare and advancement, but like many bright hopes, it is blasted. We supposed these men were coming among us as messengers of peace and prosperity who would think it was better to give than to receive, but it seems they like it better to take all they can and give none. it [sic] seems their study is to make all the money they [can] . . . and make a family affair of the advantage they have.[37]

Fontenelle's words on behalf of the chiefs expressed the despair of many Omahas over the poverty which engulfed them and their disillusionment with their Quaker agent. But this acrimony did not bring on Jacob Vore's dismissal. Instead, the consolidation of the Omaha and Winnebago agencies ended Vore's administration. At first, it appeared that Jacob Vore would take control of the new consolidated agency. The Winnebago agent, Howard White, informed his father, Barclay White, that he had received instructions to that effect. Jacob Vore planned to accept this new appointment, but, to his own embarrassment, he discovered that the Friends in the New York Yearly Meeting, which oversaw the Winnebagos, would not underwrite the expanded bond for the consolidated agency. Vore's own Yearly Meeting, Indiana, agreed to take only its part of the financial burden. In addition, the New York Hicksites said that they preferred to nominate someone of their own choosing. Vore felt that he would be excluded because he had differed with Barclay White during his annual visits as "special agent" and because "I have not hesitated to express views differing from those entertained by some of the Eastern Friends." Vore's premonitions proved correct. On April 30, 1879, Howard White became the new Omaha and Winnebago agent.[38]

Howard White served as the Omahas' agent for little more than a year. The infuriating policies of the commissioner of Indian Affairs, Ezra Hayt, especially the notorious spy system, which bedeviled Indian agents regardless of religious affiliation, produced Howard White's resignation on July 15, 1880. A letter from members of the Central Executive Committee of the Hicksite Yearly Meetings informed the secretary of the interior, Carl Schurz, that the Friends would not suggest a replacement because no one was "willing to serve under the present rulings of the secretary [supporting Hayt]." The news that White would leave prompted a request for a separate agent from a group of Omaha leaders that included members of both the chiefs' and young men's parties. As usual, Washington officials did nothing.[39]

The last two Quaker agents saw little improvement among the Omahas. Only a few weeks before Howard White left his office, J. Owen Dorsey summarized what he considered the limited progress under the two most recent Quaker administrations. The Reverend Mr. Dorsey sent his letter to the commissioner of Indian Affairs in care of his friend, the famous scientist and explorer Maj. John Wesley Powell, who was director of the Bureau of American Ethnology. Dorsey's philological study of the Omahas eventually would be published by Powell's bureau, but his letter of March, 1880, centered on the state of Omaha agriculture. Dorsey reported that 125 Omahas had five acres apiece under cultivation. Fewer than 50 members of the tribe worked from seven to twenty acres each. Only one man cultivated over twenty acres. Wild buckwheat and morning glories overran some of the fields that were supposedly in agricultural production. The agent did not supply enough seed to plant a full wheat crop, and the plows purchased to break new lands were too heavy for the Indian ponies to pull. To make ends meet, the Omahas cut timber on their reservation and sold it to white neighbors. In addition, Dorsey reported that the Winnebagos stole Omaha horses.[40]

Dorsey did not mention the agency schools because in 1880 there was nothing to report. The year before, the Quakers had given up their educational efforts, and the Presbyterians had reopened their boarding school. Some Omahas were eager for a second school, but one would not open until 1881. Literacy had progressed very little since 1875. In that year the agent reported that 120 Omahas could read. In 1879 the figure had risen to 155, but the next year, the new, non-Quaker agent reported 131 literate Omahas.

In his only annual report on the Omahas, Howard White revealed that in 1879 very few good houses existed on the reservation, so many Omahas camped on their allotments in summer and moved to the woods in winter. White did report that Indians now held most of the agency jobs, but he showed little confidence in the Omahas' fiscal responsibility. White wrote: "Many of the Indians are clamoring for the rights and privileges of citizenship. As these are generally the most thriftless, I doubt the propriety of conferring any more privileges upon them at present. They certainly should not be granted the opportunity of disposing of their lands and trust funds."[41]

The Quakers had become part of the Indian service in 1869 with the idea of turning the Indians into responsible, "civilized" farmers. When the Hicksites came to work with the Omahas, they found many members of the tribe willing to follow this ideal, but through accommodation to Omaha traditions, not through assimilation to white ways. During the 1870s, Omaha accommodation brought, if not prosperity, at least stability, especially in comparison to the Pawnees and the Otos. The Omahas did not undergo removals and schisms. They did not experience drastic declines in population. Still, the Omahas refused to fully mimic the white way of life, even though they took allotments, built houses, and sent their children to school. This refusal frustrated the Quakers, who continued to see a paternalistic role for the agent as long as the Omahas retained some native traits. Because of this paternalism, the Omahas' last two Quaker agents refused to support the peoples' desire for new land titles and for new status as U.S. citizens. After the exit of the Quakers, both these goals were obtained by 1887. Yet this success severely challenged the central concept of "uki'te," which the Omahas hoped to maintain.

The story of the Omahas' acquisition of their land titles and their recognition as citizens is full of the spirit of misguided good intentions which had characterized the Quakers' work as part of the Peace Policy. Alice Fletcher, a pioneer anthropologist and social reformer, played a central role in this story. Fletcher first visited the Omahas in September of 1881. Her hosts were Thomas Tibbles and Susette La Flesche, soon to become Susette Tibbles. This visit began a lifelong association between Fletcher and the Omahas which, with the collaboration of Francis La Flesche, a son of Joseph La Flesche, would produce the definitive study of Omaha ethnography. As Fletcher began her fieldwork among the Omahas, she also became a strong advocate of these native people's legal rights. Like many social reformers of her day, including the Quakers, Fletcher believed in the inevitable rise of culture from "savagery" to "civilization." She saw the Omahas' desire to have clear title to their farms and to have the rights of citizenship as part of this "upward" mobility. Fletcher formulated a plan which, through the efforts of her influential friends in Washington, became the Omaha Allotment Act of 1882. This act in turn became the model for the Dawes Severalty Act of 1887. This law, also known as the General Allotment Act, included a clause which made all allotted Indians, such as the Omahas, citizens of the United States.[42]

In the 1880s, allotment in severalty became the leading theory of reform in Indian affairs, just as "war without, peace within" had led the way in the 1870s. The Omahas had been one of the first native societies to undergo allotment in the early 1870s, and their fate typified that of many of the tribes who found themselves on individual farmsteads after the Dawes Act of 1887. The Omaha Allotment Act of 1882 modified the Omahas' individual holdings so that every member of the society could own eighty acres of land. This modification was precisely the acreage allotment to which the Omahas had first agreed in the treaty of 1854. Lands left over after the allotment under the 1882 act were sold and the money used to support development of the Omahas' farms. As would be the case in the Dawes Act, the government held the Omahas' new allotments in trust for twenty-five years. This quarter-century of trusteeship would, supposedly, prevent speculators from buying up individual holdings while allowing ample time for the Omahas to transform themselves into farmers. This anticipated transformation, however, did not occur.

In the summer of 1930, another important and energetic anthropologist, Margaret Mead, visited with the Omahas. The period of government trust had long passed, but the Omahas had not amalgamated into white society. Many of the Omahas had received their fee patents, sold their land, and quickly spent the money. All the Indian tribes who came under the Dawes Act (which included the Pawnees and the Otos) fell prey to this pattern. At the end of the trust period, after the granting of fee patents, approximately two-thirds of the allotted Indian lands passed into white ownership. Among the Omahas, these sales made their reservation a crazy quilt of white and Indian landholdings. In addition, many of the Omahas' remaining lands were leased to white farmers. Some Omahas had inherited bits and pieces of the original eighty-acre allotments, but the effective land base for the establishment of a "new" Omaha culture patterned on farming had disappeared. Because only a few still held tracts large enough to support a productive farm, many Omahas rented their lands. Independent farming, therefore, never became the basis of the Omahas' economy. Instead, income came primarily from rental fees, land sales, and wage labor.[43]

Another later observer noted only one Omaha in the 1960s who farmed full-time for a living. By the 1970s, none did.[44] Thus the Quaker dream of changing the Omahas into white farmers, which was shared by Alice Fletcher and other nineteenth-century reformers, had failed. But this failure did not mean that the Omahas and their culture had been destroyed. Indeed, Margaret Mead titled her study of the Omahas *The Changing Culture of an Indian Tribe*. Although many of Mead's overly negative conclusions can be questioned, she did perceive a dynamic of change, even if she did not realize the depth of this dynamic. The Omahas had recognized the role of change in their society, even in their society's origins.

In the words of their Sacred Legend, which explained the origin of the "uki'te," the Omahas learned that "the people thought . . . what shall we do? . . . How shall we better ourselves?"

This tradition of self-determined change informed the spirit of accommodation to white ways which began in the 1850s. Omaha leaders like Joseph La Flesche willingly accepted some aspects of white culture, but they wished to control these acquisitions just as the people had done in the Sacred Legend. In the 1870s this independent accommodationist attitude at first delighted, and then befuddled, the four Hicksite agents who worked with the Omahas. But the velocity of change outside their society was too great to be controlled by the "uki'te." The end of the buffalo hunt began the collapse of the Omahas' social economy. Small-scale subsistence farming, which held great hardship for white farmers in Nebraska, held greater hardships for a native people new to many of its forms. Eventually, whites controlled much of the Omahas' reservation through purchase or lease. The native people remained mired in poverty.

In 1930, Margaret Mead compared the Omahas' condition to a house partly destroyed by a wrecking crew. Although this image accurately conveyed the reality of the Omahas' economic condition, it also revealed the persistence of Omaha cultural identity. For although aspects of their native culture had altered, the Omahas themselves had not disappeared into white society. In 1976, nearly fifty years after Margaret Mead's observations, John Turner, the husband of the granddaughter of Joseph La Flesche, explained how the Omahas could cope with the problems of the modern world: "I believe that's going to be dependent on how well we can maintain our culture. Personally, I feel that the Omaha people have a culture that is far more sophisticated than any other culture that I know of in relation to how a human being should live, and get along and cooperate with his environment."[45] These words underscore the Omahas' retention of a distinct identity and their desire to maintain cultural self-determination. Or, more simply put, John Turner's words testify to the survival, despite economic hardships, of the Omahas' "uki'te."

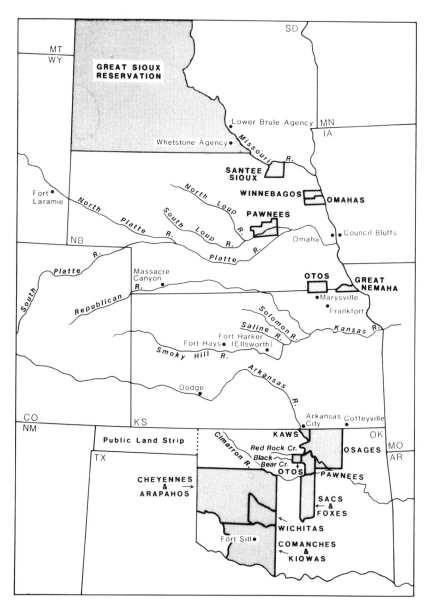

The Central Plains and Indian Territory

CHAPTER SEVEN

Quaker Exit

The end of the Hicksite Friends' work with the Indians of Nebraska came in stages, as the agents resigned their positions and the Yearly Meetings refused to submit new nominations. By 1882, Quakerly "assistance and oversight" were limited to the Santee Sioux reservation. There, two Friends agents, Isaiah Lightner and then Charles Hill, retained control until 1890.[1] The Quaker corollary to U. S. Grant's Peace Policy began its decline in the mid-1870s, when the office of the Northern Superintendency first came under attack. Then, in 1877, a new administration of the Department of the Interior under Carl Schurz began its irritating oversight of the Nebraska agencies. Schurz desired to improve the quality and efficiency of the government workers under his control. To the Quakers, this new administration seemed based on strict adherence to regulations and on expressions of loyalty to Secretary Schurz or to Ezra Hayt, his personally appointed commissioner of Indian Affairs. Hayt, in turn, wished to purge all the inefficient agents who had been part of President Grant's program of church nominees. He established a network of informants at various Indian agencies which produced numerous investigations and resignations. Hayt, like Schurz, prized bureaucratic competence and routine above religious affiliation. All denominations suffered under Hayt's policies, but the Quakers sometimes felt that they had been singled out for special mistreatment.

Between 1877 and 1882, the reform efforts of Carl Schurz and Ezra Hayt forced the resignations of all except one of the Quaker agents. During these five bitter years, Friends strove to maintain the Quakers' reputation for honesty and integrity in the face of captious Washington officials. In the midst of this struggle, the Hicksites took little time to evaluate critically their efforts to "civilize" the seven Indian tribes of Nebraska. Their commitment to a program of assimilation remained firm even as their government work among the Indians ended. The Quaker experience did not, therefore, provide an important caveat for future government officials charged with making American Indian policy. The Quakers would continue to support the ideal of assimilation even though their own efforts, over thirteen years, had produced disparate results.

The man most responsible for the "Quaker Policy" had departed early in the Grant administration. Ely S. Parker resigned his position as commissioner of Indian Affairs in February of 1871. Political figures in Congress, some of whom were eager to prevent any signs of corruption, had pilloried Parker before the House Appropriations Committee. After an examination of charges that Parker had neglected to consult with the Board of Indian Commissioners when he contracted for supplies, the committee announced that Parker's actions showed "irregularities, neglect, and incompetency" but "no evidence of any pecuniary or personal advantage." Disheartened and disgusted, Parker had returned to private business in New York.[2] Future commissioners of Indian Affairs would seem, by turns, indifferent or hostile to the Quakers' work.

In June of 1873, Commissioner Edward P. Smith informed Barclay White that in order to save money, the Northern Superintendency would be one of four closed by the Office of Indian Affairs. White suspected the intervention of Nebraska's two senators, who wanted control of all Indian agency appointments in their state. Letters and visitations to Washington from members of the seven Hicksite Yearly Meetings could not reverse the proposed closing, so delegates from Philadelphia, Baltimore, and Indiana came to Omaha to consult with White about the bleak future of the Quakers' work. But where Quaker entreaties had failed, an Omaha banker and an army general came to the rescue.

Augustine Kountze of the First National Bank, the government depository in Omaha, had come to rely on the large funds for the operation of the Northern Superintendency that were left on deposit at his bank. The nationwide economic panic of 1873 had swept west to Omaha after the collapse of Jay Cooke and Company, an important New York banking firm which had become overinvolved in railroad financing. The fact that Augustine Kountze controlled the most powerful bank in Omaha did not prevent a run on his institution's deposits. During this crisis, Barclay White kept $60,000 of federal money on deposit with Kountze, which allowed the bank to survive the raid. Out of financial shrewdness and personal gratitude, Kountze then asked his good friend, Gen. Philip Sheridan, to intervene with authorities in Washington to save the Northern Superintendency. Shortly thereafter, Barclay White received notification that the California Superintendency, rather than the Northern, would be closed.[3]

General Sheridan's influence had brought only a three-year reprieve. A renewed emphasis on economy in the operation of government took hold during the depression which followed the panic of 1873. By 1876, only the two Quaker superintendencies, the Central and the Northern, remained. Then another commissioner of Indian Affairs, John Q. Smith, closed these superintendencies as well. In place of the superintendents, federal inspectors appointed by the commissioner oversaw the work of the Indian agents. This shift in the chain of command removed the church-appointed superintendent as a buffer between federal officials and church-appointed agents. The change in organization greatly aided the next commissioner of Indian Affairs, Ezra Hayt, as he began to dismantle the denominational participation in the Peace Policy.

Barclay White closed his office on June 30, 1876, and sent all his records, documents, and files to Washington. Thereafter, the six Indian agents in Nebraska reported directly to the Office of Indian Affairs. In 1877 and 1878, for a hundred days each year, White served as a "special agent" under the pay of the Central Executive Committee of the seven Hicksite Yearly Meetings. He visited the Indian agencies in Nebraska and wrote a report on their condition for the Yearly Meetings. While he retained no official government position, the secretary of the interior approved of his visits. White appreciated this special status beyond bureaucratic control. In a moment of reflection about the closing of the Northern Superintendency, he wrote in his journal: "I have since congratulated myself that my Indian service to the Government did not extend into the term of the next Presidential administration."[4]

Barclay White's words indicate that the Quakers desired some degree of independence in their administration of Indian affairs. Both Orthodox and Hicksite Friends saw their work at the Indian agencies as an undertaking controlled by the Quakers with the cooperation of the federal government. Carl Schurz and Ezra Hayt reversed this concept. Hayt, most especially, insisted that all agents, Quakers included, served under the government first. The infamous spies sent out to numerous agencies across the West were a means of regaining government control over an Indian service which, in Hayt's view, President Grant had given away to various churches. Ezra Hayt wished to root out inefficiency, incompetency, and corruption. His spies, often the agency clerk or doctor, supplied the information vital for this purge. To his victims, Hayt appeared to be an antireligious zealot, but his policies were motivated by a zeal for the reform of government services, not by a hatred of certain denominations.

Among the Orthodox Friends of the Central Superintendency, Hayt's purge produced fuller results than with the Hicksites. The investigation and dismissal of the Quapaw agent, Hiram W. Jones, resulted in a strong protest from the Associated Executive Committee of Friends on Indian Affairs. The executive committee examined the charges and replies from the investigation. It considered Agent Jones to have been "exonerated" and the charges proven "false," yet Jones had been dismissed. The role of a government "spy" in this affair led the executive committee to demand "that no appointee of the department be retained in agencies under agents nominated by us, who shall in the judgment of the committee prove a positive hindrance to the work of solid improvement of the Indians." Interviews with Commissioner Hayt produced no assurances that he would comply with this demand, so in May of 1879 the Orthodox Friends informed President Hayes that they resigned "all further responsibility for the Indian work."[5]

At its annual meeting, the Board of Indian Commissioners learned that the Orthodox Friends, as a body, had withdrawn from the Indian Service. The Hicksite Yearly Meetings had not yet taken this final step, although they had already given up the Pawnee Agency and Hayt's informers, plus the embarrassment of investigations, continued to plague their Winnebago and Oto agents. At the next annual meeting, on January 13, 1881, in New York City, Barclay White informed Gen. Clinton Fisk, the board's chairman, that the Hicksite Friends had withdrawn from all but the Great Nemaha and Santee Sioux agencies. White also said that Hicksite Friends would no longer nominate agents. Fisk seemed surprised, and sought an explanation.

General Fisk: You formerly had more agencies?
B. White: We commenced with six. Two of these, the Winnebago and Omaha, were consolidated in one.
General Fisk: As vacancies occurred, did your society nominate new agents?
B. White: Yes, as long as we could consistently do it with self-respect. Our agents have resigned for cause, and, that cause remaining, we could not nominate others to take their places.
General Fisk: And that cause was the same as was communicated to us last year? You desired that your agents should have the privilege of selecting their own clerks?
B. White: We would prefer that they should have that privilege, but we did not press that; but we did object to have subordinate officers placed there who should communicate directly to the department, unknown to the agent, which gave them superior powers to the agent. The agents were compelled, under these circumstances, to resign, and we could not place others in their places.[6]

By 1882, Agent Mahlon B. Kent had left his post at Great Nemaha to care for his aged parents, and Isaiah Lightner of the Santee Sioux agency remained as the only Hicksite agent. The Central Executive Committee considered nominating a

Friend to replace Kent, but the issue became moot when the government consolidated Great Nemaha with the Potawatomi agency of Kansas. The Potawatomi agent took charge of all administrative duties.[7] With the exception of the Santee Sioux, the Hicksite Friends in 1882 had ended the commitment that they had first undertaken in 1869 at President Grant's invitation. Significantly, this termination was not brought on by Quaker doubts about the success of their work with the Indians. Indeed, the issue of success or failure in advancing Indian "progress" had been obscured by the feud between the Quakers and Ezra Hayt. The issue had shifted from who *could* control Indian assimilation to who *should* control. This shift in emphasis left both reformers within the government, like Schurz and Hayt, and reformers from religious groups, such as the Quakers, in the position of favoring assimilation, with neither asking whether they *could* control the process.

Each side in this feud believed that the road to assimilation and citizenship lay through the allotment of Indian lands in severalty. "Progress," it was assumed, would continue if individual Indians farmed their own private acreage. This idea of turning Indians into farmers ignored the frustrations of white agriculturalists across the United States. From the 1870s into the 1890s, the decline in agricultural profits resulted in a series of agrarian protest movements. Indeed, by the late 1880s, corn in Kansas, for example, was selling at such a low price that many farmers burned it for fuel. The individuals trapped in this economic slump did not understand how an expanded world market, the increased application of farm machinery, and the overproduction of crops had helped create their plight. They knew that times were bad, however, and they blamed their situation on such factors as the freight rates of railroad companies or the monetary policies of the federal government. Regardless of the economic explanations, the "friends of the Indian" had ample opportunities to note the woes of America's farmers. By the mid-1870s, one agrarian protest organization, the Patrons of Husbandry, or Grangers, had a membership estimated at 1.5 million. During the 1880s, the Farmers' Alliance of the plains states, Midwest, and South had members in excess of 4.5 million.[8]

In the face of such massive expressions of agrarian discontent, social reformers retained their belief in the benefits of placing Indians on individual farms. The allotment concept had appeared in many treaties of the 1850s, but by the late 1870s it had become a point of consensus among reformers, both inside and outside of the government. In 1879, Ezra Hayt, with the approval of Carl Schurz, had drawn up legislation for a general allotment of Indian lands similar to the later Dawes Act, but Congress did not vote on Hayt's proposal. The Quakers, on the other hand, continued to support the concept of allotment, as they had from the beginning of their work under the Peace Policy. The frustrating experiences of Hicksite Friends among the Nebraska Indians did not cause them to question this consensus over allotment. In 1887, with direct Hicksite influence limited to efforts among the Santee Sioux, the Central Executive Committee rejoiced at the passage of the Dawes Act, "a measure Friends have long advocated." The committee believed that "this law, if faithfully and honestly administered, will . . . solve the Indian problem and be the means ultimately of elevating the Indian to the high plane of American citizenship."[9]

Despite their support of allotment in severalty, the Hicksite Friends did not use the resignations of Ezra Hayt or Carl Schurz as an opportunity to reestablish their full participation in the Indian Service. Schurz had dismissed Hayt in January of 1880 because of a scandal which involved Hayt's son's purchase of a silver mine in return for the withdrawal by the commissioner of charges against an Indian agent in Arizona. Less sensationally, Schurz himself left the Department of the Interior in March of 1881, at the inauguration of a new president. Despite this change of command, the Hicksite Friends did not seek, nor were they offered, an expanded role in the administration of Indian affairs. Ezra Hayt had effectively ended the denominational appointment of agents, and the Hicksites seemed content to support their remaining agents until each chose to leave his position.

By 1888, as a report of the Baltimore Yearly Meeting's Committee on Indian Affairs indicated, the cooperation among the Hicksite Yearly Meetings, exemplified by the Central Executive Committee, had begun to dissipate. An effort to support financially the appointment of a matron for the Santee Sioux agency had failed. The Philadelphia Yearly Meeting had declined to participate, as had Ohio and Indiana. Genesee had not even responded to the idea. The Baltimore committee explained the decline in Quakerly concern for the Indian with some self-serving rationalizations:

We find . . . that the field of philanthropic labor in this cause by the Society of Friends is narrowing year by year. There are several reasons for this. One is that other religious denominations have gone into the work so largely and have had such abundant means, that they have in a measure crowded out those who have not been able to bring such facilities to bear. Another reason is that those Indians in whom we have been especially interested and for whom we have been working more particularly, are themselves very nearly self-supporting, and so almost beyond the need of outside help.

There is no ground for discouragement in this outlook except in the fact that the Society of Friends is perhaps not contributing its full quota of usefulness in a cause wherein it has been a pioneer. But the work is going on and great good is being done the Indians by the different religious denominations engaged in it.[10]

This statement by the Baltimore Friends suggests the possibility of a weary disillusionment on the part of the Hicksites. The bright image of the "unique" heritage of Quaker friendship toward the Indians had faded as humanitarian reformers and proselytizing denominations continued to work for Indian progress. Among Orthodox Friends, by the late 1870s, the impact of Quaker revivals in the Midwest had produced missions and efforts for religious conversion among some of the smaller tribes in the Indian Territory. The Hicksites, however, retained the traditional Quaker avoidance of proselytizing. Thus no revival meetings were held to stimulate an interest in creating Indian converts. Instead, during the 1880s the Hicksite Yearly Meetings talked more of the social issues found nearer their homes, such as public vice, intemperate drink, improvement of prisons, and charity for orphans.[11]

The Yearly Meetings may have ended their formal program for social benevolence toward Indian tribes, but individual Hicksites had not abandoned all interest in plans for Indian improvement. Lt. Richard H. Pratt's Indian boarding school at Carlisle, Pennsylvania, which opened in 1879, received much support from local members of both branches of the Society of Friends. During its four decades of operation, several Quaker women served as teachers at the school, and wealthy Friends, such as Susan Longstreth of Philadelphia, made important financial contributions. In addition, many Quaker families in the farm counties between Carlisle and Philadelphia took in Indian students as part of the school's "outing" system.[12]

Only two Hicksite leaders, Edward Hicks Magill, the president of Swarthmore College, and Joseph J. Janney, chairman of the Baltimore Yearly Meeting's Indian Committee, regularly attended what became the spiritual heir to denominational participation in the Peace Policy, the annual Lake Mohonk Conference in New York state. Organized in 1883 by the Orthodox Quaker Albert K. Smiley, these gatherings brought together each fall the major Christian reformers who wished to improve the government's program toward the Indians. Papers were presented, issues discussed, and policies considered. Sen. Henry L. Dawes, the author of the General Allotment Act of 1887, often appeared, as did Indian students from Richard Pratt's Carlisle boarding school. With the exception of Smiley, Orthodox Quaker leaders were not among the inner circle that guided these conferences. Instead, men like Senator Dawes, General Clinton Fisk, and Merrill E. Gates, the president of Amherst College provided the annual leadership.[13]

Although only Magill and Janney participated, veterans of the Hicksites' work with the Indians would have approved the consensus on reform goals which emerged from the meetings at Lake Mohonk. Most especially would they have agreed with the emphasis on the "Christianization" and "Americanization" of the Indians through the establishment of schools and the allotment of lands which these conferences stressed. The Hicksites' own efforts had centered on education and farming, so their plans for Indian reform in the 1870s were consistent with the mainstream of humanitarian reform that helped produce the Dawes Act in 1887. Barclay White underscored this congruence in a retrospective report on the Hicksites' work which he wrote in 1885 at the request of the commissioner of Indian Affairs.

In late 1882 White had been stricken with "an obscure nervous condition" which produced pressure on his spinal cord, excessive pain in his back, and partial paralysis of his right leg. He declared himself "unfit for desk work" and retired from all his official Quakerly duties, which included the posts of assistant clerk of the Philadelphia Yearly Meeting, secretary of the Philadelphia Indian committee, and secretary-treasurer of the Central Executive Committee. Despite his infirmities, however, White could not resist the opportunity to provide an historical sketch of his Society's efforts "to civilize and Christianize American Indians through commissioned officers of the United States."[14]

White's report, written at his home in Mount Holly, New Jersey, reviewed the condition of each of the seven Nebraska tribes at the time of the arrival of their Hicksite agents in 1869. Only the Omahas and the Iowas had made any "progress" in agriculture. The Sacs and Foxes, Santee Sioux, and Winnebagos were dependent on federal funds for their subsistence. The Pawnees and the Otos, "stubborn Indians," clung to traditional ways. White listed eight measures "adopted by Friends to promote civilization." The appointment of "moral" employees, each of whom, along with his or her family, was expected "to be a missionary for good in precept and example," headed the list. The next six points emphasized education, farming, and the establishment of households. White's list concluded with a restatement of the Friends' ultimate desire: "to speedily advance the condition of the Indians under their care to the status of Christian, educated, self-supporting American citizens, living in comfortable houses on lands held by them in fee simple."

In assessing the progress of the seven native societies as of 1885, White concluded that four, the Santee Sioux, the Omahas, the Winnebagos, and the Iowas, were "in such a status of civilization, education and self-support as qualified them for the duties and responsibilities of American citizenship." All four societies had settled on family homesteads and all except the Iowas held their allotments by certificate. White recommended laws to protect the property of each Indian homesteader for "one generation." The "retarded" advance of the remaining societies White attributed to several factors: drink and a large cash annuity among the Sacs and Foxes; the opposition of hereditary chiefs among the Otos; and the high mortality rate among the Pawnees after their move to the Indian Territory.

In the case of four of the tribes under their care, the Hicksites had moved in advance of the Dawes Act. After that law established general allotment for most Indian lands, the three "retarded" tribes would have their reservations broken up as well. In 1885 neither Barclay White nor the "friends of the Indian" who gathered at Lake Mohonk could foresee the long-term implications of allotment in severalty. In 1887, Indian lands comprised 138 million acres, 60 million of which would be declared surplus and sold to whites. A few native societies, such as the Navajos and the Senecas, managed to escape allotment entirely, but for those who did not, 27 million acres, or two-thirds of their lands, would be sold after the period of government trust expired. Between 1887 and 1934, when new laws reversed the process, approximately 60 percent of the original 138 million acres was lost. This deterioration of the Indian land base probably would have occurred even if Senator Dawes had not produced his General Allotment Act.[15] The Hicksite agents in Nebraska had already shown before 1887 how allotment could be carried out with individual native societies. These Quakers, as well as Dawes and his fellow reformers, did not anticipate the massive sales of allotments which would occur after the period of government trust. Nor did they anticipate the general leasing of Indian-owned lands to white farmers which also occurred in the aftermath of allotment.

What Dawes, the Quakers, and other humanitarian reformers expected was an Indian "either/or." Either the Indians would become successful farmers on individual homesteads, or they would pass away as outmoded relics of a "savage" culture. These reformers did not foresee the middle ground of poverty and piecemeal acculturation which lay between the either/or. They felt they must kill the native society to save the individual native.

The words of Barclay White, written in 1877, expressed the idealism of this plan:

Agricultural life is the grand panacea for all nomads, anchor them to the soil, make the cultivation of it profitable to them, and they will gradually build up homes convenient to their tillage, and as their wealth accumulates each dweller in the home will endeavor to adorn and make it comfortable, so, little by little they will gather around them all the comforts and conveniences of civilized life, and before they are aware of much change, have adopted "the white man's ways," and such customs and habits as fit them to become useful citizens.[16]

As White's words make clear, the Hicksite Friends who worked with the Nebraska Indians wished the best for these natives, but only in terms of white cultural values. The Quakers wanted to end the influence of traditional native culture. Yet the Pawnees, the Otos, and the Omahas had all shown that they wished to retain a core of native identity even if it meant removal, schism, or allotment. These three native societies showed that in the desperate decade of the 1870s, native peoples could act to determine their own future.

Perhaps that future might have included more acceptance of white ways if, as Barclay White assumed it would, the government policy of assimilation had actually produced prosperity. Historically, such aspects of white culture as the horse, the gun, and the fur trade had been accepted, in part, because they brought new wealth and prosperity in Indian terms. The government's insistence in the 1870s on a broader assimilation of white culture ultimately would have the opposite effect, for farming held no ready economic answers for either white settlers or Indian natives. In addition, the loss of the buffalo and the ravages of disease, plus depredations by red and white neighbors and devastations by drought and grasshoppers, all helped to create poverty, not prosperity, on the reservation.

Such hard times caused native societies to react conservatively in order to ensure their physical as well as their cultural survival. What changes did occur, such as schisms, removals, or even allotments, retained this conservative impulse. As was the case with the Otos, the Pawnees, and the Omahas, these actions had some destructive consequences, but they nonetheless represented Indian solutions to adverse conditions in the 1870s. These three native societies demonstrated that hard times could produce change based on cultural conservation rather than on the sort of wholesale cultural transformation that the humanitarian reformers desired.[17]

As for the Quakers, although their agents sometimes demonstrated a heavy-handed paternalism in the exercise of their authority, corrupt dealings and personal pecuniary profits never characterized the Friends' administration of Indian affairs in Nebraska. The Quakers did not come to do evil to the Indians; they came to do good. But this benevolent attitude did not guarantee that the Quakers would have any special talent for solving the problems which confronted the Native Americans of Nebraska. Indeed, the Quakers' good intentions merely demonstrated that they were part of the broader humanitarian reform movement of the day. Although Friends proudly referred to their special heritage in Indian affairs, Quaker ideas of Indian progress in the 1870s were part of a general consensus shared by other well-intentioned whites. This white consensus insisted on Indian assimilation to white ways and signaled an intolerance for Indian culture which, at least for Friends, seemed in stark contrast to the romantic, popular image of William Penn and the tradition of Quaker friendship toward America's Indians.

In fact, however, the Lenapes of colonial Pennsylvania with whom Penn made his treaties had been helped along in the loss of their lands by fraudulent land purchases, some carried out by the sons of William Penn. Penn's sons had acted out of evil intentions, but in the 1870s and 1880s it was the good intentions of Penn's religious descendants which helped set the stage for the massive loss of Indian lands brought on by allotment in severalty. Unfortunately, the Hicksite Friends could not see beyond the humanitarian consensus of their time for the greater benefit of the Nebraska Indians. The actions of these Quakers precipitated, rather than prevented, the decimation of the Indians' land base. The good intentions of the Friends had not been good enough.

Abbreviations in Notes

AR	Annual Reports
BIC	Board of Indian Commissioners
BYM	Minutes of the Standing Committee on Indian Concerns, Baltimore Yearly Meeting (Hicksite)
CEC	Minutes of the Central Executive Committee of Delegates from the Indian committees of the Seven Hicksite Yearly Meetings
CrIA	Commissioner of Indian Affairs
F	Frame (microfilm)
FHL	Friends' Historical Library, Swarthmore College
LR	Letters Received
M	Microcopy
MC	Minutes of Councils between Pawnees and their agents
MS	Manuscript
N	Nebraska agencies
NA	National Archives
NS	Northern Superintendency
NSHS	Nebraska State Historical Society
O	Omaha agency
OIA	Office of Indian Affairs
OHS	Oklahoma Historical Society
OSI	Office of the Secretary of the Interior
Ot	Oto agency
P	Pawnee agency
QC	Quaker Collection, Haverford College
R	Reel (microfilm)

Note:
With the exception of certain thoroughly revised sections, the endnotes of this book are a reduced selection from the footnotes in the author's doctoral dissertation, "With Good Intentions: Quaker Work and Indian Survival; the Nebraska Case, 1869-1882" (Yale, 1979). If readers wish to see a more extensive set of annotations, the dissertation should be examined.

Notes

Chapter One

1 *Boston Daily Advertiser*, 2/25/
1869; also reprinted in *New
York Times*, 2/26/1869.

2 Sherman's report published in
Report of the Secretary of War,
40th Cong., 3rd sess., 1868-69,
House Executive Documents,
no. 1, pt. 1, 3:7-8.

3 *Friends' Intelligencer*
(Philadelphia), 2/15/1868,
p. 793; 4/3/1869, pp. 72-73.
Friends' Review (Philadelphia),
2/6/1869, p. 378.

4 The letter to the *Baltimore
American* is reprinted in
Benjamin Hallowell,
*Autobiography of Benjamin
Hallowell*, pp. 265-69. The
emphasis is Hallowell's.

5 James D. Richardson, *A
Compilation of the Messages
and Papers of the Presidents,
1789-1897*, 7:39.

6 Ellen Starr Brinton, "Benjamin
West's Painting of Penn's
Treaty with the Indians,"
*Bulletin of Friends' Historical
Association* 30 (Autumn 1941):

99-131; Mary H. Child (of the
Hicksite Philadelphia Yearly
Meeting's Indian committee) to
Otos and Missourias, Albert
Green Papers, FHL. The appeal
of West's painting would not die
with Grant's "Quaker Policy."
The original would again be on
display at the peace exhibit of
the Columbian Exposition in
Chicago in 1893. In the late
nineteenth century, educational
publishing companies made
many inaccurate copies
(Brinton, "West's Painting,"
pp. 107, 120-21).

7 This division, which began in
1827 in Philadelphia, had both
theological and sociological
origins. By 1828, Pennsylvania,
New York, Baltimore, Ohio, and
Indiana had experienced
separations, so that "Hicksite"
and "Orthodox" Yearly
Meetings existed in each state.
Elias Hicks (1748-1830), a Long
Island farmer who traveled and
preached widely among Friends,
had attacked the so-called
Orthodox for overemphasizing

discipline and tenets of faith at the expense of the "true" belief in the Inner Light. Hicks did not wish to create a schism, but the targets of his criticism generally coincided with the largely urban, more prosperous leadership of the Society. Those attracted to Hicks' views were, with some exceptions, the rural, less economically successful Friends. In Pennsylvania and New York, two-thirds of the membership went over to the Hicksite side. An even greater number became Hicksites in the Baltimore Yearly Meeting. Ohio split nearly in half, whereas only a small group in Indiana joined the schism. New England, North Carolina, and Virginia, which later merged with Orthodox Baltimore, escaped division altogether. Edwin B. Bronner, "An Historical Summary," in Edwin B. Bronner, ed., *American Quakers Today*, pp. 18-20. The definitive sociological study of the schism is Robert W. Doherty, *The Hicksite Separation.*

8 Hugh Barbour, *The Quakers in Puritan England*, pp. 8-30, 163-89.

9 Peter Brock, *Pioneers of the Peaceable Kingdom*, pp. xi-xvi and passim.

10 Rayner W. Kelsey, *Friends and the Indians, 1655-1917*, pp. 19-24. An account of the Mayhews' work may be found in Francis Jennings, *The Invasion of America*, pp. 230-32.

11 Red or black membership in the Society of Friends never became widespread until after an evangelical revival in the 1870s and 1880s increased midwestern Orthodox Quakers' concern for proselytism. This new outreach eventually produced Quaker membership among Indians in Oklahoma and Africans in Kenya.

12 Howard H. Brinton, *Friends for 300 Years*, pp. 101-3.

13 BYM, AR, FHL, 10/31/1867, pp. 189-91; Robert Winston Mardock, *The Reformers and the American Indian*, p. 32 and pp. 1-46, passim.

14 BYM, AR, FHL, 10/22/1868, pp. 217-18.

15 *Friends' Intelligencer*, 12/21/1867, pp. 665-68.

16 *House Miscellaneous Documents*, no. 29, 40th Cong., 3rd sess., vol. 1: Louis Thomas Jones, *The Quakers of Iowa*, pp. 205-8. The new schisms involved the conservative "Wilburites" and the evangelical "Gurneyites." The first schism occurred in 1845 in New England after John Wilbur (1774-1856) was disowned by the Yearly Meeting because of his opposition to the preachings of Joseph John Gurney (1788-1846), an English Friends minister who had made a great impression on the American Orthodox Quakers during his tour of the United States in 1837. The Wilburites wished to maintain Quakerly traditions whereas the Gurneyites seemed willing to accommodate Quakerism to other Protestant sects by such means as a paid pastoral system of ministry. Wilburite withdrawals from Orthodox Yearly Meeting occurred up until 1903 (Bronner, "Historical Summary," pp. 20-21).

17 *Friends' Review*, 9/18/1869, p. 56; Philip S. Benjamin, *The Philadelphia Quakers in the Industrial Age, 1865-1920*, pp. 8, 19; *Friends' Intelligencer*, 12/15/1877, pp. 673-74; *The Friend*, 12/28/1867, pp. 143-44; 6/26/1869, p. 349; 6/12/1869, p. 335-36.

18 BYM, FHL, 3/6/1869, pp. 221-22.

19 Ibid., 3/25/1869, pp. 223-24 and misc. papers; Journals of Thomas Wistar, QC.

20 Gail Brooks Gerlach, "Samuel McPherson Janney: Quaker Reformer" (M.S. thesis, University of Utah, 1977), pp. 114-15.

21 Ibid., pp. 1-118, passim; report of Committee on Indian Affairs in AR of Philadelphia Yearly Meeting (Hicksite), p. 37, FHL, Hallowell, *Autobiography*, passim.

22 *Friends' Review*, 3/4/1871, pp. 435-36.

23 Gerlach, "Samuel Janney," p. 124; *Omaha Daily Herald*, 5/28/1869.

24 Samuel Janney to Elizabeth Janney, 5/30/1869; 6/11/1869; 6/19/1869, Samuel Janney Papers, FHL; Gerlach, "Samuel Janney," pp. 125-26.

25 *Friends' Intelligencer*, 5/8/1869, p. 146; 6/12/1869, p. 230; NA, OIA, Agency Employees, Service Record Book No. 2, 1865-69, pp. 3, 6, 19, 29, 106-7. Religious preference was not noted in the Service Record, but a collation of state of origin and the author's research index of Quaker names produced an accurate enumeration.

26 CEC, FHL, 12/19/1870, pp. 9-10. The Orthodox Associated Executive Committee of Friends on Indian Affairs, as originally organized, had no female members. *Friends' Review*, 7/10/1869, pp. 721-24.

27 Albert Green to J. Russell Hayes, Swarthmore College, 9/23/1935, Albert Green Papers, FHL. Green, agent to the Otos and Missourias, was the Lightfoots' son-in-law.

Chapter Two

1 Richard White, "The Winning of the West: The Expansion of the Western Sioux in the 18th and 19th Centuries," *Journal of American History* 65 (September 1978): 319-43.

2 My information on Pawnee epidemics comes from Richard White's typescript of his chapter "The Pawnees: Politics, Ecology and Technology on the Plains," which will appear in a forthcoming book from the University of Nebraska Press.

3 Gene Weltfish's ethnography of the Pawnees, *The Lost Universe*, contains details on the yearly cycle of events as well as the architecture of the earthlodges. She uses 1867 as her base year.

4 Peter Nabokov, in a forthcoming coauthored book from Oxford University Press, will have a chapter on the religious encoding of the Plains earthlodge. He graciously allowed me to read a draft of that chapter.

5 Wendell H. Oswalt, *This Land Was Theirs*, pp. 245, 248, 257-58, 265-67. The South bands are often called the Republicans, Grandes, and Topages in white sources. To the Hicksite administrators' credit, they used the aboriginal name for

the bands, but the phonetic spelling of these bands as well as the spelling of personal names varies greatly from source to source. I have tried to standardize my spellings, in the few cases where possible with those in Weltfish, *Lost Universe,* and George E. Hyde, *The Pawnee Indians.*

6 A melee which occurred in 1859 was called the Pawnee War by the Nebraska newspapers. The total casualties were one settler wounded and one Pawnee killed.

7 Samuel Allis to David Greene, 7/21/1843, in "Letters concerning the Presbyterian Mission in the Pawnee Country, near Bellevue, Nebraska, 1831-1849," *Collections of the Kansas State Historical Society* 14 (1915-18): 730.

8 NA, OIA, LR, M 234, Council Bluffs Agency, R 216, Daniel Miller to D. D. Mitchell, 12/24/1843; Daniel Miller to Th. H. Harvey, 5/2/1844; St. Louis Superintendency, R.754, F 335, T. Harvey to Wm. Medill, 10/17/1847; John Dunbar to David Green, 1/24/1845 and 6/30/1846, in *Collections of the Kansas State Historical Society* 14 (1915-18): 672, 686.

9 The significance of the Pawnees' change to primarily upland agriculture in the 1860s is the discovery of Richard White. The crops which survived drought and grasshoppers tended to be from the riverbottom plots.

10 Charles H. Whaley, *Annual Reports of the Commissioner of Indian Affairs, 1868,* pp. 234-35 (hereafter cited as AR of CrIA with year of report).

11 NA, OIA, LR, M 234, P, R 660, F 663, Jacob Troth to Samuel M. Janney, 7/3/1869; F 631, Janney to Ely S. Parker, 7/5/1869; *Friends' Intelligencer,* 8/7/1869, p. 358; *Report of the Joint Delegation of Baltimore, Philadelphia and New York Yearly Meetings in their Visit to the Northern Superintendency, 7th and 8th Months, 1869.* Hyde claimed no summer hunt in 1869 (*Pawnee Indians,* p. 296). As with many events and details in his history, Hyde's account is unreliable. His work is lightly documented and highly opinionated. He seems to have rarely used the letters received by the Office of Indian Affairs from the Pawnee Agency, relying instead on annual reports by the agent and superintendent or the personal accounts of his contemporary informants.

12 *Friends' Intelligencer,* 8/7/1879, p. 358.

13 NA, OIA, LR, M 234, P, R 660, F 51-70, Testimony from the murder trial of Yellow Sun et al., transcribed for Samuel M. Janney, 11/5/1869; F 625-28, Samuel M. Janney to Ely S. Parker, 7/4/1869; F 634, Janney to Parker, 7/5/1869; F 636, Janney to Parker, 7/15/1869; *Friends' Intelligencer,* 8/7/1869, p. 358.

14 NA, OIA, LR, M 234, P, R 661, F 133, Jacob Troth to Samuel M. Janney, 5/21/1870; F 147, Janney to Ely S. Parker, 6/22/1870; F 162, Capt. D. C. Poole to Janney, 6/28/1870.

15 NA, OIA, LR, M 234, P, R 660, F 651, Samuel M. Janney to Ely S. Parker, 9/1/1869; R 661, F 94, Janney to Parker, 2/17/1870; F 13, telegram, Gen. John Pope to Gen. Wm. T. Sherman, 6/2/

1870; telegram, Gen. E. D. Townsend to Gen. John Pope, 6/3/1870.

16 NA, OIA, LR, M 234, P, R 661, F 286, Samuel M. Janney to Ely S. Parker, 1/13/1871; F 328, Janney to Parker, 4/24/1871; F 355, Janney to Parker, 6/8/1871; F 382, Janney to CrIA, 8/5/1871; F 424, Jacob Troth to Barclay White, 10/10/1871; F 422, Barclay White to H. R. Clum, Acting CrIA, 10/13/1871; Troth, in *AR of CrIA, 1871*, p. 452.

17 NA, OIA, LR, M 234, P, R 661, F 309, Samuel M. Janney to Ely S. Parker, 2/23/1871; F 336, Janney to Parker, 5/3/1871; MC, OHS, pp. 3-20 and passim.

18 BYM, FHL, 6/12/1871, p. 265; NA, OIA, LR, M 234, P, R 661, F 369-73, Samuel M. Janney to Ely S. Parker, 7/10/1871, and Resolutions of Pawnee Council, 7/8/1871; F 391, Resolutions of Pawnee Council, 9/25/1871. Troth's and Janney's complaints about rates charged by Dr. S. A. Bonesteel and their efforts to hire a physician for the agency are revealed in NA, OIA, LR, M 234, P, R 660, F 679-81, Troth to Janney, 11/8/1869; Janney to Parker, 11/8/1869; R 661, F 116, Janney to Parker, 4/21/1870; F 292, Troth to Janney, 1/24/1871; F 339, Samuel Townsend (Baltimore Indian committee) to Parker, 5/14/1871; *Friends' Intelligencer*, 12/31/1870, pp. 694-95, letter from Troth dated 12/9/1870. The workings of the Pawnee Council are described in Journal of Barclay White, 2:151, FHL.

19 Weltfish, *Lost Universe*, pp. 6-7, 19; Preston Holder, *The Hoe*

and the Horse on the Plains, pp. 44-47; personal conversation and correspondence with Martha Royce Blaine, 6/12/1979 and 9/17/1979.

20 NA, OIA, LR, M 234, NS, R 600, F 569-70, Samuel M. Janney to H. R. Clum, 8/7/1871; P, R 661, F 427, Barclay White to Clum, 10/27/1871; Journal of Barclay White, 1:285, 298-99, 320; Council, 10/16/1871, MC, OHS, pp. 31-34.

21 Journal of Barclay White, 1:286; 2:149-51. Of the four chiefs, Tirawahut-lasharo was killed by the Sioux and Pitalesharo died in a strange "accident" before the Pawnees moved to the Indian Territory. Ter-re-kaw-wah expired soon after the removal.

22 Personal conversation and correspondence with Blaine, 6/12/1979 and 9/17/1979.

23 John B. Dunbar, "Pitalesharo – Chief of the Pawnees," *Magazine of American History* 5 (November 1880): 343-45.

24 NA, OIA, LR, M 234, P, R 666, F 263-65, Joseph Hertford to E. A. Hayt, CrIA, 4/10/1878. Weltfish often mentions "Man Chief" (Pitalesharo) in her anthropological characterization of the Pawnees circa 1867. She presents a council meeting where Bayhylle instructed the chiefs before a meeting with the agent and told Man Chief to talk first (*Lost Universe*, pp. 412-13).

25 Journal of Barclay White, 2:148-52.

26 Ibid., pp. 158-59.

27 Ibid., 1:305-7; 2:230; NA, OIA, LR, M 234, P, R 661, F 486-88,

Sidney Barnett to U. S. Grant, 7/18/1872; F 584, Wm. F. Cody to Francis A. Walker, CrIA, 12/3/1872; F 589, Barclay White to Walker, 12/12/1872.

28 Barclay White, in *AR of CrIA, 1872*, p. 214; *Friends' Intelligencer*, 6/17/1876, pp. 263-64; Journal of Barclay White, 2:230.

29 The speeches at the council of 6/8/1872 are in MC, OHS, pp. 52-55.

30 Journal of Barclay White, 1:318-20; BYM, FHL, Report of Committee of Visitors to Pawnee Agency, 6/21/1872, pp. 275-76; BYM, FHL, 7/8/1872, p. 277; 9/7/1872, pp. 277-78; NA, OIA, LR, M 234, P, R 661, F 473, Columbus Delano, Sec. of the Interior, to CrIA, 10/11/1872; OSI, Appointments Division, LR, P, Record Group 48, Samuel M. Janney, Benjamin Hallowell, B. Rush Roberts, and Richard T. Bentley to Delano, 12/4/1872.

31 NA, OIA, LR, M 234, P, R 661, F 163-80, Petitions from Platte, Boone, Madison, and Hall counties in Nebraska, some dated 8/12/1872.

32 NA, OIA, LR, M 234, P, R 662, F 158-61, Petition from citizens of Platte County, 3/29/1873.

33 *Platte Journal*, 5/14/1873.

34 NA, OIA, LR, M 234, P, R 662, F 30-153, Transcript of testimony and report of William J. Haddock, Special Agent, 6/2/1873.

35 In the summer of 1873, Samuel Janney reported to the Baltimore Yearly Meeting's Indian committee that the secretary of the interior, commissioner of Indian Affairs, and Central Executive Committee of the Hicksite

Friends' Indian committees considered Haddock's report a complete vindication of Agent Burgess and the employees under his care. Later that year a similar statement was made before the Board of Indian Commissioners. In his journal, Barclay White dismissed the Nebraskans' complaints as "trivial" and "groundless" – the product of politicians "dissatisfied with the recent change in agents" (BYM, FHL, 6/n.d./1873, p. 282; *Annual Reports of the Board of Indian Commissioners*, [hereafter cited as *AR of BIC*, with year of report]; *1873*, p. 41; Journal of Barclay White, 1:366-67).

36 A close analysis of migration and settlement patterns in this region of Nebraska has not yet been done, but other studies, such as William A. Bowen, *The Willamette Valley*, have shown the important role of prefrontier kinship ties and neighborly relations.

37 *Platte Journal*, 8/21/1872; 9/4/1872; 5/14/1872; OHS, P, letterpress book, letters sent (microfilmed), R 3, F 158, Jacob Troth to J. H. Painter, 6/18/1872.

38 NA, OIA, LR, M 234, P, R 661, F 575-77, Jacob Troth to Barclay White, 11/11/1872; F 507 Troth to White, 7/18/1872; F 568, Troth to White, 10/29/1872; Jacob Troth, in *AR of CrIA, 1872*, p. 223.

Chapter Three

1 NA, OIA, LR, M 234, P, R 662, F 362, William Burgess to Barclay White, 2/20/1873; F 401ff., White to H. R. Clum, Council

Petition enclosed, 3/22/1873; F 347, White to Clum, 2/20/1873; F 360, White to Clum, 2/22/1873. Pitalesharo was not claiming exclusive hunting rights, because the Pawnees' major buffalo range along the western Republican River and its tributaries was a prime hunting ground for most central and even some southern Plains tribes.

2 NA, OIA, LR, M 234, P, R 662, F 319, William Burgess to Barclay White, 1/2/1873; F 347, White to H. R. Clum, 2/20/1873; F 851-52, White to Edward P. Smith, 5/26/1873; Jacob Troth, in *AR of CrIA, 1872*, p. 223; Journal of Barclay White, 1:321, FHL; Minute of conversation with Frank White, Chaui soldier, and another Chaui, 1/24/1873, MC, OHS, p. 76. Acting Commissioner Clum did approve a white "overseer" for the winter hunt of 1872/73, but his letter was not sent until January 19, 1873, after the Pawnees had returned. An article in the Lowell (Neb.) *Weekly Register* quoted John G. Ralston, who claimed he and "Wild Bill" Hickok killed the three Brulé leaders. Afraid the Brulés might take revenge on white settlers, Barclay White asked the U.S. marshal to arrest the two murderers. No arrests and no Sioux raids against the settlers followed (Journal of Barclay White, 2:22-26, FHL).

3 NA, OIA, LR, M 234, P, R 662, F 396ff., Report of John W. Williamson to William Burgess, 8/12/1873; F 427ff., Report of Capt. Charles Meinhold, 8/17/1873; F 378-79, Barclay White to Edward P. Smith, 8/11/1873. L. B. Platt, who had come west from Baltimore on his vacation from college, had Barclay White's permission to go on the hunt (Journal of Barclay White, 1:371). He was captured by the Sioux early in the fight. They took his revolver and released him unharmed. Subagent Antoine Janis said that Little Wound's Oglala band, which was under Janis's charge, had news about the Pawnee buffalo hunters on August 2 and joined up with the Brulés on August 3. The subagent for Spotted Tail's Brulés, Stephen F. Estes, tried to blame Janis, the military, and the Pawnees for the attack. Janis should have stopped Little Wound, Estes claimed, and, besides, the Pawnees were on Sioux hunting grounds (which was not the case). In addition, Estes stated that he had heard that some military officers had assured the Pawnees that there would be no danger from the Sioux in the eventual battle area north of the Republican. Estes's self-serving explanations aside, Brulés apparently did dominate among the Sioux attackers — which perhaps indicated some connection to the unresolved issue of the murders of Whistler, Fat Badger, and Hand Smeller (P, R 662, F 200, Antoine Janis to J. W. Daniels, 8/5/1873; F 182, Stephen F. Estes to Maj. E. A. Howard, 8/6/1873; F 189, Estes to Howard, 8/28/1873).

Paul D. Riley, in the most complete study of the incident, "The Battle of Massacre Canyon" (*Nebraska History* 54

[Summer 1973]: 221-49), says the
Sioux raids against the Pawnees
during the winter of 1872/73
may have been in retaliation for
the murder of Whistler et al.
Pawnee oral traditions also
indicate that Sky Chief did not
die early in the battle, as
reported by Williamson, but
lived to rally the Pawnee
warriors against the Sioux. In
his later years John Williamson
set himself up as the leading
authority on what many
considered the last great battle
among Indians on the Plains.
But some old Pawnee men who
survived the battle had the last
say with Williamson when they
asked him, "How would you
know what happened there?
You ran off and left us"
(Garland James Blaine and
Martha Royce Blaine, "Pa-re-su
A-ri-ra-ke: The Hunters That
Were Massacred," *Nebraska
History* 58 [Fall 1977]: 353-54,
356).

4 Journal of Barclay White, 1:379-
81.

5 OHS, P, letterpress book, letters
sent, R 3, F 618-19, William
Burgess to Barclay White, 10/8/
1873; Journal of Barclay White,
1:382-84. The speeches are in
Council, 10/18/1873, MC, OHS,
pp. 83-86. These minutes
misstate the number of
emigrants as 485. White's
journal misdates the council as
10/1/1873.

6 NA, OIA, LR, M 234, P, R 663, F
174, Barclay White to Edward
P. Smith, 5/25/1874; White in
Ar of CrIA, 1874, p. 200. George
Bird Grinnell learned from
Indian informants that a
Kitkehaxki named Lone Chief
and a Chaui soldier called

Frank White were active
leaders along with Big Spotted
Horse in the October, 1873,
removal. Grinnell's account had
two-thirds of the Pawnees
attempting to leave in October
of 1873 before runners brought
the party back. Grinnell also
reported a large conference in
the summer of 1873 at the
Wichita camp with other
Indians (Comanches, Kiowas,
and Kiowa-Apaches) besides
those of the Wichita agency. An
invitation to the Pawnees, by
this account, was then made.
Grinnell does not mention the
February, 1874, council at the
Wichita agency. Neither his
two-thirds figure nor the
summer council of 1873 is noted
in National Archives'
documents for the Pawnees and
Wichitas (Grinnell, *Pawnee
Hero Stories and Folk Tales*,
pp. 391-96).

7 NA, OIA, LR, M 234, NS, R 600,
F 1000-1004, Barclay White's
report to the CEC, 4/28/1874; P,
R 664, F 129, Gen. Philip
Sheridan to Secretary of War,
1/30/1874; OSI, Indian Division,
LS, M 606, R 14, p. 136, C.
Delano to Secretary of War, 1/
23/1874.

8 NA, OIA, LR, M 234, P, R 663, F
148ff., William Burgess to
Barclay White, signed
resolutions of chiefs' council
enclosed, 3/18/1874.

9 BYM, FHL, Annual Report of
Standing Committee, 10/23/
1874, p. 299; John B. Dunbar,
"Lone Chief and Medicine Bull,"
Magazine of American History
8 (November 1882): 754-56.

10 NA, OIA, LR, M 234, P, R 663, F
202ff., Transcript of meeting
with Pawnee chiefs sent by

Barclay White to Washington, n.d.

11 NA, OIA, LR, M 234, P, R 663, F 93ff., Lester W. Platt to CrIA, 5/20/1874.

12 NA, OIA, LR, M 234, P, R 663, F 86ff., Lester W. Platt to Edward P. Smith, 7/7/1874.

13 NA, OIA, LR, M 234, P, R 663, F 88, Petition of Pawnee chiefs, 8/7/1874; R 665, F 241, William Burgess to William Nicholson, 1/3/1877.

14 Council, 2/12/1874, MC, OHS, p. 87; NA, OIA, LR, M 234, P, R 663, F 96, Pawnee chiefs (via B. T. Spooner) to Edward P. Smith, 8/21/1874; John Williamson Collection, NSHS, (microfilm). On one petition Spooner named people in Michigan who could attest to his character. Baptiste Bayhylle got into a brief fight without injury after a Kitkehaxki soldier called the Skidi interpreter a "thief and liar" during a council held 9/8/1874 (MC, OHS, p. 94).

15 NA, OIA, LR, M 234, P, R 663, F 204, William Burgess to Barclay White, 9/15/1874; F 208, White to CrIA, Edward P. Smith, 9/21/1874; B. Rush Roberts, "Special Report on Condition of Indians in Northern Superintendency," 11/9/1874, *AR of BIC 1874*, p. 55.

16 NA, OIA, LR, M 234, P, R 663, F 213-22, resolutions of Pawnee council, 10/8/1874; William Burgess, in *AR of CrIA, 1875*, p. 321; Roberts, "Special Report." The reason for Pitalesharo's death remains mysterious. Neither National Archives nor Quaker sources refer to it. The earliest published reference is in John Dunbar's 1880 article,

"Pitalesharu — Chief of The Pawnees" (*Magazine of American History* 5 [November 1880]: 344), which said the Chaui chief died in the summer of 1874 of a wound in the thigh: "The common report makes the shot purely accidental from his own pistol; but it is quite confidently asserted, also, that the shot was from another hand and with malicious intent." Dunbar said that Pitalesharo vacillated over supporting or opposing removal and that "agitators" for removal desired the chief's death lest he defeat their scheme. The wound itself, however, was not fatal, but "the perverse treatment of a medicine man" produced gangrene and eventual death. George Bird Grinnell (*Pawnee Hero Stories*, p. 396) repeated nearly the same story, but said Pitalesharo definitely opposed removal and that a white man may have fired the shot. Grinnell claimed that Pitalesharo received good care from a "white surgeon" but "was induced to put himself in a care of a Pawnee doctor, under whose treatment he died." Elvira Gaston Platt ("Some Experiences as a Teacher among The Pawnees," *Collections of The Kansas State Historical Society* 14 [1915-18]: 792) reported an accident, mentioned no conspiracy, and blamed summer heat, personal corpulence, refusal of white medicine, and use of native doctors. George Hyde (*The Pawnee Indians*, pp. 320-31) had Pitalesharo alive at the October 8 council and opposing removal. Hyde claimed that the Chaui leader received his wound fording the Loup Fork on the first day of the southward exodus. Besides the old explanations of accidental discharge or attempted murder by whites, Hyde claimed, "some" believed the chief "had shot himself so he might be buried in the land of his fathers." Hyde probably got his account from Luther H. North, who had heard this story from John W. Williamson (see L. H. North to W. H. Fowler, 9/10/1925, Luther Hedden North Collection, NSHS). National Archives materials present Pitalesharo as an advocate of removal.

17 Journal of Barclay White, 2:28-29; Roberts, "Special Report."

18 Journal of Barclay White, 2:29-30.

19 NA, OIA, LR, P, R 663, F 87, Note to CrIA from "Terekowah" (writer not shown), 10/10/1874; F 89, Petition from 16 Chiefs, 10/12/1874. Also see F 88, Petition of Pawnee Chiefs, 8/7/1874. Lester Platt died in 1875. The Pawnees had called him "kitskotoos," which was also their name for the Platte River. Elvira Platt lived until 1911. In the mid-1880s she taught for three and a half years at the Carlisle Indian School in Pennsylvania. Her final years were spent in Oberlin, Ohio (Elvira Gaston Platt, "Written by Amelia's Request: Mere Hints of My Changeful Life," typescript, circa 1900, MS Collection, NSHS).

20 John Williamson, "The Story of the Pawnees' Removal South," typescript, n.d., John William Williamson Collection, NSHS, p. 6.

Chapter Four

1 NA, OIA, LR, P, R 663, F 39, William Burgess to Edward P. Smith, 12/12/1874; F 33, Burgess to Smith, 12/18/1874; F 273, Burgess to Barclay White, 2/19/1875; F 275-77, Burgess to Smith, Petition of 12 chiefs enclosed, 3/9/1875.

2 NA, OIA, LR, Wichita Agency, R 929, F 1521-23, Jonathan Richards to Enoch Hoag, 3/12/1875; OHS, Kiowa Agency (microfilm), R 47, F 92-95, William Burgess to Richards, 4/15/1875; AR of BIC, 1875, p. 37, Edward P. Smith to Secretary of the Interior, 3/6/1875.

3 Report of F. H. Smith and B. Rush Roberts, AR of BIC, 1875, p. 41. Congress would not authorize the sale of the old reservation until April 10, 1876, at which time it also advanced $300,000 to cover the expenses of removal and resettlement.

4 George E. Hyde, The Pawnee Indians, p. 335; George Bird Grinnell, Pawnee Hero Stories and Folk Tales, p. 391.

5 Jacob Troth, in AR of CrIA, 1872, p. 222; NA, OIA, LR, P, R 665, F 55, William Nicholson to John Q. Smith, CrIA, 7/31/1877; F 126ff., Report of S. A. Galpin to CrIA, 1/26/1877; R 666, F 767, Dr. J. W. York to CrIA, 8/8/1878; F 770, York to CrIA, 8/15/1878; F 773, York to Ezra A. Hayt, CrIA, 9/11/1878; William Burgess, in AR of CrIA, 1876, pp. 55-56; OHS, Kiowa Agency, R 39, F 260-61, Burgess to Jonathan Richards, 12/1/1875.

6 Journal of Barclay White, 2:48-49, FHL.

7 NA, OIA, LR, P, R 666, F 234, O. P. Haughton to CrIA, 3/8/1878.

8 Recollections of Captain L. H. North, typescript, Luther Hedden North Collection, NSHS, p. 135.

9 *Friends' Intelligencer*, 11/3/1877, pp. 577-81.

10 George A. Dorsey, *Traditions of the Skidi Pawnee*, n. 234, pp. 352-53.

11 NA, OIA, LR, P, R 666, F 62, Charlie Tatiah to CrIA, 5/30/1878. The Pawnees and the Cheyennes had established a mutual peace in the summer of 1876 without white intermediaries. Horse stealing between these two peoples ended. Overtures to establish a similar peace with the Osages failed (Charles Chapin, "Removal of Pawnee and Peace with their Neighbors: A Memoir of Charles Chapin," *Nebraska History* 26 [January–March 1945]: 43-48).

12 Francis Paul Prucha, *American Indian Policy in Crisis*, pp. 61-62; Stanley Clark, "Irregularities at the Pawnee Agency," *Kansas Historical Quarterly* 12 (November 1943): 370.

13 NA, OIA, LR, M 234, P, R 666, F 337-54, Report of D. W. Dunnett to Charles Devens, Attorney General of the U.S., 1/21/1878. Dunnett, a lawyer from Coffeyville, Kansas, had been retained as an investigator by the federal attorney for Kansas, George R. Peck. Dunnett interviewed Burgess in December of 1877, in Columbus, Nebraska.

14 NA, OIA, LR, M 234, P, R 665, F 126-30, Report of S. A. Galpin to CrIA, 1/26/1877; F 158-60, William Nicholson to George R. Peck, U.S. Attorney, Kansas, 8/22/1877. This was the report which became the basis for Galpin's dismissal.

15 NA, OIA, LR, M 234, P, R 665, F 167, George R. Peck to Charles Devens, Attorney General of the U.S., 10/24/1877; Clark, "Irregularities," pp. 373-76. After leaving the Pawnee Agency, Burgess returned to Columbus, Nebraska, for a while and then lived for several years in California. Eventually he came back to Millville, Pennsylvania. Burgess died November 1, 1905, in Chicago, Illinois (William Bacon Evans, ed., "Dictionary of Quaker Biography," typescript, QC). The Pawnees reopened the question of fraud by their Quaker agent as part of a petition filed on October 3, 1913, under Senate bill no. 10830 of the sixty-first Congress, which permitted suits that concerned "misappropriation of any funds." Hearings on this petition were not held until October 19, 1920. On December 6 of that year the Court of Claims of the United States decided in *The Pawnee Tribe of Indians* v. *The United States* (No. 17324, Congressional) that there was "no competent testimony to establish any frauds charged against the Indian agent [i.e., William Burgess]."

16 NA, OIA, Employee Roster 7, 1877-78, Entry 978, Register 975; LR, M 234, P, R 666, F 235-60, Joseph Hertford to Ezra A. Hayt, 12/8/1877, 12/25/1877, 1/5/1878; F 213, Hertford to Hayt, 1/3/1878. Twelve letters from Hertford to Hayt were filed in one wrapper (F 235-60).

Hertford carried on his correspondence so zealously that on Christmas Day of 1877, he wrote four separate letters to the commissioner of Indian Affairs.

17 NA, OIA, LR, M 234, P, R 666, F 322-28, Joseph Hertford to Ezra A. Hayt, 6/20/1878; F 235-60, Hertford to Hayt, 1/3/1878; F 147, Samuel S. Ely to Hayt, 7/25/1878.

18 NA, OIA, LR, M 234, P, R 666, F 34, Baptiste Bayhylle to Ezra Hayt, 3/26/1878; F 263-65, Joseph Hertford to Hayt, 4/10/1878.

19 NA, OIA, LR, M 234, P, R 666, F 83, Samuel S. Ely to Ezra Hayt, 2/14/1878; F 78-80, Ely to CrIA, 4/18/1878; LS, M 21, R 138, pp. 474-75, C. W. Holcomb, Acting CrIA, to Ely, 2/25/1878; R 142, p. 20, Hayt to Ely, 3/18/1878; R 143, pp. 15-16, William M. Leeds, Acting CrIA, to Ely, 4/16/1878.

20 NA, OIA, LS, M 21, R 142, p. 326, Ezra Hayt to Samuel Ely, 6/8/1878; p. 327, Hayt to Charles Searing, 6/8/1878; LR, M 234, P, R 666, F 137, Ely to CrIA, 7/17/1878; CEC, FHL, Report of Barclay White, p. 257, 10/18/1878; Journal of Barclay White, 3:265, 271, 274-75. Carl Schurz was informed of Barclay White's appointment and gave authorization for his visit to the Pawnee — and other Hicksite-controlled — agencies. That it sought such authorization showed how carefully the Central Executive Committee of the Hicksite Yearly Meetings tried to avoid conflicts with the new political powers in Washington.

21 NA, Reports of Inspection of the Field Jurisdictions of the OIA, M 1070, P, R 35, F 38-58, E. C. Watkins to E. A. Hayt, 1/10/1878.

22 All speeches and descriptions of the council meetings are taken from Journal of Barclay White, 3:271-98. Barclay White's accounts obscure the dates of the councils. In his journal, White places both meetings in May. His report to the Central Executive Committee dated the meetings in July (which could be a printer's error). Two letters from Joseph Hertford to Ezra Hayt (NA, OIA, LR, M 234, P, R 666, F 322, 6/20/1878, and F 272, 7/10/1878) reliably place the first council on June 19, 1878, and the second on June 27, 1878. Marianna Burgess, a teacher at the agency school, made the original notes of the meetings.

23 White's journal does not specify which Ter-re-re-cox spoke. Two Pawnee chiefs, one a Skidi, the other a Pitahawirata, went by this name.

24 Journal of Barclay White, 3:43; NA, OIA, LR, M 234, P, R 666, F 263-65, Joseph Hertford to Ezra Hayt, 4/10/1878. In his statement before government inspector John McNeil about the June 27 council, Dick Lushabaugh, a former Pawnee Scout, said that a fight almost broke out between the Kitkehaxkis and the Skidis. He also said that Agent Ely threatened no more extra pay for the chiefs and soldiers if the old annuity receipts were not signed. Peter H. Woodward, the agency blacksmith, told McNeil that "Mr. Bayhille said that sooner than see his brothers

going to fight if Mr. Searing would bring on his papers, he would sign anything for him to go, as he was the Pawnee's great enemy." Merrit Sherman, a full-blood Pawnee, reported a similar speech by Bayhylle. All three statements were witnessed before McNeil by Joseph Hertford (NA, Reports of Inspection, M 1070, P, R 35, F 104-34, John McNeil to E. A. Hayt, 7/8/1878).

25 NA, OIA, LR, M 234, P, R 666, F 150-51, Samuel Ely to CrIA, and resolutions of council, 7/31/1878; Journal of Barclay White, 3:61.

26 NA, OIA, LR, M 234, P, R 666, F 322, Joseph Hertford to Ezra Hayt, 6/20/1878; F 272, Hertford to Hayt, 7/10/1878.

27 NA, OIA, LR, M 234, P, R 666, F 129, unsigned note, n.d.; F 281, Joseph Hertford to Ezra Hayt, 8/8/1878.

28 NA, OIA, LR, M 234, P, R 666, F 528-38, five petitions from Pawnee agency, 8/1878. Rousseau Pappan, a Skidi who had taken up farming, told Inspector John McNeil that Nelson Rice held a feast for the Pawnee chiefs and soldiers on Sunday, August 18, opposite Stacy Matlock's store. The repast consisted of one calf, a hog, three washboilers of coffee and three sacks of flour cooked-up as loaves of bread. After the feast, Rice asked the chiefs and soldiers to sign a petition for the removal of the agency clerk and doctor because their "good agent" had not chosen these men, but instead they had been sent from Washington. Pappan said that Baptiste Bayhylle spoke out against the petition

and that the chiefs refused to sign. Pappan assumed that Agent Ely and Matlock's clerk, William Bishop, had encouraged Rice and had supplied the food (NA, Reports of Inspection, M 1070, P, R 35, F 185-86, Rousseau Pappan's statement before John McNeil, 9/30/1878).

29 NA, OIA, LR, M 234, P, R 667, F 85-115, B. Rush Roberts to Carl Schurz, 8/31/1878; Roberts to Ezra Hayt, 8/15/1878; Petition from Pawnee agency, 8/22/1878.

30 NA, OIA, LS, M 21, R 166, F 431, Ezra Hayt to John McNeil, 9/11/1878; LR, M 234, P, R 666, F 469, McNeil to Hayt, 9/12/1878; F 476, McNeil to Hayt, 9/19/1878; M 348, Report Book, R 31, p. 548, Hayt to Secretary of the Interior, 12/3/1878. More than a month before he suspended the Quaker agent, McNeil wrote to Commissioner Hayt that in his opinion, "if Matlock had been out of the way, and the quarrel had not been fomented by a set of intriguing women, these men [Ely and Hertford] might have pulled together" (NA, Reports of Inspection, M 1070, P, R 35, F 154-57, John McNeil to E. A. Hayt, 8/10/1878). Although he presented no concrete evidence, McNeil often claimed that Matlock was a dishonest trader who was protected by his coreligionists, Searing and Ely.

31 BYM, FHL, misc. papers, 10/27/1879; NA, OIA, LR, M 324, P, R 667, F 280, B. Rush Roberts to Carl Schurz, 3/2/1879. The Central Executive Committee of the Hicksite Yearly Meetings assigned Baltimore the joint care of the Santee Sioux agency along with the Genesee, Ohio,

and Illinois Yearly Meetings.
32 Hayt's espionage system and
his purge of agents was not
limited to the Hicksite Quakers
at the Pawnee agency. A wave
of dismissals swept through the
Indian Service because Hayt
refused to retain any agent in
whom he did not have full
confidence. Hayt's actions
proved disruptive and led to the
resignation of Chief Clerk
William Leeds (who had
replaced Samuel Galpin). Leeds
told a Senate committee that
Hayt's administration had been
a "positive obstruction" to the
business of the Indian
department (Loring Benson
Priest, *Uncle Sam's
Stepchildren*, pp. 70-71).
33 Alexander Lesser, *The Pawnee
Ghost Dance Hand Game*, pp.
33-34, 45-49.

Chapter Five

1 During the eighteenth century,
the Missourias occupied one
village near the mouth of the
Grand River in the present
state of Missouri. They may
have numbered nearly a
thousand at the start of the
century. By the end of the
century, disease and warfare
had greatly reduced their
population. This remnant of the
Missourias joined other friendly
native societies. The largest
number, less than a hundred,
affiliated with the Otos but
retained their own chiefs. In the
nineteenth century, along
tributary rivers of the Missouri
in present-day Nebraska, the
Otos and Missourias functioned
as one society. Unless otherwise
stated, the term Otos includes

the Missourias. Berlin Basil
Chapman, *The Otoes and
Missourias*, pp. xiii-xiv; William
Whitman, *The Oto*, pp. xi-xii.
2 *Chapman, Otoes and Missourias*,
p. 113; Whitman, *The Oto*, p. xii;
NETV, Lincoln, Nebraska,
videotape and transcript of Jim
Cleghorn. Robert F. Berkhofer,
Jr., *Salvation and the Savage*,
discusses the role of factions in
American Indian history,
specifically as a product of
divisions between Christian
converts and "pagan"
traditionalists within a society.
Both Berkhofer and P. Richard
Metcalf have considered the
political dimensions of Indian
factions in journal articles. See
Berkhofer, "The Political
Context of a New Indian
History," *Pacific Historical
Review* 40 (August 1971): 57-82;
and Metcalf, "Who Should Rule
at Home? Native American
Politics and Indian-White
Relations," *Journal of
American History* 61 (December
1974): 651-65. Although each of
the two Oto factions
demonstrated a capacity for
independent action, they also
continued to recognize the role
of the federal government's
authority. Because of such
political behavior, and because
of the very low incidence of
religious conversions among
them, the two Oto factions
differ significantly from the
models and case studies
presented by Berkhofer and
Metcalf.
3 NA, OIA, LR, M 234, Ot, R 654,
F 173, Albert Green to Samuel
M. Janney, 6/5/1869; Chapman,
Otoes and Missourias, p. 86.
4 Chapman, *Otoes and Missourias*,

pp. 42, 86. The names of the Oto
chiefs in Washington in
February of 1869 are listed on a
petition for $600 in presents
(NA, OIA, LR, M 234, Ot, R 654,
F 138, 2/15/1869). The
description of Medicine Horse
comes from William H.
Jackson's *Descriptive Catalogue
of Photographs of North
American Indians* (published in
1877; Chapman, *Otoes and
Missourias*, n. 8, pp. 100-101).
William Whitman discusses the
nine Oto gentes in his
anthropological monograph
(*The Oto*, pp. 15-35). The eight
other gentes are Eagle, Beaver,
Elk, Buffalo, Pigeon, Hoot Owl,
Snake, and Coyote. The last two
no longer exist. See also NETV,
Lincoln, Nebraska, transcript of
Jim Cleghorn (Pah-grund-gee of
the Otos).

5 Albert Green to J. Russell
Hayes of Swarthmore,
Pennsylvania, 2/15/1935, Albert
Green Papers, FHL; NA, OIA,
LR, M 234, Ot, R 654, F 248-49,
petition of chiefs and braves, 1/
1870; Chapman, *Otoes and
Missourias*, pp. 90-91.

6 Whitman, *The Oto*, pp. 1-37;
Albert Green to J. Russell
Hayes, 2/21/1955, Albert Green
Papers, FHL; Albert Green in
Friends' Intelligencer, 11/2/
1872, pp. 575-76.

7 NA, OIA, LR, M 234, N, R 521,
F 233-39, Jesse Griest to John
Q. Smith, CrIA, 7/19/1877.

8 NA, OIA, LR, M 234, Ot, R 655,
F 75-76, Barclay White to
Medicine Horse and other
Chiefs, 7/5/1875.

9 NA, OIA, LR, M 234, Ot, R 655,
F 11-14, Sen. P. W. Hitchcock to
Francis Walker, CrIA, 2
petitions enclosed, 8/9/1872; F

43, resolution of Oto Council, 9/
6/1872; F 42, Barclay White to
Walker, 9/11/1872; F 73-74,
White to Walker, 12/19/1872;
Chapman, *Otoes and Missourias*,
p. 94.

10 NA, OIA, LR, M 234, Ot, R 655,
F 44, draft of act submitted by
Secretary of Interior, 12/19/
1872; F 212, Barclay White to
Francis Walker, 1/13/1873; F
139, Joint Resolution . . . to U.S.
Congress, 1/26/1873.

11 NA, OIA, LR, M 234, Ot, R 655,
F 182, Barclay White to Edward
P. Smith, CrIA, 4/21/1873; F
200-202, resolutions of Oto
Council, 5/26/1873. On June 5,
1873, the editor of the *Beatrice
Express* stated his displeasure
over the news that only 80,000
acres, and not the entire
reservation, were to be sold.
The editor preferred to see
settlement by whites on all the
reservation lands and the
removal of the Otos from
Nebraska.

12 NA, OIA, LR, M 234, Ot, R 655,
F 224, Barclay White to Edward
P. Smith, 7/14/1873; F 244,
Jesse Griest to White, 7/29/
1873.

13 *Friends' Intelligencer*, 11/22/
1873, pp. 592-93; NA, OIA, LR,
M 234, Ot, R 655, F 133, Jesse
Griest to Edward P. Smith, 10/
28/1878. The transcripts of the
three meetings are on National
Archives microfilm (R 655, F
147-67).

14 NETV, Lincoln, Nebraska,
transcript of Jim Cleghorn;
Whitman, *The Oto*, pp. 42, 47.

15 C. Vann Woodward, *The Origins
of the New South: 1877-1913*,
p. 223.

16 Whitman, *The Oto*, pp. 63, 70-73.

17 Chapman, *Otoes and Missourias*,

p. 95; *Beatrice Express*, 1/15/
1874; Benjamin Rush Roberts,
in *AR of BIC, 1874*, p. 56; NA,
OIA, LR, M 234, Ot, R 655, F
369, Jesse Griest to Gen. John
Pope, 10/8/1874; F 370-71,
J. H. Sands, 6th Cavalry, to
Ass't Adjutant General,
Department of Missouri, 10/10/
1874 and 10/12/1874; F 465-66,
Barclay White to Edward
P. Smith, 4/21/1875; F 499-501,
Jesse Griest to John Q. Smith,
CrIA, 1/17/1876; OSI, Indian
Division, LS, M 606, R 14, p.
407, C. Delano to Secretary of
War, 10/30/1874; *Beatrice
Express*, 10/15/1874 and 10/22/
1874.

18 NA, OIA, LR, M 234, Ot, R 655,
F 362-65, Jesse Griest to
Barclay White, 10/26/1874; F
359, Griest to White, 10/17/
1874.

19 NA, OIA, LR, M 234, Ot, R 655,
F 465-66, Barclay White to
Edward P. Smith, 4/21/1875.

20 *Friends' Intelligencer*, 7/3/1875,
p. 301; *Beatrice Express*, 7/13/
1876; NA, OIA, LR, M 234, N, R
519, F 134-39, Jesse Griest to
John Q. Smith, 11/7/1876; R
525, F 172-74, Griest to Ezra
A. Hayt, CrIA, 1/14/1879.
Council petitions with the
names of new chiefs and
headmen began appearing in
October of 1875 (Ot, R 655, F
439-41, 10/11/1875). Big Soldier
at first participated in the
agent's new council. After 1875,
his name disappeared from this
list. On January 1, 1876, his
name appeared on an
"unofficial" petition addressed
to Congress by the Coyotes
(Chapman, *Otoes and
Missourias*, p. 102). In later
years, his name would appear

on various letters and petitions
from either faction. Big Soldier
seems to be an example of one
individual who could move
between the two groups.

21 NA, OIA, LR, M 234, Ot, R 655,
F 503-6, Resolutions against
sale of reservation, 1/1/1876; F
499-501, Jesse Griest to John
Q. Smith, 1/17/1876.

22 The petition of 1/17/1876 is in
NA, 44 Cong., 1st sess., no. 35,
Senate 44, A-H 11, box 198. All
quotations and references are
from Chapman, *Otoes and
Missourias*, pp. 102-3.

23 NA, OIA, LR, M 234, Ot, R 655,
F 482, Jesse Griest to John
Q. Smith, 6/20/1876; F 485,
Griest to Smith, 6/23/1876; N, R
519, F 8, Mary L. Barnes to
CrIA, 7/16/1876; F 742-46,
F. O. Wallis to Zachariah
Chandler, Sec. of Int., 7/22/
1876.

24 NA, OIA, LR, M 234, N, R 519,
F 110-12, Jesse Griest to John
Q. Smith, 9/25/1876.

25 NA, OIA, LR, M 234, N, R 520,
F 208-10, Oto Council
resolutions, 12/23/1876.

26 NA, OIA, LR, M 234, N, R 520,
F 232-34, petition of Oto chiefs,
2/1/1877; F 236, Jesse Griest to
John Q. Smith, 2/2/1877; F 583-
84, Secretary of Interior to
CrIA, 2/19/1877; R 522, F 84,
Headquarters, Department of
Missouri, to Ft. Leavenworth, 3/
8/1877; R 520, F 607-8,
Secretary of Interior to CrIA,
4/19/1877; R 525, F 204-5,
George Fink to Griest, 2/13/
1879; Journal of Barclay White,
2:371; 3:204-5, FHL; *Beatrice
Express*, 3/1/1877 and 3/29/
1877.

27 Chapman, *Otoes and Missourias*,
p. 123.

28 NA, OIA, LR, M 234, N, R 521, F 598-97, B. Rush Roberts to Ezra Hayt, 12/19/1877; R 520, F 99, Samuel S. Ely to Hayt, 12/5/1877; P, R 666, F 83, Ely to Hayt, 2/14/1878.

29 NA, OIA, LR, M 234, N, R 522, F 750-54, petition of council, 3/13/1878; F 748-49, Jesse Griest to Ezra Hayt, 3/30/1878; F 917-18, petition of Oto chiefs, 4/23/1878. The official agency interpreter, Battist Deron, witnessed both petitions.

30 NA, OIA, LR, M 234, N, R 522, F 807-8, Jesse Griest to Ezra Hayt, 5/27/1878; F 821-22, Griest to Hayt, 6/11/1878; P, R 666, F 110, Samuel Ely to CrIA, 6/27/1878.

31 NA, Reports of Inspection, M 1070, N, R 29, F 26-45, John McNeil to E. A. Hayt, 11/25/1878; OIA, LR, M 234, N, R 522, F 895-900, letter from Oto chiefs and leading men, 11/23/1878; Chapman, *Otoes and Missourias*, pp. 113-14, 138. At the council on November 15, Medicine Horse claimed that for a decade the young men of Otos, Iowas, Kickapoos and Potawatomis had planned to move to the Indian Territory. No doubt this statement was meant to impress Inspector McNeil as well as to sway the vote of the other faction.

32 NA, OIA, LR, M 234, N, R 525, F 172-74, Jesse Griest to Ezra Hayt, 1/14/1879; F 343-45, Griest to CrIA, 9/25/1879; R 527, F 1225-31, Griest to CrIA, 12/26/1879. Between December, 1878, and December, 1879, at least five letters and two petitions from the "wild" faction arrived in Washington. The name of E. L. Begun appeared often in this correspondence. In one letter (N, R 525, F 32-35, Begun to Hayt, 7/15/1879), Begun said that the Otos wanted to have a private contract with him to pay for their removal. Begun expected to be repaid by the federal government after, one assumes, he made his middleman's profit. Jesse Griest said Begun had "stolen or forged" names on one petition (R 525, F 255-56, 5/7/1879). At least five letters and three petitions from the "progressives" also arrived in Washington. Most of this correspondence had been overseen by Jesse Griest.

33 NA, OIA, LR, M 234, N, R 527, F 610, James Arkeketah to CrIA, 4/9/1880.

34 NA, OSI, Appointments Division, LR, Ot, Record Group 48, F. M. Munroe to CrIA, 4/7/1880; Jesse Griest to William J. Pollock, 5/10/1880.

35 Minutes and speeches of councils on 5/3/1880 and 5/5/1880 are from NA, OSI, Appointments Division, LR, Ot, Record Group 48.

36 NA, OSI, Appointments Division, LR, Ot, Record Group 48, Testimony of Jesse Griest to William J. Pollock, 5/14/1880; Pollock to Carl Schurz, 5/15/1880; Pollock to Schurz, 5/16/1880.

37 NA, OIA, LR, M 234, N, R 528, F 78, Jesse Griest to CrIA, 5/18/1880; F 159-60, John S. Shorb, agent at Sac and Fox to Robert S. Gardner, special agent at Oto, 7/6/1880; Chapman, *Otoes and Missourias*, pp. 138-40.

38 OHS, Indian-Pioneer History,

vol. 66, pp. 143-44, Interview with W. D. Barnes, 6/25/1937; OHS, Ot, letterpress books (microfilmed), LS, R 23, F 336-37, Lwellyn B. Woodin to CrIA, 11/9/1881; F 415, Woodin to CrIA, 5/15/1882.

39 Minutes of CEC, 5/10/1881, pp. 146-48, FHL; NA, OIA, LR, M 234, N, R 528, F 103, Robert S. Gardner to CrIA, 6/17/1880; OSI, Appointments Division, LR, Ot, Record Group 48, Report of John Saunders, Barclay White, and Samuel Jeanes, 3/19/1881.

40 Journal of Barclay White, 3:194; Jesse Griest, in *AR of CrIA, 1878*, p. 98.

41 OHS, Sac and Fox-Shawnee Agency, LR, R 37, F 734-35, John H. Oberly, CrIA, to Moses Neal, Indian agent, 11/24/1888; F 741-43, R. V. Belt, Acting CrIA, to Neal, 5/13/1889; F 747, witnessed document for adoption of Medicine Horse by Iowas, 8/31/1889; F 825, Belt to D. J. M. Wood, Indian agent, 2/11/1892. The Iowas were close traditional friends of the Otos. Apparently Medicine Horse left the Iowas in 1892, taking his granddaughter and her two children with him, because the granddaughter's Iowa husband abused her.

Chapter Six

1 Alice C. Fletcher and Francis La Flesche, *The Omaha Tribe*, 2:623-24, 629-30, 633; Journal of Barclay White, 1:290, FHL.

2 Fletcher and La Flesche, *Omaha Tribe*, 1:84, 202; 2:631-32, 495; Frederick J. Dockstader, *Great North American Indians*, p. 143; Margaret Mead, *The Changing Culture of an Indian Tribe*, p. 26. Mead called the Omahas "Antlers" in her study. Francis La Flesche was a son of Joseph La Flesche. He earned a law degree from National University (Washington, D.C.) in 1893 and became a noted anthropologist with the Bureau of American Ethnology, where he worked from 1903 to 1930.

3 Fletcher and La Flesche, *Omaha Tribe*, 2:632-33.

4 Ibid., 1:35-36. In their South Siouan language, the term "Omaha" was a descriptive word for "against the current" or "upstream," a designation which distinguished the Omahas from the Quapaws, who at some time in the past had divided from the Omahas and gone "quapaw," "with the current" or "downstream."

5 Ibid., 1:70-71, 141; 2:608-10; Lawrence J. Evers, "The Literature of the Omahas" (Ph. D. diss., University of Nebraska, 1972), pp. 19, 54-56.

6 Fletcher and La Flesche, *Omaha Tribe*, 2:630, 618-19; Quaker observers noted the continuation of the robe, the buffalo hunt, and the pipe dance in the 1870s; see Journal of Barclay White, 1:290; Thomas Lightfoot to Howard White, n.d., Thomas Lightfoot Papers, FHL. Lightfoot served as agent at Great Nemaha until September of 1873.

7 NA, OIA, LR, M 234, O, R 605, F 810-11, petition of chiefs' council, 2/8/1868; F 827-28, petition of Omaha council, 5/20/1868; F 880-81, petition of Omaha council, 10/19/1868; *Friends' Intelligencer*, 8/21/1869, pp. 285-86; Fletcher and

La Flesche, *Omaha Tribe*, 1:212; 2:635.

8 Presbyterian Board of Foreign Missions (microfilm), R 2, series 1, Robert W. Furnas to Lowrie, 7/29/1866 (available at NSHS); Fletcher and La Flesche, *Omaha Tribe*, 2:635.

9 NA, OIA, LR, M234, O, R 605, F 1029, Loyalty Oath (affirmed) of Edward Painter, 5/6/1869; F 962, Painter to Samuel M. Janney, 6/3/1869; F 976-78, Painter to Janney, 6/14/1869.

10 NA, OIA, LR, M 234, O, R 605, F 812-14, H. B. Denman to Nathaniel G. Taylor, CrIA, 2/8/1868; F 962, Edward Painter to Samuel Janney, 6/3/1869; F 1004-7, Painter to Janney, 8/16/1869; F 67-77, allotment roll of Omaha tribe, n.d. The exact incidence of polygyny among the Omahas is not known. Fletcher and La Flesche (*Omaha Tribe*, 2:326) report that a majority of families had one wife and that polygynous families rarely had more than two wives.

11 Theodore T. Gillingham, in *AR of CrIA, 1876*, pp. 97-98; Fletcher and La Flesche, *Omaha Tribe*, 2:363; NETV, Lincoln, Nebraska, videotape and transcript of interview with John Turner and Suzette La Flesche Turner.

12 Edward Painter, in *AR of CrIA, 1870*, p. 714; NA, OIA, LR, M 234, O, R 605, F 1065, petition of Omaha Council, 2/24/1870; F 1080, petition of Omaha council, 4/12/1870; F 1081, Painter to Samuel Janney, 4/14/1870; F 1092, petition of Omaha council, 5/5/1870; F 1112, Janney to Ely S. Parker, 8/11/1870; R 606, F 135-36, petition to sell 50,000

acres, 10/27/1871; Painter, in *AR of CrIA, 1871*, pp. 445-47; ibid., *1873*, p. 191. The quality of the western part of the reservation was noted by Arthur Edwards, in *AR of CrIA, 1881*, pp. 129-30.

13 NA, OIA, LR, M 234, O, R 606, F 200-203, Edward Painter to Barclay White, 3/25/1872; F 204-5, White to Francis A. Walker, 4/1/1872; N, R 524, F 175, Jacob Vore to CrIA, 1/12/1878; R 529, F 1063-64, Howard White to CrIA, 7/10/1880.

14 NA, OIA, LR, M 234, O, R 605, F 1055, budget request of Edward Painter for fiscal year 1871; O, R 606, F 33-35, Painter to Samuel Janney, 2/1/1871; table of statistics in AR of CrIA, *1880*, p. 248; Painter in *Friends' Intelligencer*, 5/6/1871, pp. 152-54; Society of Friends, *Second Annual Report of the Joint Delegation . . . 1870*; "Report of Delegation of Indiana Indian Committee . . . ," in *Friends' Intelligencer*, 11/13/1875, pp. 594-98.

15 NA, OIA, LR, M 234, O, R 606, F 435, O. A. Pearson, Acting Chief Clerk, OIA, to CrIA, 8/26/1873; NS, R 600, Edward Painter to Samuel M. Janney, 12/10/1870; O, R 606, F 925, Theodore T. Gillingham to Edward P. Smith, CrIA, 7/10/1875; F 1177, Barclay White to John Q. Smith, 6/17/1876; F 1084, Zachariah Chandler, Secretary of Interior, to CrIA, 5/15/1876; N, R 519, F 107, Gillingham to John Q. Smith, 9/20/1876; F 105-6, Gillingham to Smith, 9/19/1876.

16 NA, OIA, LR, M 234, N, R 519, F 653-54, Jacob Vore to John Q. Smith, 10/5/1876; O, R 606, F

929-32, Theodore T. Gillingham
to Edward P. Smith, 7/20/1875.
17 Gilbert C. Fite, *The Farmers'
Frontier, 1865-1900*, pp. 55-62;
Dorothy Huse Nyberg, *History
of Wayne County, Nebraska*, p.
52; Theodore T. Gillingham, in
AR of CrIA, 1876, pp. 97-98;
table of statistics in *AR of
CrIA, 1875*, p. 123; *1876*, p. 231;
NA, OIA, LR, M 234, N, R 521,
F 871, Jacob Vore to John Q.
Smith, 1/17/1877.
18 NA, OIA, LR, M 234, N, R 522,
F 06, Report of H. E. Stansburg,
19th Infantry, Company K, 1/
11/1877, R 520, F 07-08. Gen.
Philip Sheridan to CrIA, 2/7/
1877; R 522, F 34, Sheridan to
Gen. William T. Sherman, 2/23/
1877; F 93, list of rations and
cost, 3/6/1877; R 521, F 74,
Jacob Vore to CrIA, 3/29/1877;
F 142-43, Vore to CrIA, 5/9/
1877; Stansburg's report called
"Estenobbe" the "general
supervisor" of the Omahas'
hunt. Stansburg probably had
named the "watho^n'" or
"director of the hunt." This
position of full authority over
all activities of the hunt was
granted a select individual at a
special council called by the
"Hon'ga" or "first people" gens.
The "watho^n'" was the most
important individual in the
organization of the traditional
hunt (Fletcher and La Flesche,
Omaha Tribe, 1:275-83).
19 Table of statistics in *AR of
CrIA, 1877*, p. 312; *1880*, pp. 248,
266-67; *1879*, p. 255.
20 Fite, *Farmers' Frontier*, pp. 65-
73.
21 David A. Baerreis, Foreword to
The Middle Five, by Francis La
Flesche, pp. ix-x. This book is a
classic account of life at a

missionary boarding school.
22 H. B. Denman, in *AR of CrIA,
1868*, p. 227.
23 NA, OIA, LR, M 234, N 526, F
209ff., Samuel M. Janney to Ely
S. Parker, 9/22/1869; John H.
Lowrie to Parker, 8/26/1869.
24 Table of statistics in *AR of
CrIA, 1871*, p. 610; Theodore T.
and Elizabeth H. Gillingham in
ibid, p. 448.
25 NA, OIA, LR, M 234, O, R 606,
F 521-23, Questionnaire on
agency and schools, 1/1873;
Edward Painter in *AR of BIC,
1872*, p. 193.
26 NA, OIA, LR, M 234, O, R 606,
F 471-73, John M. Peebles to
Edward P. Smith, 6/10/1873; F
584-85, Barclay White to Smith,
7/8/1873.
27 NA, OIA, LR, M 234, O, R 606,
F 582-83, Edward Painter to
Barclay White, 7/5/1873.
28 NA, OIA, LR, M 234, O, R 605,
F 960-61, Omaha council
petition, 6/3/1869; R 606, F 663-
64, joint council of Poncas and
Omahas, 11/6/1873. The nine
members of the agent's council
in June, 1869, were: Fire Chief,
Yellow Smoke, Standing Hawk,
White Horse, No Knife, Hard
Walker, Ga-huga, Eba-hom-ba,
and Lion. In November, 1873,
White Horse and No Knife were
recorded under their aboriginal
names, Ma ha ninga and
Shonga skah, or, as Fletcher
and La Flesche spelled them,
Mon hin thinge (*mon hin,* stone
knife; *thinge,* none) and *Shon' ge
cka* (*Shon' ge,* horse; *cka,* white)
(*Omaha Tribe*, 1:145, 155, 164).
29 Table of statistics in *AR of
CrIA, 1874*, pp. 98-99; *1875*, p.
113; *1876*, pp. 214-15; *1877*, p.
297; *1878*, p. 291; *1879*, p. 237;
Theodore T. Gillingham, in *AR*

of CrIA, 1876, p. 98. The budget restriction was section five of the appropriation bill of March 3, 1875, which allowed only $6,000 per year to pay for labor at Indian agencies. At some agencies — for example, those of the Winnebagos, Otos and Omahas — such labor included salaried teachers. Barclay White had many complaints about this measure because it continued as a financial policy after 1876 (see NA, OIA, LR, M 234, NS, R 600, F 1201, White to Edward P. Smith, 7/9/1875; White in *AR of BIC, 1877*, pp. 57–58).

30 Jacob Vore in *AR of BIC, 1876*, p. 70; Dockstader, *Great American Indians*, p. 143; NA, OIA, LR, M 234, N, R 519, F 411-12, N. C. Read, Principal, Elizabeth Institute, to S. A. Galpin, Acting CrIA, 11/4/1876; F 378-79, Susette La Flesche to CrIA, 10/16/1876.

31 NA, OIA, LR, M 234, N, R 519, F 690-91, Jacob Vore to John Q. Smith, 11/28/1876; F 393, Smith to Vore, 12/26/1876; Thomas Henry Tibbles, *Buckskin and Blanket Days*, p. 205.

32 Ibid., pp. 193-235; Francis Prucha, *American Indian Policy in Crisis*, pp. 114-18.

33 James Owen Dorsey, *Omaha and Ponka Letters*, Bureau of American Ethnology Bulletin no. 11, pp. 20-33, 52-54.

34 Jacob Vore in *AR of CrIA, 1877*, pp. 144-45. In a letter of 5/14/1878 (NA, OIA, LR, M 234, N, R 524, F 302-3), Vore told the commissioner of Indian Affairs of two parties among the Omahas, "the Chiefs' party and the young men's party — so called — consisting of the more intelligent, industrious and

progressive portion of the tribe."

35 NA, OIA, LR, M 234, N, R 524, F 14-22, petition of fifty-one Omahas to president of U.S., 1/12/1878.

36 Ibid.; NA, OIA, LR, M 234, O, R 606, F 445, Edward Painter to Samuel M. Janney, 4/8/1871; N, R 521, F 300-301, Jacob Vore to CrIA, 8/30/1877; R 524, F 351, Vore to CrIA, 7/3/1878; R 526, F 777-78, Vore to CrIA, 12/27/1878.

37 NA, OIA, LR, M 234, N, R 525, F 110-16, Henry Fontenelle to CrIA, 1/16/1879. Other letters against Vore attributed to the Omaha chiefs include R 526, F 775, Shoor ga skah and Eba Hom ba to CrIA, 12/27/1878, and F 573-74, L. D. Hamilton to CrIA, received 3/10/1879.

38 Journal of Barclay White, 3:158; NA, OIA, LR, M 234, N, R 524, F 463-64, Jacob Vore to CrIA, 10/18/1878; F 545-47, Vore to CrIA, 12/20/1878; R 527, F 05-07, Vore to CrIA, 2/3/1879; Edward E. Hill, *The Office of Indian Affairs, 1824-1880*, p. 105.

39 Howard White's troubles with Ezra Hayt's policies are evident in two letters: NA, OIA, LR, M 234, N, R 529, F 256-59, S. M. Yeatman, special agent, to Ezra Hayt, 1/21/1880; R 528, F 842-43, Howard White to E. J. Brooks, chief clerk, OIA, 2/3/1880. On White's resignation and the Omahas' petition, see R 527, F 917, Arthur Edwards to CrIA, 8/30/1880; F 808-11, J. Owen Dorsey to CrIA, 3/18/1880; Appointment papers, O, Record Group 48, B. Rush Roberts, Aaron Wright, Barclay White, Stephen R. Hicks, to Carl Schurz, 2/25/1880; Dorsey, *Letters*, pp. 82-85.

40 NA, OIA, LR, M 234, N, R 527, F 826-28, J. Owen Dorsey to CrIA, 5/26/1880. The Omahas also often complained about the Winnebagos stealing their horses.

41 Howard White, in *AR of CrIA, 1879*, pp. 108-9.

42 Nancy Oestreich Lurie, "The Lady from Boston and the Omaha Indians," *The American West* 3 (Fall 1966): 31-33, 80-85; Tibbles, *Buckskin Days*, pp. 236-61. Tibbles referred to Fletcher by her Omaha gift-name, "Highflyer." Lurie believes that the Omahas desired a legal guarantee for their entire reservation and that Fletcher misguidedly translated this into a desire for a guarantee of individual allotments. Contrary to Lurie's impressions, many Omahas had already committed themselves to the idea of individual titles before Fletcher arrived. Neither Fletcher nor these Omahas understood at the time the full ramifications of their decision.

43 Mead, *Changing Culture*, pp. 47-53; Lurie, "Lady from Boston," pp. 81-83.

44 Personal correspondence from Paul Olson, professor of English, University of Nebraska, 8/6/1980.

45 NETV, Lincoln, Nebraska, interview with John Turner and Suzette La Flesche Turner.

Chapter Seven

1 In 1885, Charles Hill agreed to accept his appointment as agent to the Santee Sioux on the condition that the Hicksite Yearly Meetings provide "assistance and oversight," as with Isaiah Lightner. Hill, a Friend, had overseen farming operations among the Santees for several years. He was replaced by James E. Helms, a non-Quaker on July 1, 1890. Cyrus Blackburn, in *AR of BIC, 1885*, pp. 65-66; Proceedings of Indiana Yearly Meeting, 1886, p. 14, FHL.

2 William H. Armstrong, *Warrior in Two Camps*, pp. 152-60.

3 Journal of Barclay White, 1:368-70, FHL.

4 NA, OIA, LR, M 234, NS, R 600, F 1302, U.S. Grant to Secretary of Interior, 6/2/1876; Journal of Barclay White, 2:238, 254.

5 Lawrie Tatum, *Our Red Brothers and the Peace Policy of Ulysses S. Grant*, pp. 283-85. The documents of the investigation of Hiram W. Jones may be found in NA, OIA, Special Files, M 574, R 63.

6 Albert H. Smiley (Orthodox) and Richard D. Bentley (Hicksite), in *AR of BIC, 1879*, p. 92; Fisk and White, in *AR of BIC, 1880*, p. 97.

7 Report of Indian committee of Philadelphia Yearly Meeting, in *Friends' Intelligencer*, 6/11/1881, pp. 259-60; letter of Central Executive Committee, in *AR of BIC, 1882*, p. 41.

8 C. Vann Woodward, "Political Stalemate and Agrarian Revolt, 1877-1896," in John M. Blum, ed., *The National Experience*, pp. 475-79.

9 Francis Prucha, *American Indian Policy in Crisis*, pp. 241-42; Levi K. Brown of CEC to William C. Starr, in Proceedings of Indiana Yearly Meeting, 1887, p. 20, FHL.

10 Proceedings of Baltimore Yearly Meeting, 1888, pp. 19-20, FHL.

11 On the Orthodox missions to

the Indian Territory, see Tatum,
Red Brothers, pp. 297-366; on
social issues, committees on
philanthropic labor reported
regularly to the various
Hicksite yearly meetings; see
also Philip S. Benjamin, *The
Philadelphia Quakers in the
Industrial Age, 1865-1920*, pp.
73-100.

12 Everett Arthur Gilcreast,
"Richard Henry Pratt and
American Indian Policy, 1877-
1906" (Ph.D. diss., Yale
University, 1967), pp. 54-55, 88,
320.

13 *Index Rerum* to Lake Mohonk
Indian Conferences, 1885-92,
Smiley Family Papers, QC;
Prucha, *Policy in Crisis*, pp.
143-68; Larry E. Burgess, "The
Lake Mohonk Conferences on
the Indian, 1883-1916" (Ph.D.
diss., Claremont Graduate
School, 1972), pp. 19-20.

14 Journal of Barclay White, 3:334;
Barclay White, *The Friends and
the Indians*, pp. 4-5. White's
report was published and
distributed after being
presented to the convention of
the Central Executive
Committee on the Indian
Concern of the Seven Yearly
Meetings.

15 Wilcomb E. Washburn, *The
Indian in America*, pp. 243-44.

16 Journal of Barclay White, 2:328.

17 For a somewhat different and
lengthier discussion of these
concepts, see the author's
article "Off the White Road:
Seven Nebraska Indian
Societies in the 1870s, A
Statistical Analysis of
Assimilation, Population and
Prosperity," *Western Historical
Quarterly* 12 (January 1981): 37-
52.

Bibliography

Manuscripts and Archives

Friends Historical Library,
Swarthmore College, Swarthmore, Pennsylvania

Journal of Barclay White, 3 vols., microfilmed.
Minutes of the Central Executive Committee of Delegates from the Indian Committees of the Yearly Meetings (Hicksite) of Baltimore, Philadelphia, New York, Indiana, Ohio, Genesee, and (Illinois), 1869-1878.
Minutes of the Standing Committee on Indian Concerns, Baltimore Yearly Meeting (Hicksite), 1857-1877 and 1878-1919, clerk's paginated manuscript.
Albert Green Papers.
Samuel Janney Papers.
Thomas Lightfoot Papers.

Library of Congress,
Washington, D.C.

Ulysses S. Grant Papers, Manuscript Division, Reference Department, microfilmed.

Nebraska State Historical Society, Lincoln, Nebraska

Luther Hedden North Collection, partially microfilmed.
John William Williamson Collection, microfilmed.
Presbyterian Board of Foreign Missions, microfilmed.

National Archives and Records Service, Washington, D.C.

Record Group 48. Records of the Office of the Secretary of the Interior.
Appointments Division, Letters Received.
Indian Division, Letters Received. Microcopy 825.
Indian Division, Letters Sent. Microcopy 606.
Record Group 75. Records of the Bureau of Indian Affairs.
Agency Employees, Service Record, paginated work books.
Northern Superintendency, Field Office Files, Letters Received.
Northern Superintendency, Field Office Files, Letters Sent.
Office of Indian Affairs, Letters

Received, 1824-1881. Microcopy 234.

Office of Indian Affairs, Registers of Letters Received, 1824-1880. Microcopy 18.

Office of Indian Affairs, Letters Sent, 1824-1881. Microcopy 21.

Office of Indian Affairs, Special Files, 1807-1904. Microcopy 574.

Record Group 48 and Record Group 75.

Reports of Inspection of the Field Jurisdictions of the Office of Indian Affairs, 1873-1900. Microcopy 1070.

NETV, Lincoln, Nebraska

Videotape and transcript of Jim Cleghorn (Pah-grund-gee of the Otos), April 1978, for Native American Culture project of the Junior League of Lincoln.

Videotape and transcript of interview with John Turner and Suzette La Flesche Turner, April 1976, for Native American Culture project of the Junior League of Lincoln.

Oklahoma Historical Society, Oklahoma City, Oklahoma

Indian-Pioneer History. Indian Archives Division. Typescript of interviews.

Kiowa Agency letters. Indian Archives Division. Microfilmed

Minutes of Councils between Pawnees and their agents, 1870-1875. Indian Archives Division. Microfilmed.

Pawnee Agency letterpress books. Indian Archives Division. Microfilmed.

Sac and Fox-Shawnee Agency letters. Indian Archives Division. Microfilmed.

Quaker Collection, Haverford College, Haverford, Pennsylvania

Evans, William Bacon, ed. "Dictionary of Quaker Biography," compiled typescript. John B. Garrett Collection.

Enoch Hoag Papers.

Smiley Family Papers (Lake Mohonk Conferences).

Thomas Wistar Collection.

Published Reports

Federal Government

Report of the Secretary of War, 40th Cong., 3d sess., 1868-69. *House Executive Documents.* No. 1, part 1. vol. 3.

House Miscellaneous Documents, No. 29, 40th Cong., 3d. sess., 1868-69, vol. 1.

Report of Board of Inquiry Convened by Authority of Letter of the Secretary of the Interior of June 7, 1877, to Investigate Certain Charges Against S. A. Galpin, Chief Clerk of the Indian Bureau, and Concerning Irregularities in Said Bureau. Washington, D.C.: Government Printing Office, 1878.

Dorsey, James Owen. *Omaha and Ponka Letters.* Bureau of American Ethnology Bulletin no. 11. Washington, D.C.: Government Printing Office, 1891.

Annual Reports of the Board of Indian Commissioners. Washington, D.C.: Government Printing Office, beginning in 1869.

Annual Reports of the Commissioner of Indian Affairs. Washington, D.C.: Government

Printing Office, beginning in 1868.
Congressional Globe

Society of Friends

Report of the Joint Delegation of Baltimore, Philadelphia and New York Yearly Meetings in their visit to the Northern Superintendency, 7th and 8th Months, 1869 (Philadelphia, 1869).
Second Annual Report of the Joint Delegation Appointed by the Committees on the Indian Concern of the Yearly Meetings of Ohio and Genesee, and Approved by the General Conference of Delegates from the Indian Committees of the Yearly Meetings of Baltimore, Philadelphia, New York, Indiana, Ohio and Genesee respectively which met at Philadelphia 5th month, 6th, 1870. Rochester, N.Y.: Democrat Book and Job Printing House, 1870.
White, Barclay. *The Friends and the Indians.* Oxford, Pa., 1886.
Annual Reports of the Associated Executive Committee of Friends on Indian Affairs (Orthodox), beginning in 1870.
Proceedings of the Hicksite Yearly Meetings (published annually for the Yearly Meetings of Baltimore, Genesee, Illinois, Indiana, New York, Ohio and Philadelphia).

Newspapers

Boston Daily Advertiser. 1869.
Beatrice Express (Nebraska). 1868-82.
Chicago Tribune. 1868-69.

The Friend (Philadelphia). 1865-85.
Friends' Intelligencer (Philadelphia). 1865-85.
Friends' Review (Philadelphia). 1865-85.
New York Times. 1868-69.
New York Tribune. 1868-69.
Platte Journal (Columbus, Nebraska). 1870-78.
Rocky Mountain News (Denver, Colorado). 1868-69.

Articles and Unpublished Works

Berkhofer, Robert F. "The Political Context of a New Indian History." *Pacific Historical Review* 40 (August 1971): 357-82.
Blaine, Garland James, and Blaine, Martha Royce. "Pa-re-su A-ri-ra-ke: The Hunters That Were Massacred." *Nebraska History* 58 (Fall 1977): 343-58.
Brinton, Ellen Starr. "Benjamin West's Painting of Penn's Treaty with the Indians." *Bulletin of Friends' Historical Association* 30 (Autumn 1941): 99-131.
Burgess, Larry E. "The Lake Mohonk Conferences on the Indian, 1883-1916." Ph.D. dissertation, Claremont Graduate School, 1972.
Chapin, Charles. "Removal of Pawnee and Peace with their Neighbors: A Memoir of Charles Chapin." *Nebraska History* 26 (January-March 1945): 43-46.
Clark, J. Stanley. "Irregularities at the Pawnee Agency." *Kansas Historical Quarterly* 12 (November 1943): 366-77.
Dunbar, John B. "Letters concerning the Presbyterian Mission in the Pawnee Country, near Bellevue, Nebraska, 1831-1849." *Collections of the Kansas*

State Historical Society 14 (1915-18): 570-784.

———. "Lone Chief and Medicine Bull." *Magazine of American History* 8 (November 1882): 754-56.

———. "Pitalesharu – Chief of the Pawnees." *Magazine of American History* 5 (November 1880): 343-45.

Evers, Lawrence J. "The Literature of the Omaha." Ph.D. dissertation, University of Nebraska, 1972.

Fritz, Henry E. "The Making of Grant's 'Peace Policy.'" *Chronicles of Oklahoma* 36 (Winter 1959-60): 411-32.

Gerlach, Gail Brooks. "Samuel McPherson Janney: Quaker Reformer." M.S. thesis, University of Utah, 1977.

Gilcreast, Everett Arthur. "Richard Henry Pratt and American Indian Policy, 1877-1906: A Study of the Assimilationist Movement." Ph.D. dissertation, Yale University, 1967.

Illick, Joseph E. "'Some of Our Best Indians are Friends . . .': Quaker Attitudes and Actions regarding the Western Indians during the Grant Administration." *Western Historical Quarterly* 2 (July 1971): 283-94.

Jennings, Francis P. "Miquon's Passing: Indian-European Relations in Colonial Pennsylvania." Ph.D. dissertation, University of Pennsylvania, 1965.

Keller, Robert H., Jr. "The Protestant Churches and Grant's Peace Policy: A Study in Church-State Relations, 1869-1881." Ph.D. dissertation, University of Chicago, 1967.

Lurie, Nancy Oestreich. "The Lady from Boston and the Omaha Indians." *American West* 3 (Fall 1966): 31-33, 80-85.

Metcalf, P. Richard. "Who Should Rule at Home? Native American Politics and Indian-White Relations." *Journal of American History* 61 (December 1974): 651-65.

Milner, Clyde A., II. "Off the White Road: Seven Nebraska Indian Societies in the 1870s, A Statistical Analysis of Assimilation, Population and Prosperity." *Western Historical Quarterly* 12 (January 1981): 37-52.

Nabokov, Peter. "The Plains Earthlodge." Typescript. Oxford: Oxford University Press, forthcoming.

Oehler, Gottlieb, and Smith, David. "Description of a Journey and Visit to the Pawnee Indians . . . April 22-May 18, 1851." Reprint from *Moravian Church Miscellany of 1851-52* (New York, 1914), pp. 18-32.

Platt, Elvira Gaston. "Written by Amelia's Request: Mere Hints of My Changeful Life." Typescript, circa 1900. MS Collection, NSHS.

———. "Some Experiences as a Teacher among the Pawnees." *Collections of the Kansas State Historical Society* 14 (1915-1918): 784-94.

Riley, Paul. "The Battle of Massacre Canyon." *Nebraska History* 54 (Summer 1973): 221-49.

Unrau, William E. "The Civilian as Indian Agent: Villain or Victim?" *Western Historical Quarterly* 3 (October 1972): 405-20.

Utley, Robert M. "The Celebrated Peace Policy of General Grant." *North Dakota History* 20 (July 1953): 121-42.

Waltmann, Henry G. "Circumstantial Reformer: President Grant and the Indian Problem." *Arizona and the West* 13 (Winter 1971): 323-42.

Wishart, David J. "The Dispossession of the Pawnee." *Annals of the Association of American Geographers* 69 (September 1979): 382-401.

White, Richard. *The Pawnees: Politics, Ecology and Technology on the Plains.* Typescript. Lincoln: University of Nebraska Press, forthcoming.

————— "The Winning of the West: The Expansion of the Western Sioux in the Eighteenth and Nineteenth Centuries." *Journal of American History* 65 (September 1978): 319-43.

Books

Armstrong, William H. *Warrior in Two Camps: Ely S. Parker, Union General and Seneca Chief.* Syracuse, N.Y.: Syracuse University Press, 1978.

Barbour, Hugh. *The Quakers in Puritan England.* New Haven: Yale University Press, 1964.

Benjamin, Philip S. *The Philadelphia Quakers in the Industrial Age: 1865-1920.* Philadelphia: Temple University Press, 1976.

Berkhofer, Robert F. *Salvation and the Savage.* 1965. Reprint. New York: Atheneum, 1972.

Blaine, Martha Royce. *The Ioway Indians.* Norman: University of Oklahoma Press, 1979.

Blum, John M. *The National Experience: A History of the United States.* New York: Harcourt, Brace, Jovanovich, 1973.

Bowen, William A. *The Willamette Valley: Migration and Settlement on the Oregon Frontier.* Seattle: University of Washington Press, 1978.

Brinton, Howard H. *Friends for Three Hundred Years.* 1952. Reprint. Wallingford, Pennsylvania: Pendle Hill Publications, 1965.

Brock, Peter. *Pioneers of the Peaceable Kingdom.* Princeton, N.J.: Princeton University Press, 1968.

Bronner, Edwin B., ed. *American Quakers Today.* Philadelphia: Friends World Committee, 1966.

Chapman, Berlin Basil. *The Otoes and Missourias: A Study of Indian Removal and the Legal Aftermath.* Stillwater, Oklahoma: *Times Journal* Publishing Company, 1965.

De Ponceau, Peter S., and Fisher, J. Francis. *A Memoir on the History of the Celebrated Treaty Made by William Penn with the Indians under the Elm Tree at Shackamaxon, the Year 1682.* Philadelphia: M'Carty and Davis, 1836.

Dockstader, Frederick J. *Great North American Indians: Profiles in Life and Leadership.* New York: Van Nostrand Reinhold Co., 1977.

Doherty, Robert W. *The Hicksite Separation: A Sociological Analysis of Religious Schism in Early Nineteenth Century America.* New Brunswick, N.J.: Rutgers University Press, 1967.

Dorsey, George A. *Traditions of the Skidi Pawnee, Memoirs of the American Folk-lore Society,* Vol. 8. New York: Houghton, Mifflin and Co., 1904.

Drake, Thomas E. *Quakers and Slavery in America.* New Haven, Connecticut: Yale University

Press, 1950.

Fite, Gilbert C. *The Farmers' Frontier, 1865-1900.* New York: Holt, Rinehart and Winston, 1966.

Fletcher, Alice C., and La Flesche, Francis. *The Omaha Tribe.* Twenty Seventh Annual Report of the Bureau of American Ethnology to the Secretary of the Smithsonian Institution, 1905-6. 1911. Reprint. Lincoln: University of Nebraska Press, 1972.

Fritz, Henry E. *The Movement for Indian Assimilation, 1860-1890.* Philadelphia: University of Pennsylvania Press, 1963.

Grinnell, George Bird. *Pawnee Hero Stories and Folk Tales.* New York: Forest and Stream Publishing, 1889.

————— *Two Great Scouts and their Pawnee Battalion: The Experiences of Frank J. North and Luther H. North.* 1928. Reprint. Lincoln: University of Nebraska Press, 1973.

Hallowell, Benjamin. *Autobiography of Benjamin Hallowell.* Philadelphia: Friends' Book Association, 1883.

Hill, Edward E. *The Office of Indian Affairs, 1824-1880: Historical Sketches.* New York: Clearwater Publishing, 1974.

Holder, Preston. *The Hoe and the Horse on the Plains: A Study of Cultural Development among North American Indians.* Lincoln: University of Nebraska Press, 1970.

Hyde, George E. *The Pawnee Indians.* 1951. Reprint. Norman: University of Oklahoma Press, 1973.

Janney, Samuel M. *Memoirs of Samuel M. Janney.* Philadelphia: Friends' Book Association, 1881.

Jennings, Francis. *The Invasion of America: Indians, Colonialism and the Cant of Conquest.* Chapel Hill: University of North Carolina Press, 1975.

Jones, Louis Thomas. *The Quakers of Iowa.* Iowa City: State Historical Society of Iowa, 1914.

Kappler, Charles J., ed. *Indian Affairs: Laws and Treaties.* Washington, D.C.: Government Printing Office, 1904.

Kelsey, Rayner Wickersham. *Friends and the Indians, 1655-1917.* Philadelphia: Associated Executive Committee of Friends on Indian Affairs, 1917.

La Flesche, Francis. *The Middle Five: Indian Schoolboys of the Omaha Tribe.* Madison: University of Wisconsin Press, 1963.

Lesser, Alexander. *The Pawnee Ghost Dance Hand Game: A Study of Culture Change.* New York: Columbia University Press, 1933.

Mardock, Robert Winston. *The Reformers and the American Indian.* Columbia, Missouri: University of Missouri Press, 1971.

Mead, Margaret. *The Changing Culture of an Indian Tribe.* Columbia University Contributions to Anthropology 15. New York: Columbia University Press, 1932.

Meyer, Roy W. *History of the Santee Sioux: United States Indian Policy on Trial.* Lincoln: University of Nebraska Press, 1967.

Nyberg, Dorothy Huse. *History of Wayne County, Nebraska.* Wayne, Nebraska: The *Wayne Herald,* Publishing Co., 1938.

Oswalt, Wendell H. *This Land Was Theirs: A Study of the North*

American Indian. New York: John Wiley and Sons, 1966.

Parker, Arthur C. *The Life of General Ely S. Parker: Last Grand Sachem of the Iroquois and General Grant's Military Secretary*. Buffalo: Buffalo Historical Society, 1919.

Priest, Loring Benson. *Uncle Sam's Stepchildren: The Reformation of United States Indian Policy, 1865-1887*. New Brunswick, N.J.: Rutgers University Press, 1942.

Prucha, Francis Paul. *American Indian Policy in Crisis: Christian Reformers and the Indian, 1865-1900*. Norman: University of Oklahoma Press, 1976.

Richardson, James D. *A Compilation of the Messages and Papers of the Presidents, 1789-1897*. Washington: U.S. Congress, 1900.

Schmeckebier, Laurence F. *The Office of Indian Affairs: Its History, Activities and Organization*. Institute for Government Research, Service Monographs of the United States Government, no. 40. Baltimore: The Johns Hopkins Press, 1927.

Stuart, George H. *The Life of George H. Stuart*. Edited by Robert Ellis Thompson. Philadelphia: J. M. Stoddart and Co., 1890.

Stuart, Paul. *The Indian Office: Growth and Development of an American Institution, 1865-1900*. Ann Arbor, Mich.: UMI Research Press, 1978, 1979.

Tatum, Lawrie. *Our Red Brothers and the Peace Policy of Ulysses S. Grant*. 1899. Reprint. Lincoln: University of Nebraska Press, 1970.

Tibbles, Thomas Henry. *Buckskin and Blanket Days: Memoirs of a Friend of the Indians*. 1905.

Reprint. Lincoln: University of Nebraska Press, 1957.

Utley, Robert M. *Frontier Regulars: The United States Army and the Indian, 1866-1891*. New York: Macmillan Co., 1973.

Wallace, Anthony F. C. *The Death and Rebirth of the Seneca*. New York: Random House, Vintage Books, 1969.

Washburn, Wilcomb E. *The Indian in America*. New York: Harper & Row, 1975.

Weltfish, Gene. *The Lost Universe*. New York: Basic Books, 1965.

Whitman, William. *The Oto*. New York: Columbia University Press, 1937.

Woodward, C. Vann. *The Origins of the New South: 1877-1913*. Baton Rouge: Louisiana State University Press, 1951.

Index